I0900948

IMAGES
of America

FREEHOLD
VOLUME II

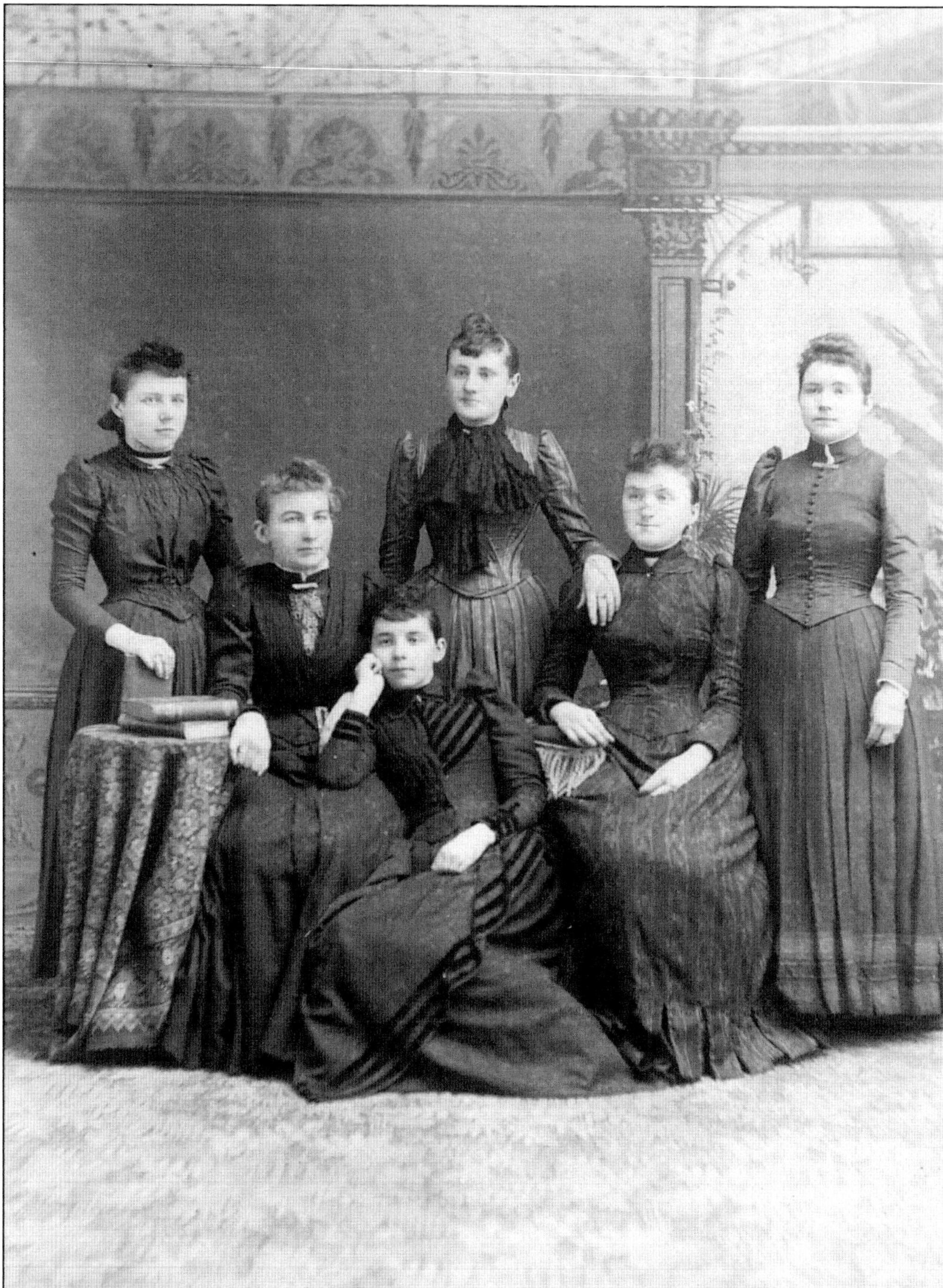

Group of Friends, c. 1890. Ella O'Connor White is the second from the right. (Scott, photographer. Collection of Kevin Coyne.)

IMAGES
of America

FREEHOLD
VOLUME II

Lee Ellen Griffith, Ph.D.

ARCADIA
PUBLISHING

ISBN 978-0-7385-9009-7

Published by Arcadia Publishing
Charleston, South Carolina

Printed in the United States of America

Library of Congress Catalog Card Number:

For all general information contact Arcadia Publishing at:
Telephone 843-853-2070
Fax 843-853-0044
E-mail sales@arcadiapublishing.com
For customer service and orders:
Toll-Free 1-888-313-2665

Visit us on the Internet at www.arcadiapublishing.com

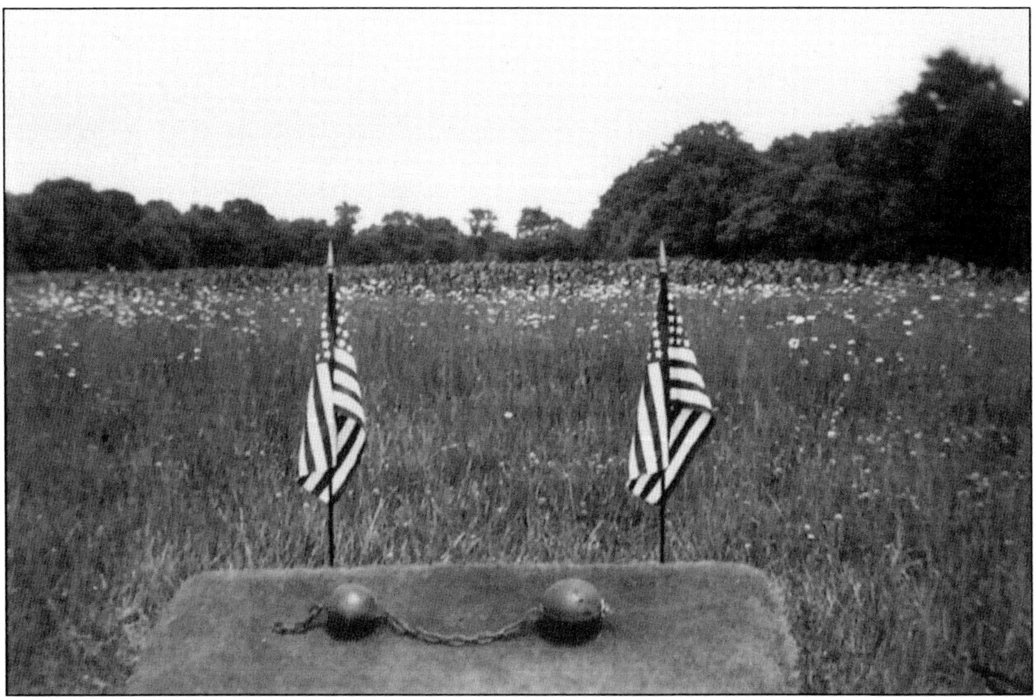

CHAIN SHOT FROM THE BATTLE OF MONMOUTH. A variation on the standard cannon ball, chain shot consisted of two cannon balls that were joined by a chain so that they would spin end over end when fired, causing considerable damage to their target. This example was found by S.V. Perrine on Henry Perrine's farm in Freehold and photographed in 1938. (MCHA Archives 1998.24.)

Contents

ACKNOWLEDGMENTS

I would like to thank all those who have assisted me in compiling this book by sharing photographs or providing information, inspiration, or moral support, including the staff and trustees of the Monmouth County Historical Association, in particular, Carla Z. Tobias, Megan Springate, and Joyce Conk; Jack Aaronson; Ezra Cohen of Perfect Photo in Freehold; Kevin Coyne; James Dorn of Dorn's in Red Bank; Rebecca L. Griffith; Joseph W. Hammond; Gail Hunton; Kenneth Kalmis; Dr. Zeff Lazinger; Harry Reed; Zack S. Roberts; Mary Jane Whalen; and Nancy DuBois Wood.

It would not have been possible to compile this second volume of Freehold photographs without the generosity of two private collectors. Carl N. Steinberg is well known as a collector of Freehold memorabilia and a resource for local history. A third-generation Freehold businessman, Carl has also contributed to our community through public service as a borough councilman, as a member of the Freehold Fire Department, and in various other civic organizations. Richard J. Dalik, as the author of Arcadia's *Manalapan* and *Englishtown*, was particularly sympathetic to this author's request for photographs. A native of Manalapan, Dick and his wife, Sally, have been actively involved with the Battleground Historical Society and collect postcards and photographs of this area.

Introduction

Freehold's Contribution to the March of Progress

From a *Guide to Historic Freehold*, compiled by the Students of Freehold High School, Class of 1924.

In the course of world events, places and people become minutely famous, renowned and glorious, and then they are forgotten. The world looks skeptically attentive while that person or place advances and tries to make itself renown in the present and future as well as past glory.

Freehold has an abundance of past glory, is taking great strides in the march of progress at the present time and looks forward to taking still greater strides in the future. The Battle of Monmouth, the glorious people and events connected with it, furnish much of Freehold's past glory . . . The noble patriots in and around Freehold who suffered and died in the cause of freedom were as brave as those from any other part of our country. They were simple God-fearing country folk whose homes were burned by the ruthless red coats and whose sons marched off to do their bit. Thus Freehold had a great share in the national birth of America.

Freehold is the nucleus of the farming district in the State of New Jersey. There are practically 25,000 acres of potatoes in the Monmouth County with an average of eighty barrels to the acre. Freehold has the best public market in the state, doing a retail and wholesale business sending out about seventy-five cars of perishables a day . . . . With a population of over 5,500, {Freehold} is tending to become a manufacturing city as well as an agricultural center. Already there are numerous factories employing hundreds of people daily . . .

Freehold has recently constructed new streets of concrete which make traveling through our city a pleasure for the tourists of our own as well as sister states. We have set a high standard of civic beauty. Our streets are shaded by huge trees which add a great touch of beauty to any community. We have surrounded our monument with a fine park thus making a fitting background for that memorial to the soldiers of the Revolution . . . .

Freehold has all the conveniences of a large city combined with the advantages of its situation, one of the richest and most productive parts of our great country, only sixty miles from Philadelphia and fifty miles from New York City. The patriots of the present as well as those of the past have combined to make our city one of which America may well be proud.

—Harry Neafie

The students of the class of 1924 wrote an informative and optimistic history of their community, presumably as a senior class project. Their appreciation of Freehold's glorious past as well as its present is clearly expressed throughout the little volume. Looking at photographs in this book that reflect the era, the same high spirits are evident. With the Karagheusian Rug Mill and other industries prospering in town, and the produce market sending agricultural products out at a remarkable rate, these were certainly some of Freehold's glory days.

Freehold, Volume II compliments its predecessor with some interesting new components: a glimpse of some more recent times, a section on the parades for which Freehold was well known, some snapshots of 20th-century farm life, and a group of family portraits that show a personal side of history. More photographs of the businesses of Freehold, large and small, are also offered. The interiors of shops are always of great interest to students of social and business history for their detail of everyday life.

The immediacy and honesty of photographs are part of their great appeal to us today. They offer a little something for everyone. These images of Freehold's early days carry personal associations for longtime residents while providing delightful discoveries to newcomers.

One

Victorian Freehold

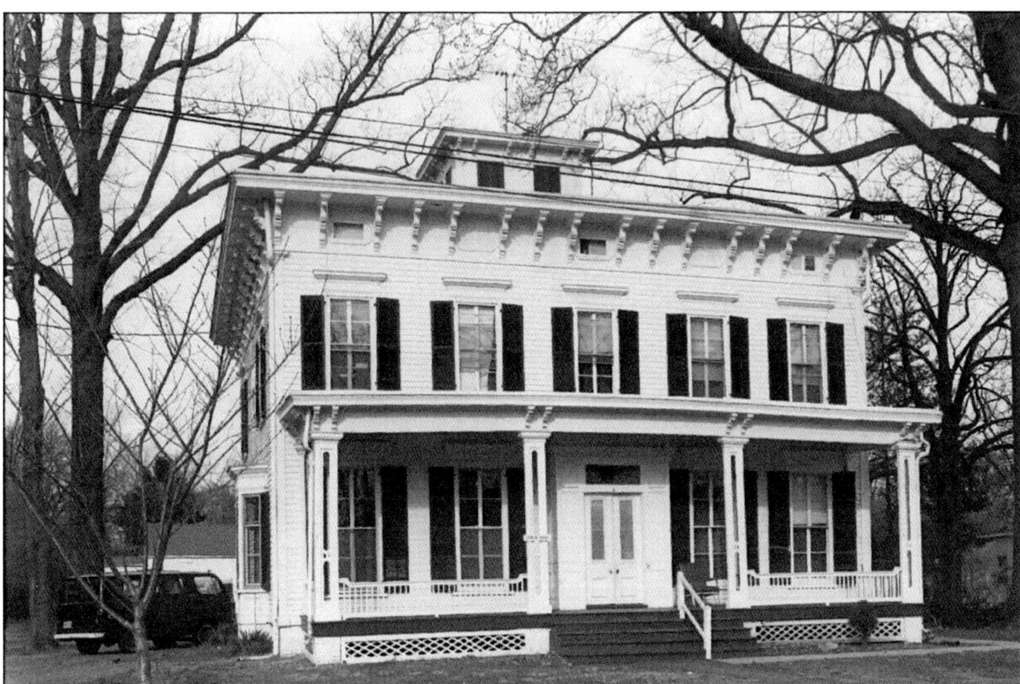

The John Dorrance House, built c. 1860. Freehold house builder Charles C. Bowne constructed this Italianate-style residence for John Dorrance, who was the director of the First National Bank of Freehold. (Monmouth County Historic Sites Inventory.)

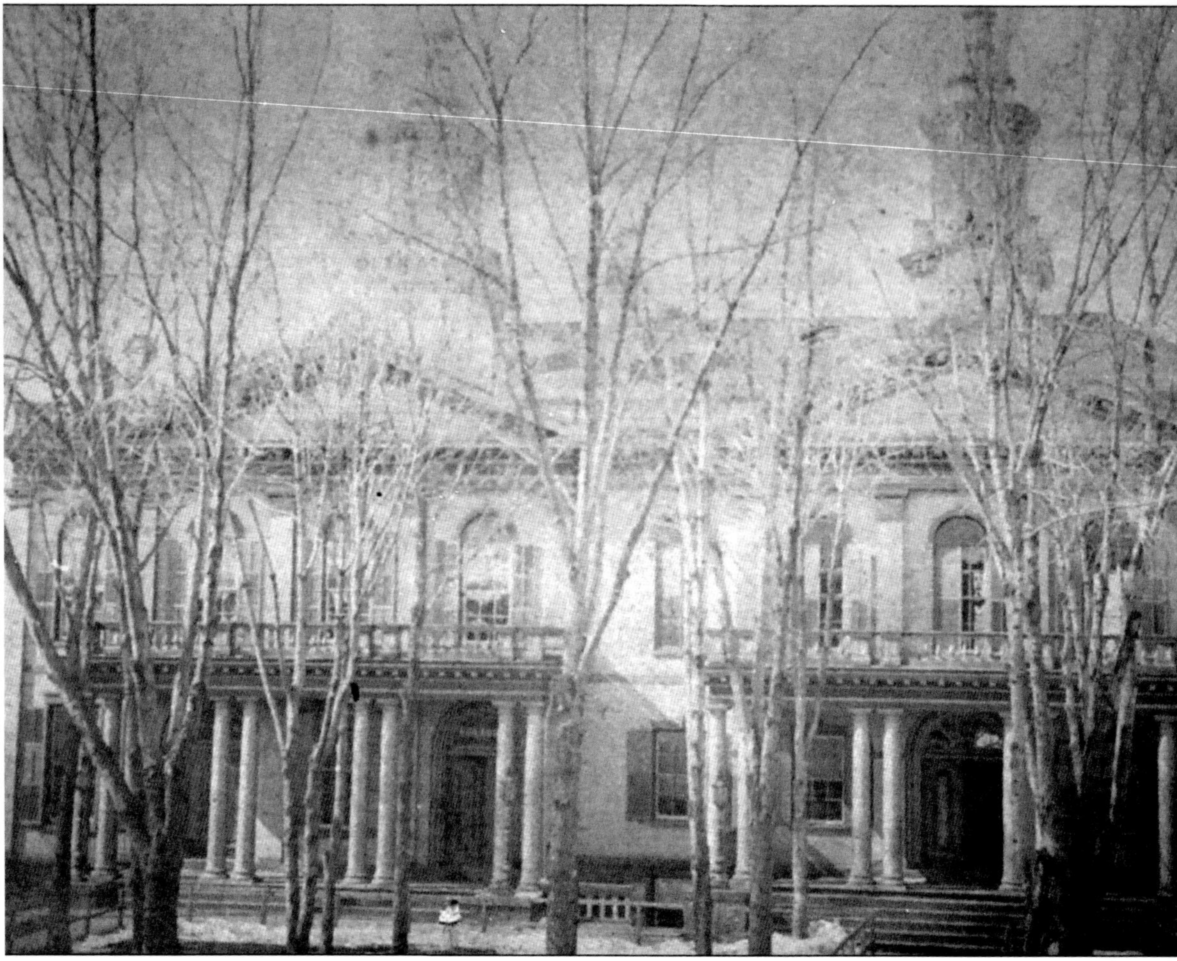

MONMOUTH COUNTY COURTHOUSE, 1873. This rare view of the Courthouse, with its original twin cupolas, was taken before the great fire of October 1873 that destroyed the Courthouse as well as a block of commercial buildings to the south. (MCHA Archives FR99.)

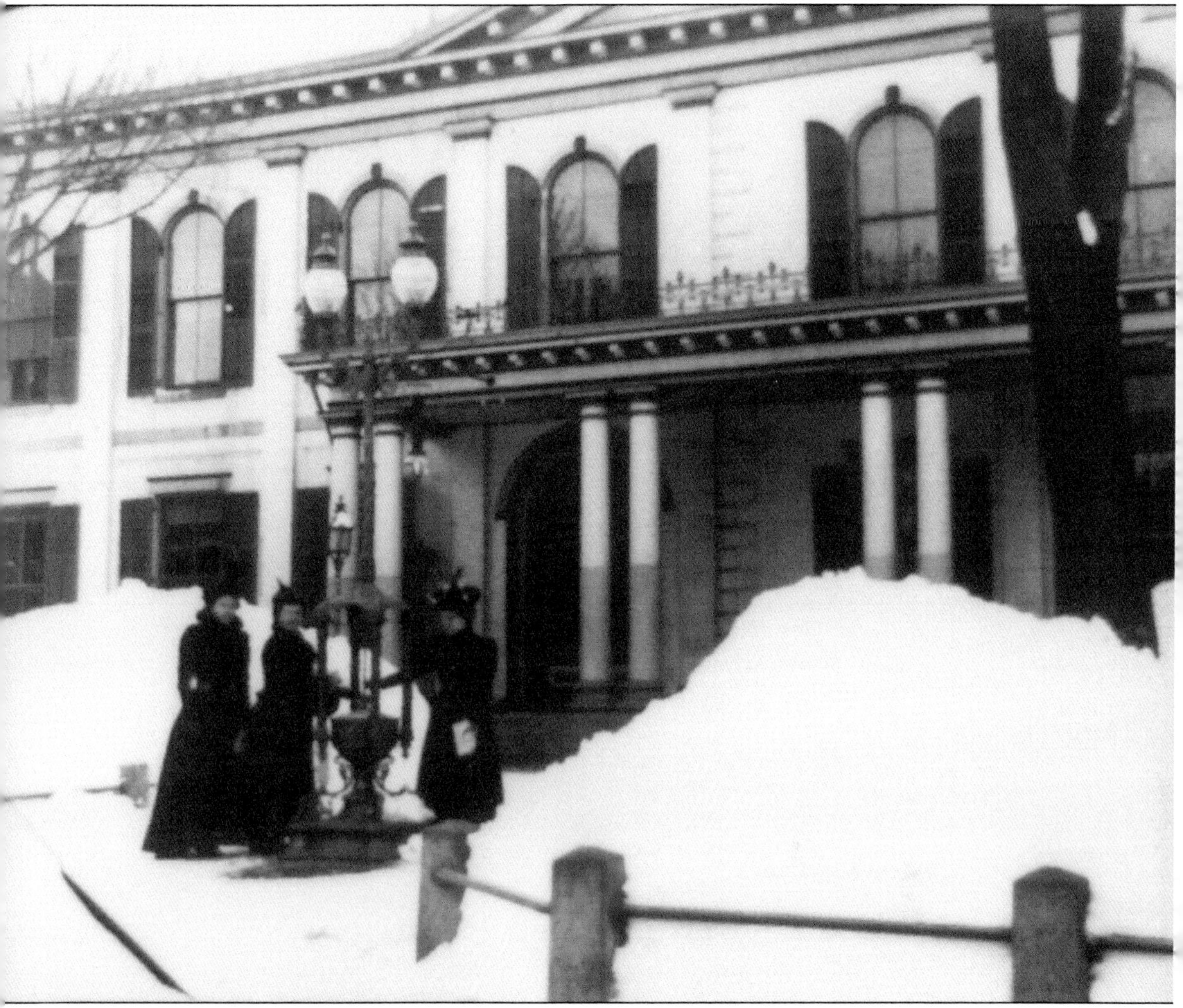

THE COURTHOUSE IN THE SNOW, 1899. A sizable snowstorm blanketed Freehold on February 14, 1899. Three ladies in stylish winter attire pose in front of the Courthouse next to the new gaslight. (MCHA Archives.)

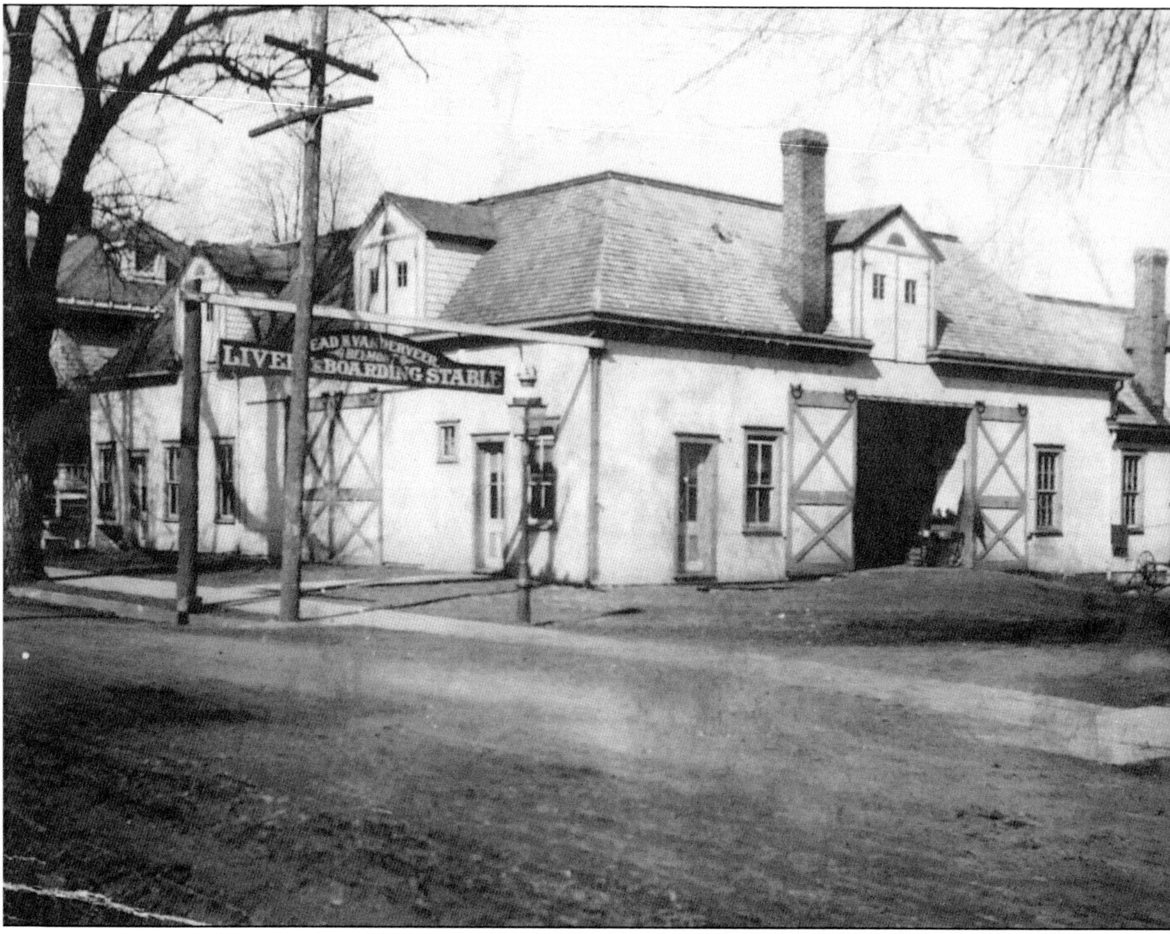

Read & VanDerveer Livery and Boarding Stable, 1900. Successors to Errickson's Livery Stable, Harry W. Read, D.V.M., and Edgar M. VanDerveer ran this establishment into the early 20th century on Court Street opposite Bennett Street. Appropriately, it is now a parking lot. (Collection of Harry Read.)

WOLCOTT'S SALOON, 1880S. On the night of November 4, 1865, this was the final stop for an angry mob that had just murdered Gilbert Perrine and injured others. The violence escalated from a heated political discussion in another Main Street bar, Frey's Lager Beer Saloon. An editorial in the *Monmouth Democrat* lamented, "The number of these saloons for a community as small as ours is astonishing." (Collection of Richard J. Dalik.)

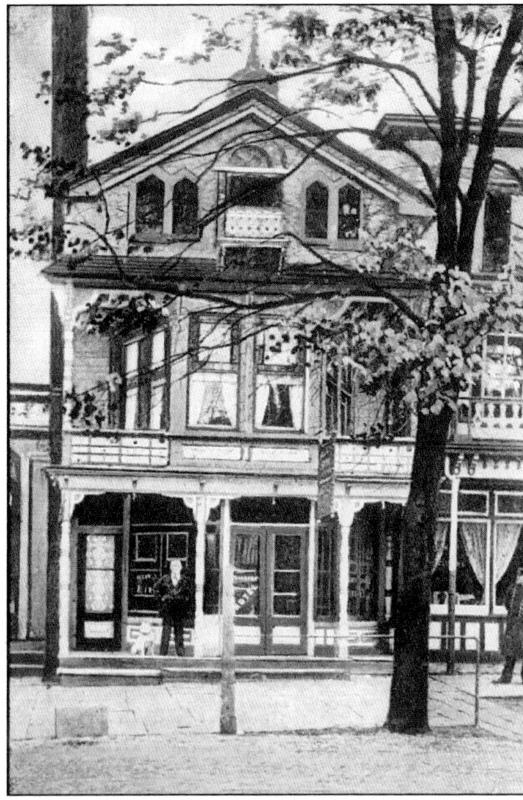

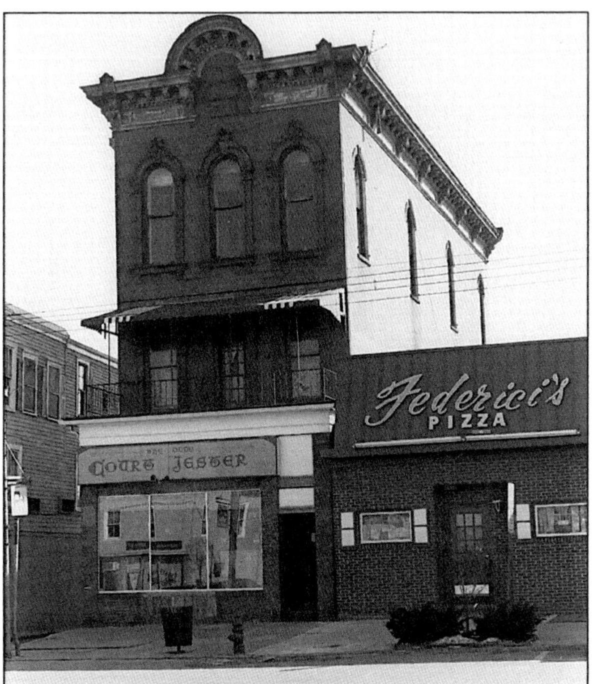

BROWN BUILDING, BUILT 1874. An elegant narrow brown sandstone building with an ornate metal cornice, this office building was constructed for Stewart Brown who proudly displayed his name and the date "1874." It now houses the Court Jester and is next door to a Freehold tradition, Federici's, formerly the site of Wolcott's Saloon. (Monmouth County Historic Sites Inventory.)

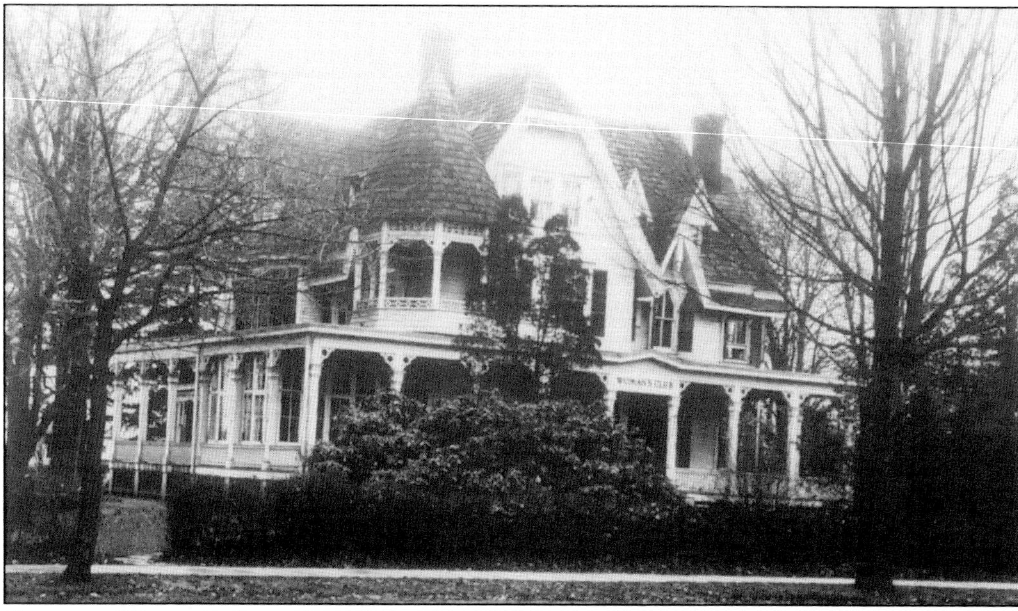

FREEHOLD WOMEN'S CLUB. This large Queen Anne–style house, which no longer stands, was located at the corner of Broad and Club Streets and was once home to the Freehold Women's Club, a social organization founded in 1909. The club purchased this house in 1921 for $11,000 and it served as its headquarters until 1949. During WW II, it was used by the American Red Cross as their headquarters. (Collection of Richard J. Dalik.)

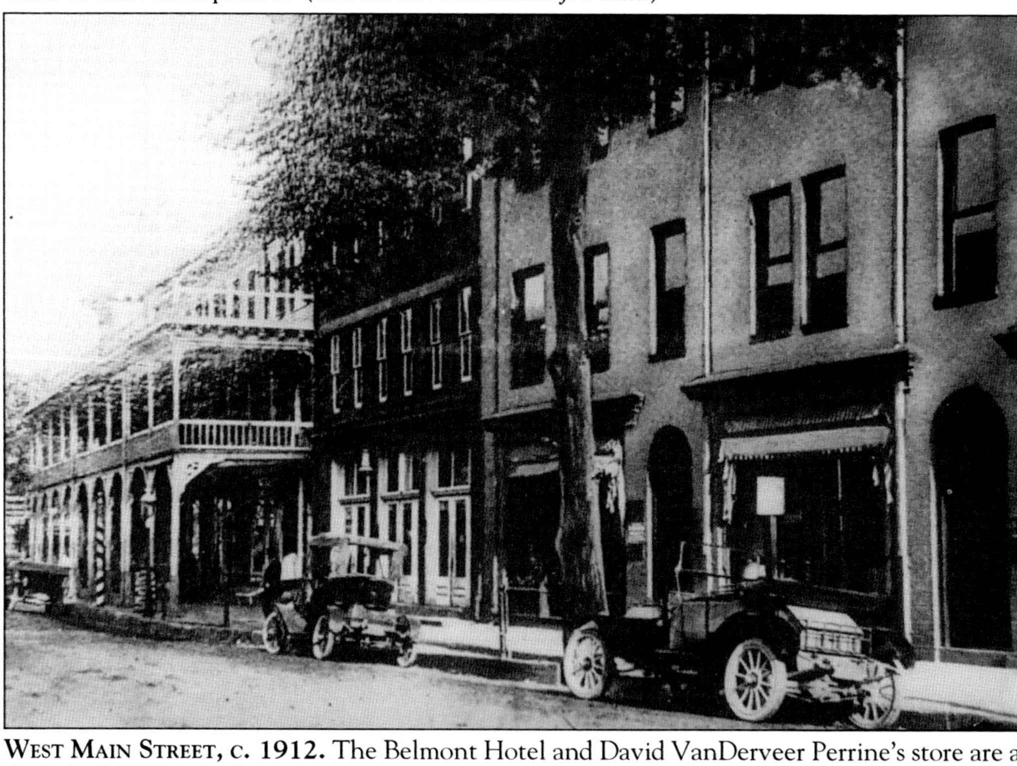

WEST MAIN STREET, C. 1912. The Belmont Hotel and David VanDerveer Perrine's store are at the left. (MCHA Archives.)

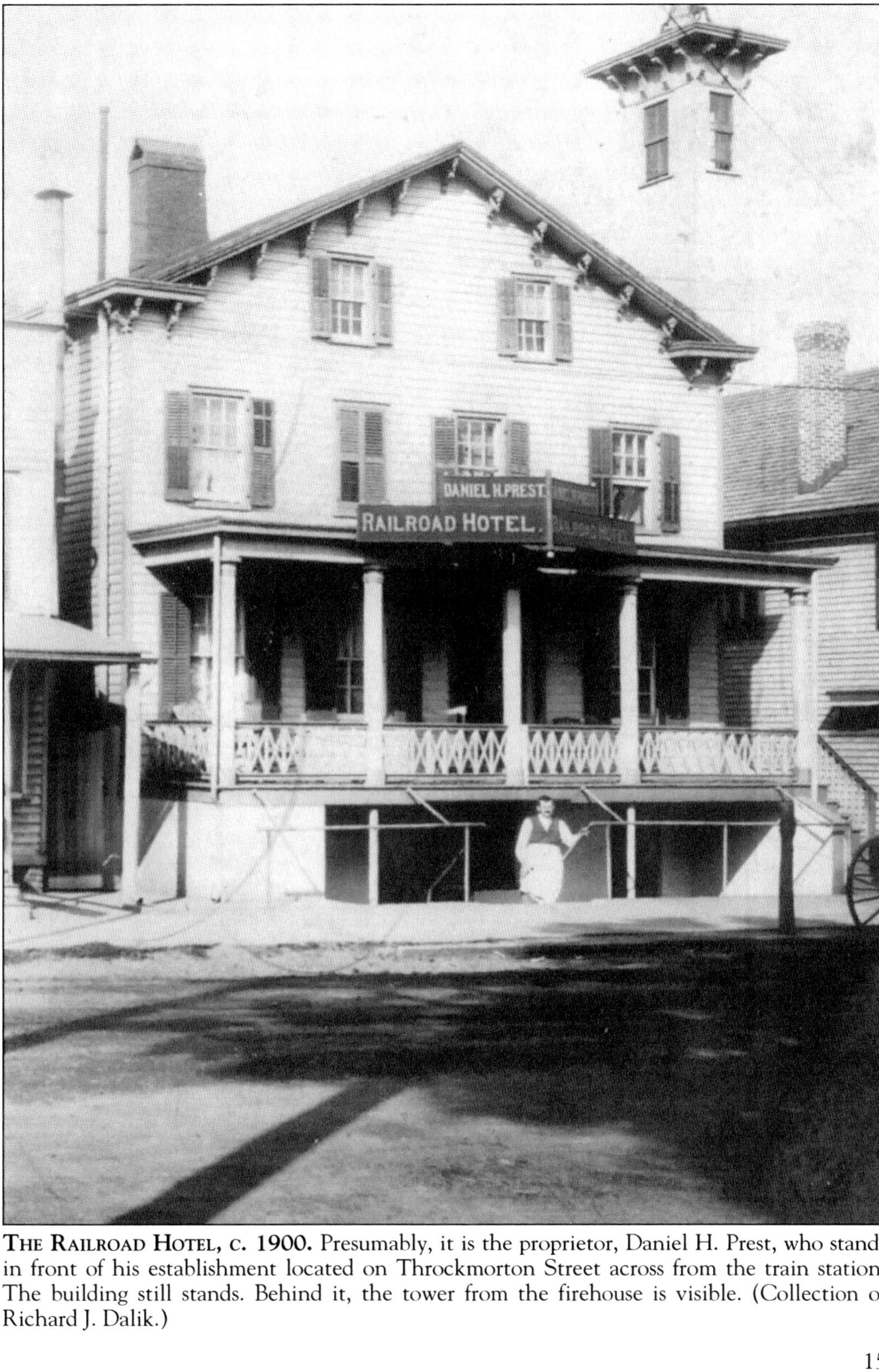

THE RAILROAD HOTEL, c. 1900. Presumably, it is the proprietor, Daniel H. Prest, who stands in front of his establishment located on Throckmorton Street across from the train station. The building still stands. Behind it, the tower from the firehouse is visible. (Collection of Richard J. Dalik.)

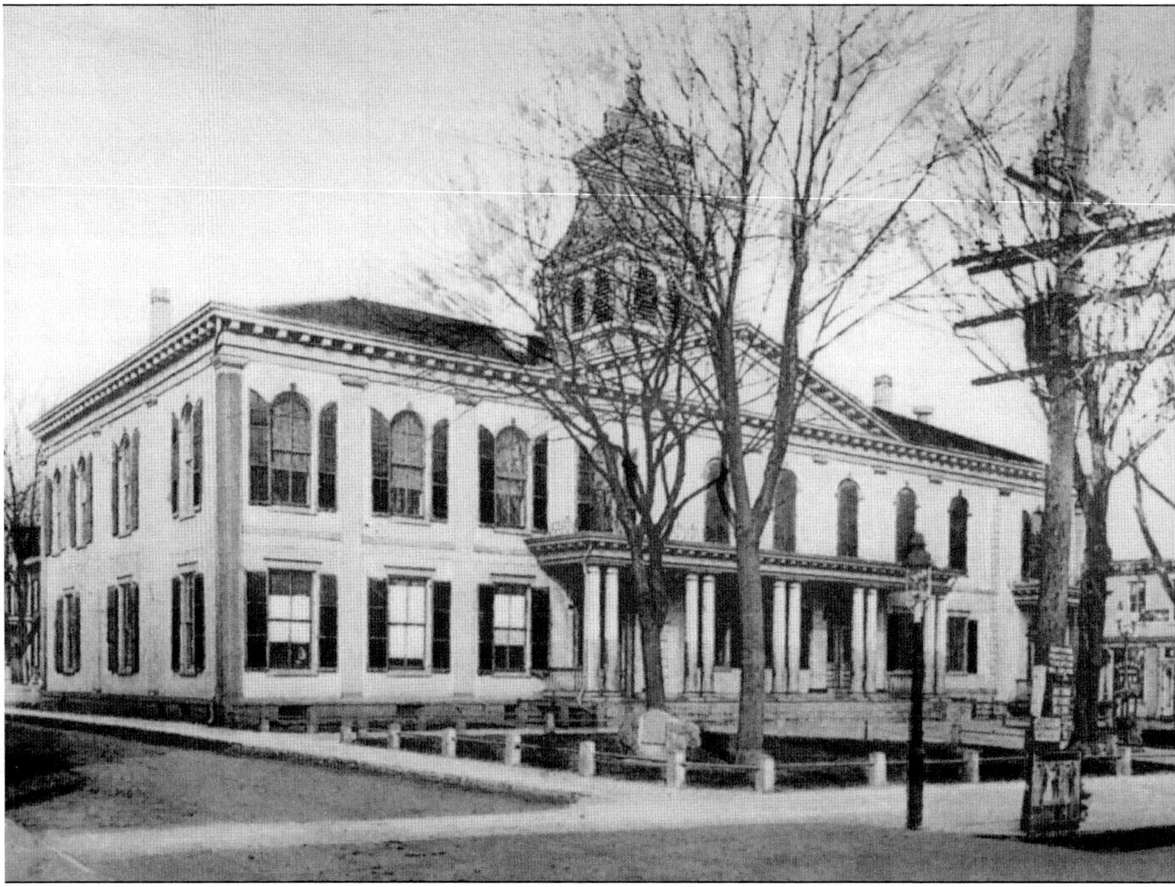

COURT HOUSE SQUARE EAST, C. 1915. This panoramic view of the Courthouse and East Main Street provides a detailed record of the center of town. It was published by J.T.

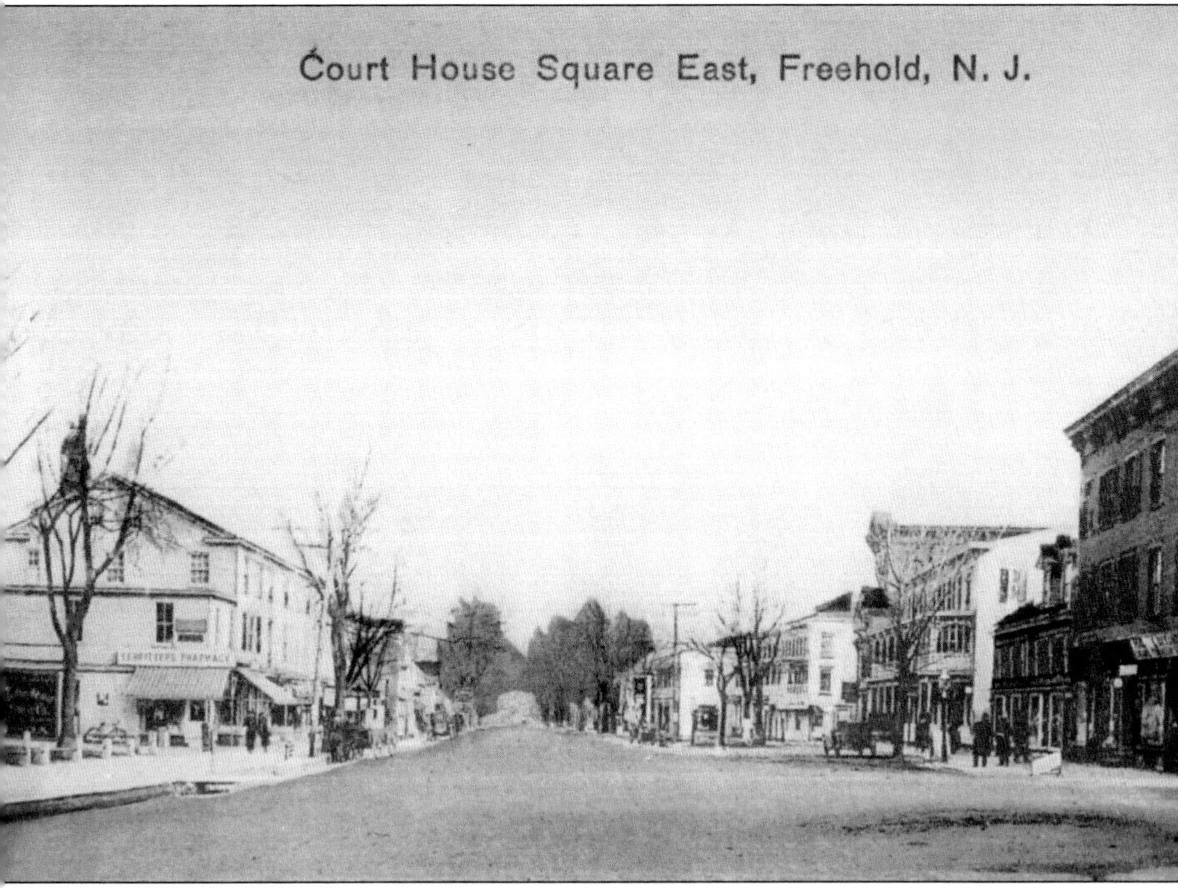

Chesney of Freehold. (Collection of Richard J. Dalik.)

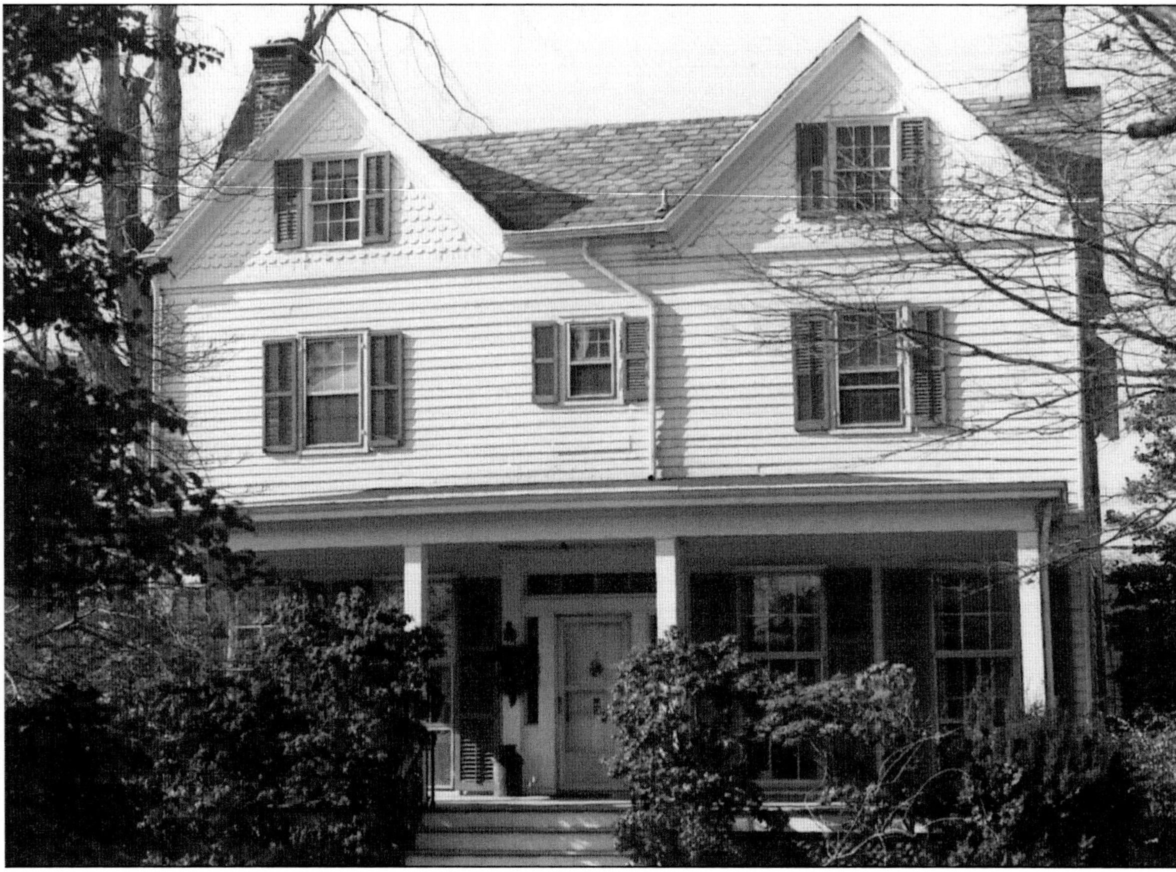

St. Peter's Rectory, built c. 1820–40. One of the earliest houses still standing in downtown Freehold, and the most intact, the rectory first appears in church records in 1843 when it was rented to a Mrs. Abigail Barclay. The building remains in use by the church as office and meeting space and is currently under restoration. (Monmouth County Historic Sites Inventory.)

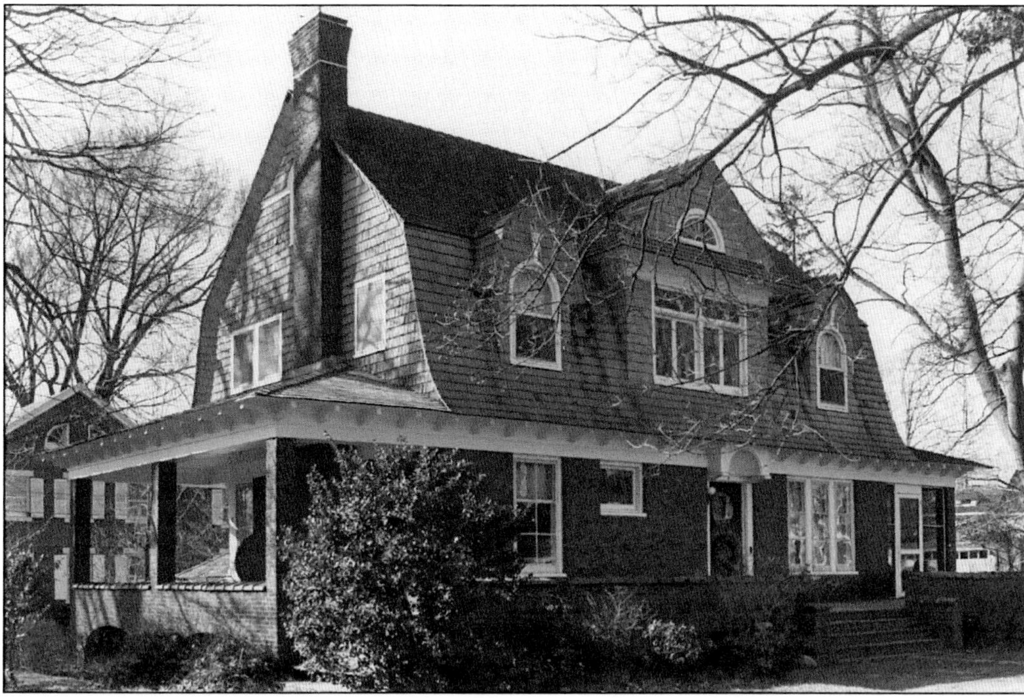

WARREN H. CONOVER HOUSE, BUILT 1897. Freehold-born architect Warren H. Conover designed and built this house for his family. Known for his colonial revival designs, Conover received his degree from Cooper Union and had an office in New York City with his son, J. Hallam Conover, until 1947. (Monmouth County Historic Sites Inventory.)

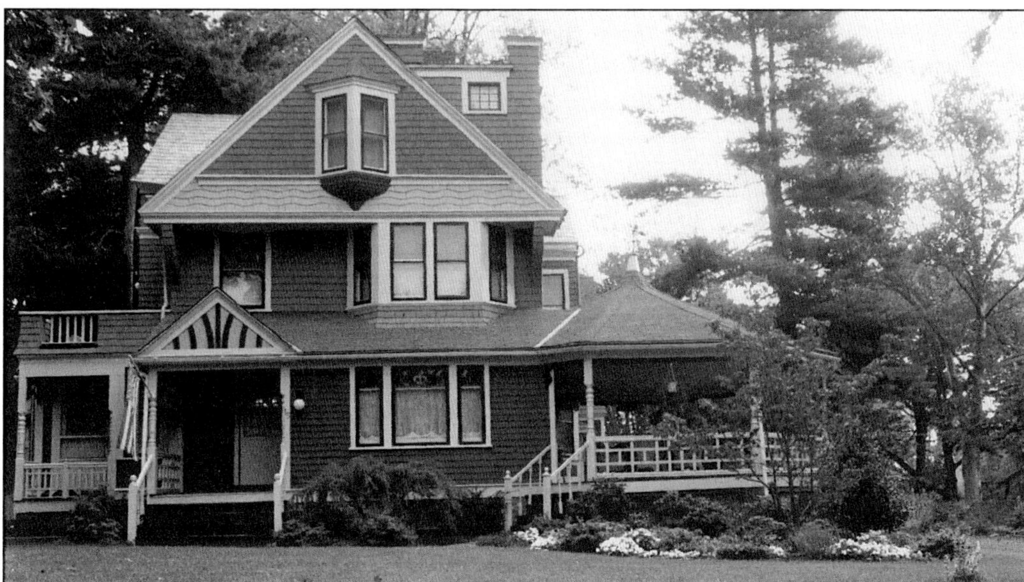

THE HEPBURN HOUSE, BUILT 1855. Dr. William Hepburn, a respected physician in the Freehold area, built this house to serve as his family residence and medical offices. It was also the home of the author "Hepburn Dinwoodie," actually Dr. Hepburn's daughter, who wrote two novels. (Photograph by Visual Expressions. Collection of Jack and Doris Horenkamp.)

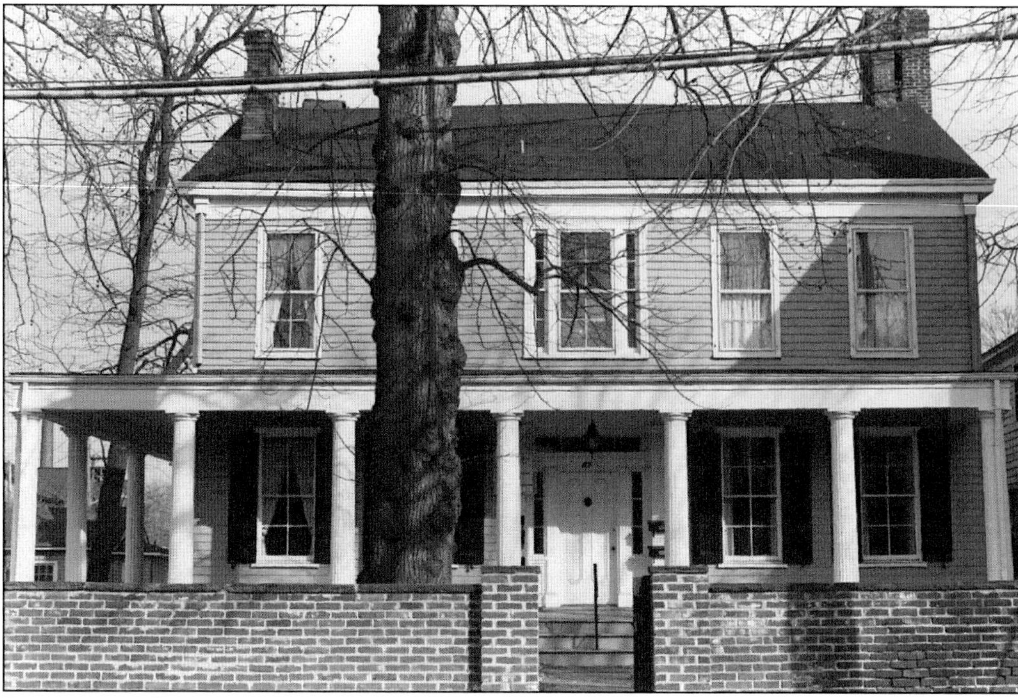

Bennington Randolph House, built c. 1850. Originally built for Bennington Randolph, an attorney and judge, this house was home to Charles Haight, also an attorney, who was elected to the New Jersey General Assembly and later to the U.S. Congress. Haight's daughter Annie married John B. Kerfoot and together they ran an antique shop there, known as "The House with the Brick Wall." (Monmouth County Historic Sites Inventory.)

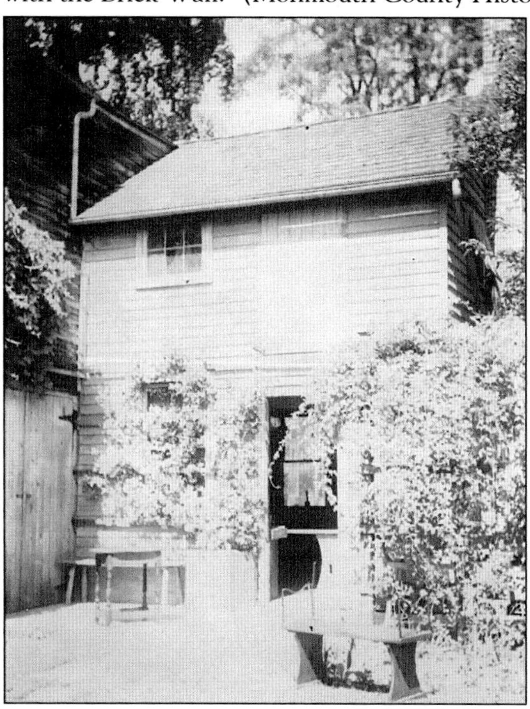

Cabinet Shop, c. 1920. Behind "The House with the Brick Wall," Richard Hornickle refinished and repaired antique furniture for the Kerfoots and for Charles VanDerveer. Freehold was noted for its number and quality of antique dealers who were active in the early 20th century. (Collection of Carl N. Steinberg.)

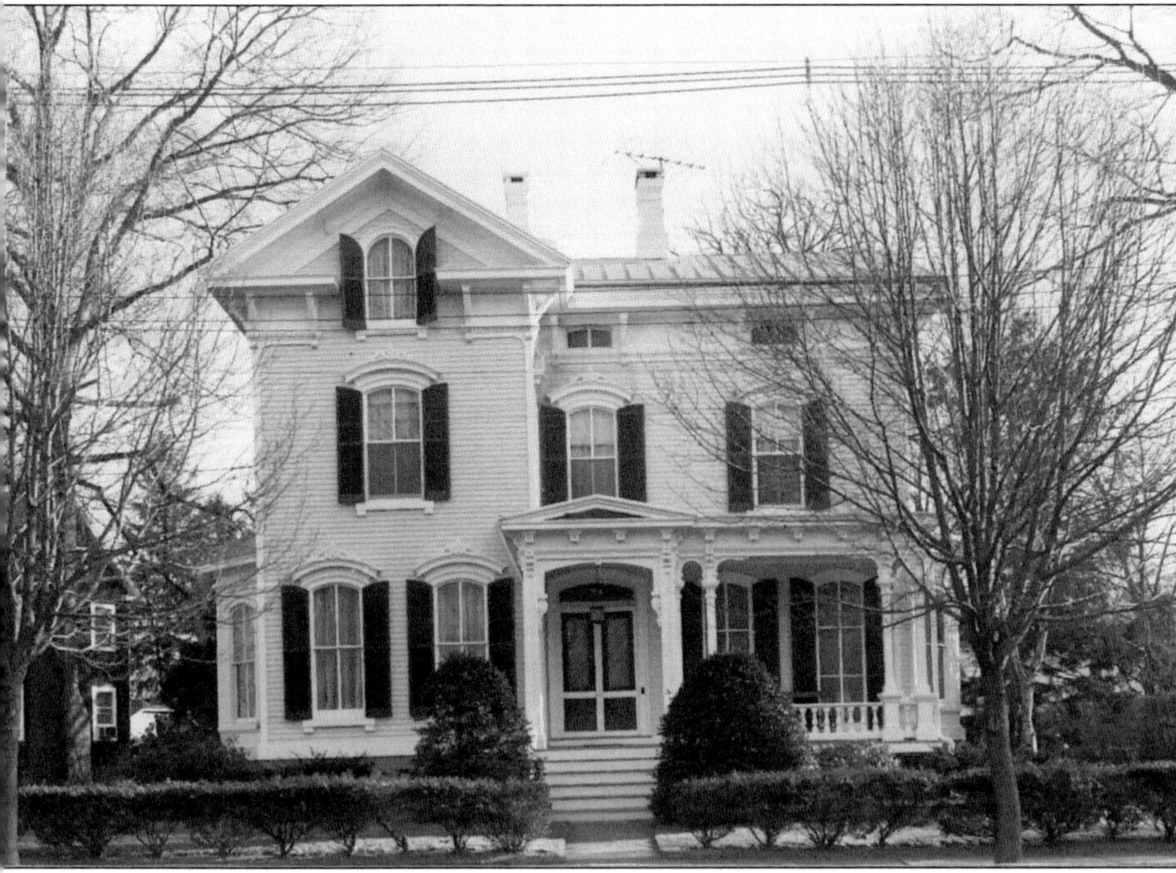

JOSEPH T. LAIRD HOUSE, BUILT C. 1872. Joseph T. Laird married Mary Evans of Fryeburg, ME, in 1872, and they settled into this grand new Italianate-style house on Main Street. Today, it is in extraordinary condition and evokes the elegance and genteel style of 19th-century Freehold. (Monmouth County Historic Sites Inventory.)

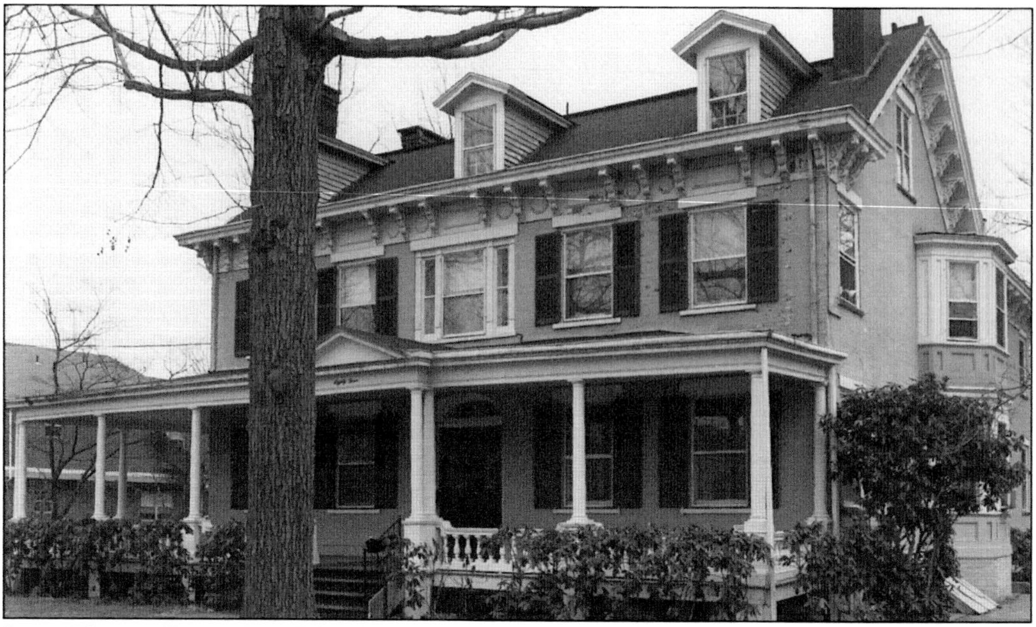

John Wesley Bartleson House, built c. 1836. This brick "mansion," as *Ellis* call it, was built for the co-owner and publisher of the *Monmouth Inquirer* (see *Freehold, Volume I*, p. 10). He was only 30 years old at the time the house was built, but one of the largest landholders in Freehold. Only 11 years later, he sold it to Charles Parker and moved to a farm on the outskirts of Freehold. (Monmouth County Historic Sites Inventory.)

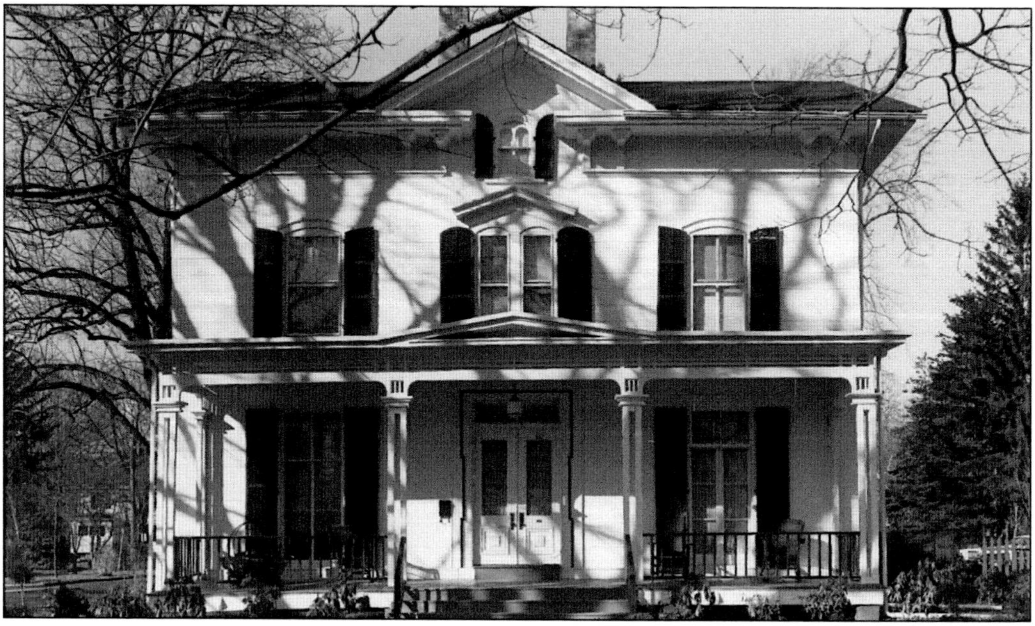

James Sterling Yard House, built 1860s. Yard was the owner and publisher of the *Monmouth Democrat* (see *Freehold, Volume I*, pp. 18 and 65), which he purchased in 1854. He later established the *Long Branch News* in 1866. Yard also served the chairman of the committee that planned and raised funds for the erection of the Battle of Monmouth Monument. (Monmouth County Historic Sites Inventory.)

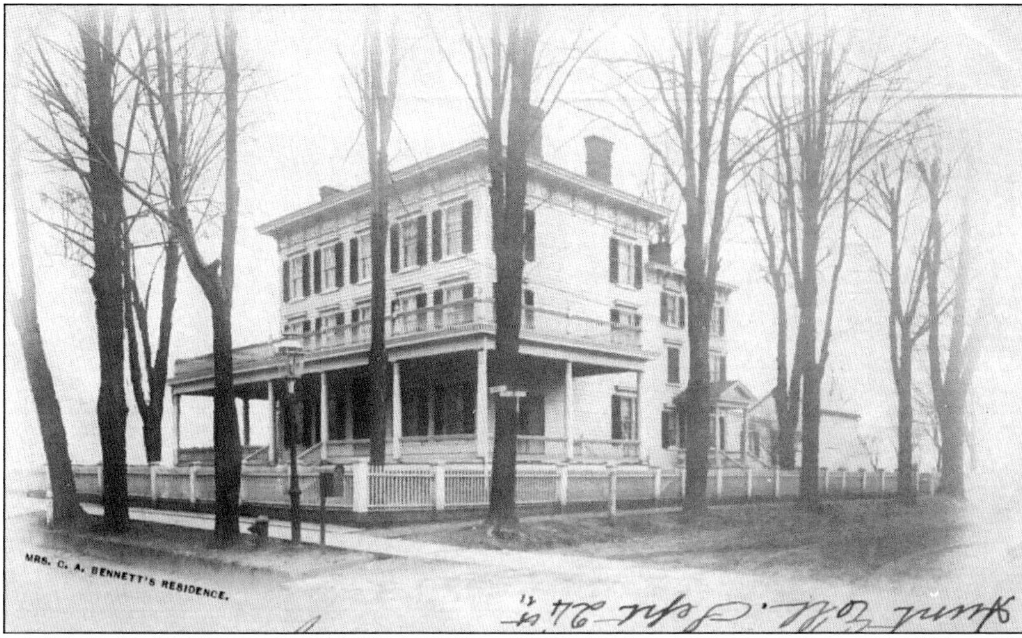

Mrs. Bennett's House, postcard view c. 1907. This house once stood at the corner of East Main and Bennett Streets where the Knights of Columbus building is now. It was not uncommon in the early 20th century to have photographic postcards of one's residence that could be used as note cards. (Collection of Richard J. Dalik.)

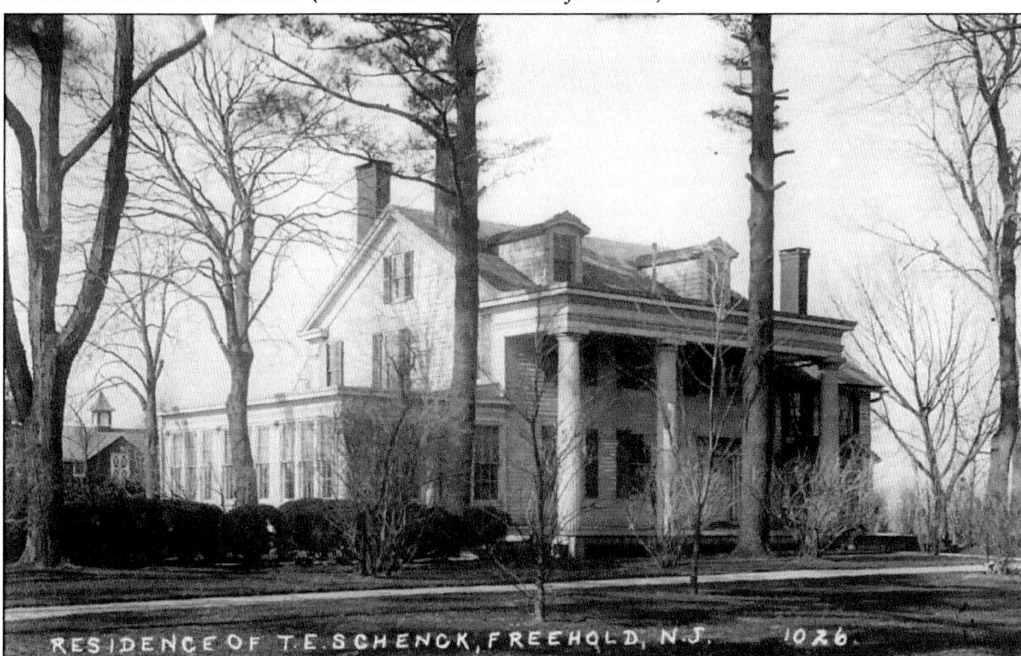

Residence of T.C. Schenck, postcard view c. 1907. Now known as Boxwood Hall, this 1830–55 Greek Revival house with its mid-18th-century wing was moved from its original location to Schenck Street in 1969 in order to make way for the new Courthouse. (Collection of Richard J. Dalik.)

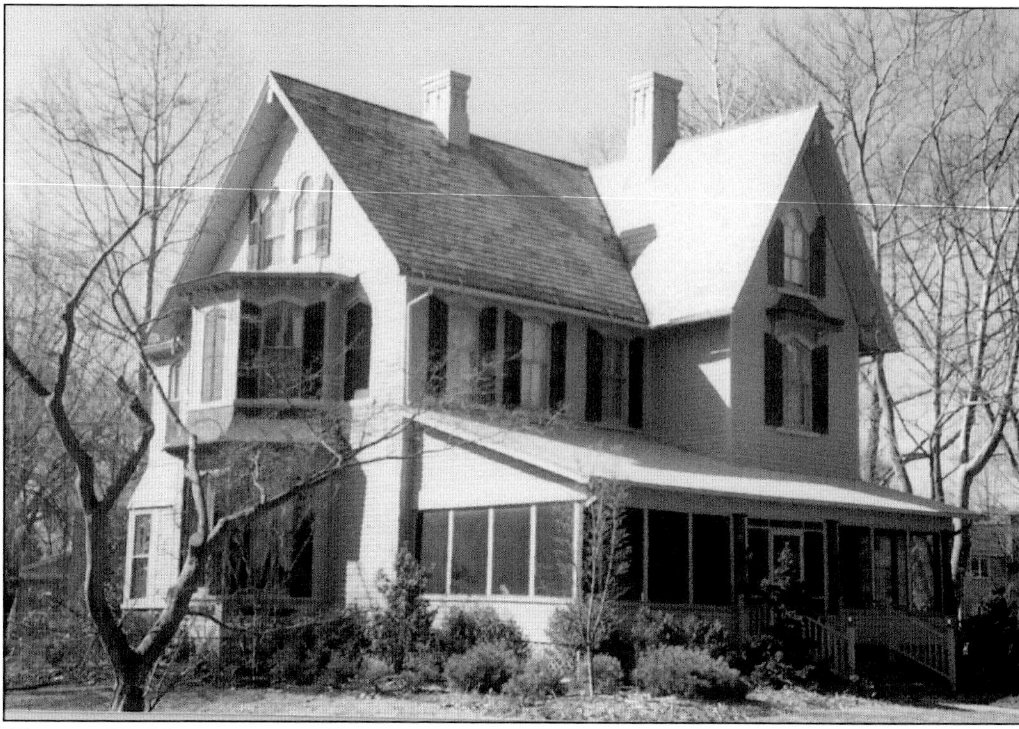

William H. Vredenburgh House, built c. 1870. The son of New Jersey Supreme Court Justice Peter Vredenburgh and the brother of local civil war hero Major Peter Vredenburgh (see *Freehold Volume I*, p. 118), William practiced law in Freehold. This Gothic-style house sits on a tract on Brinkerhoff Street that was once the Monmouth County Fairgrounds. (Collection of Kenneth Kalmis.)

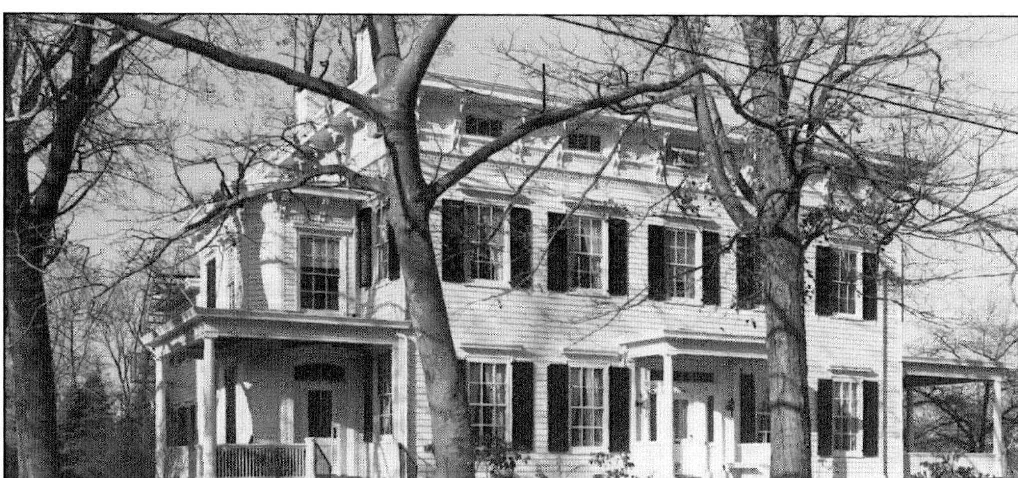

Woodhull House, built c. 1840. Freehold was well known for its institutions of learning and one of the earliest was the Woodhull School, opened in 1844 by William W. and Charles F. Woodhull. Like many of Freehold's large Victorian houses, this one has been converted into office space preserving its residential façade and contributing to the character of Main Street. (Monmouth County Historic Sites Inventory.)

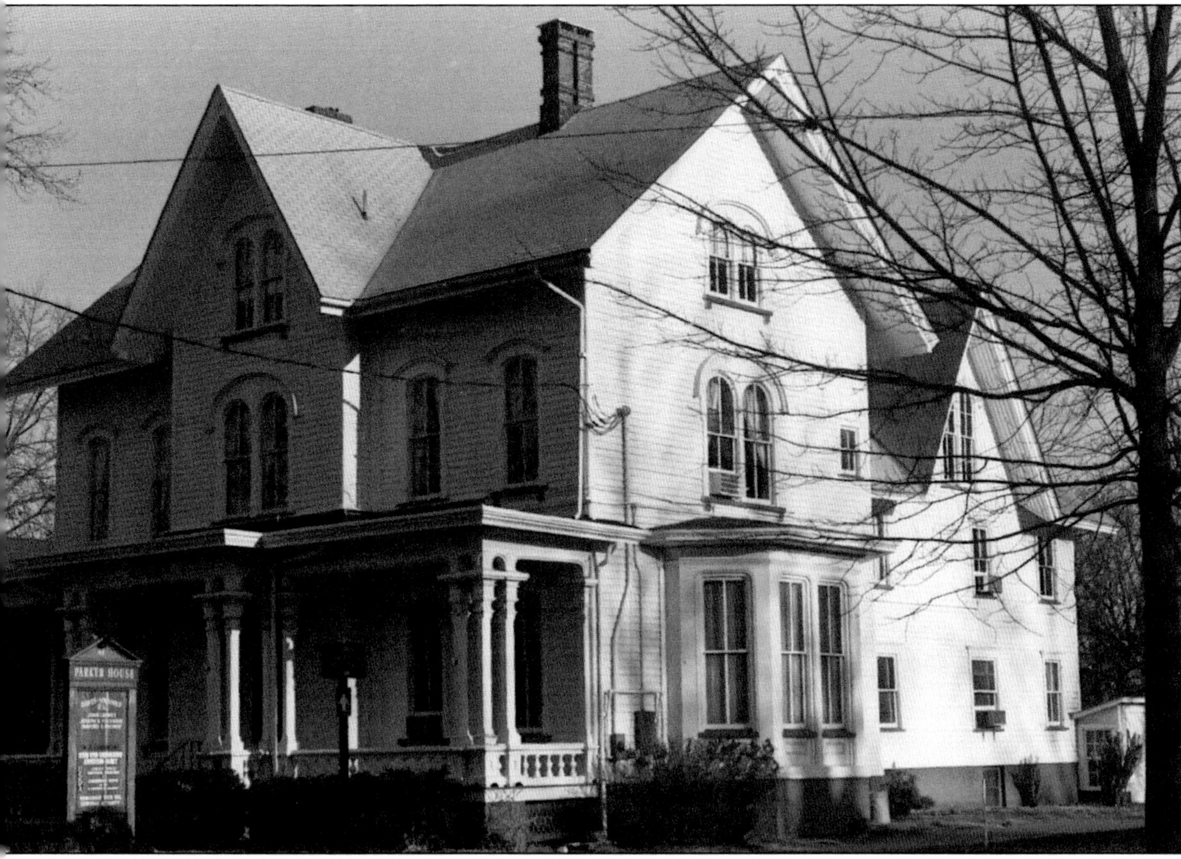

Governor Joel Parker House, built 1860s. Joel Parker, a Freehold native, graduated from Princeton and studied law with Judge Henry W. Green in Trenton. In 1842, after being admitted to the bar, he returned to Freehold to establish his practice. His interest, however, was in political life, and, after serving in the state assembly and several county offices, he was twice elected governor (1863–1866 and 1872–1875). (Monmouth County Historic Sites Inventory.)

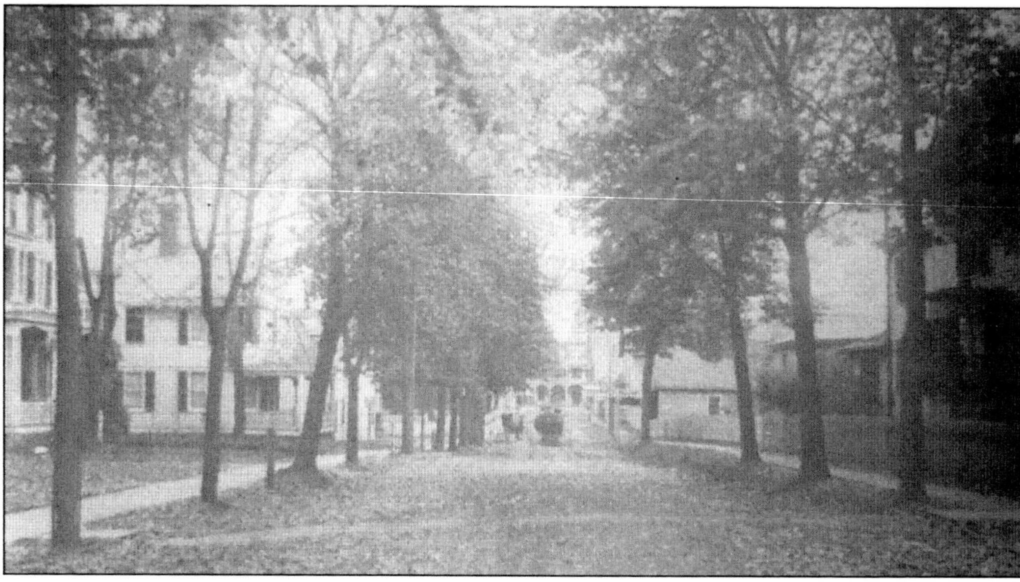

STREET SCENE, c. 1900. The streets of Freehold have long been tree-lined, and in this early view, before the streets were paved, a horse and carriage are visible. (MCHA Archives FR538.)

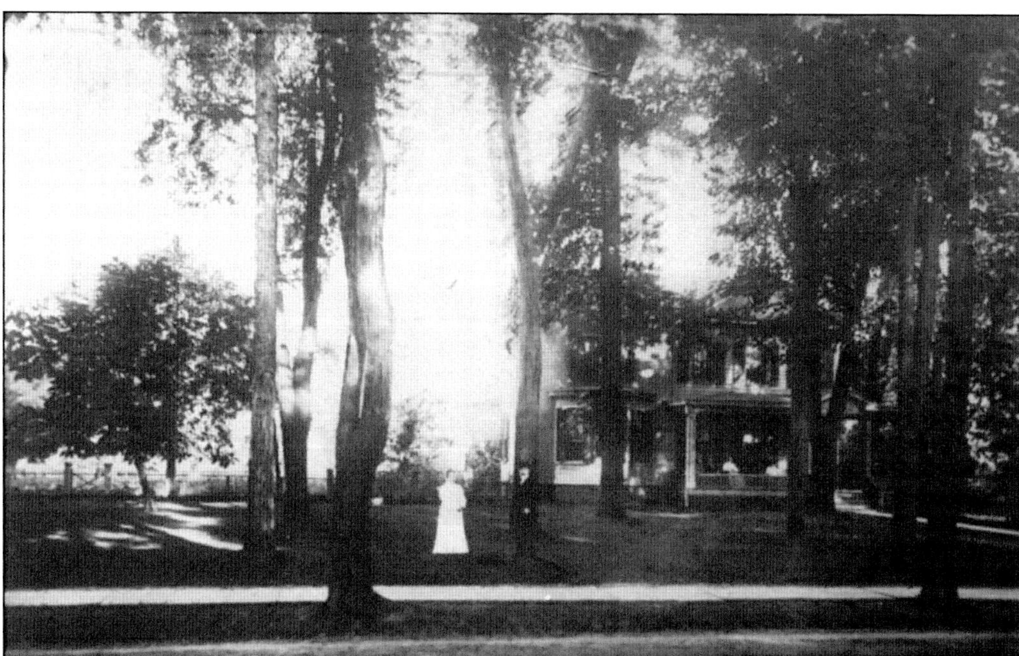

"HAPPY NEW YEAR," c. 1900. Photographer and local historian L.H. Conover took this photograph of an unidentified Freehold house with a woman standing in front of it. As noted earlier, photographic postcards found favor as note cards and were often mailed with brief messages of greetings or thanks. (Collection of Richard J. Dalik.)

Two

Sports and Leisure

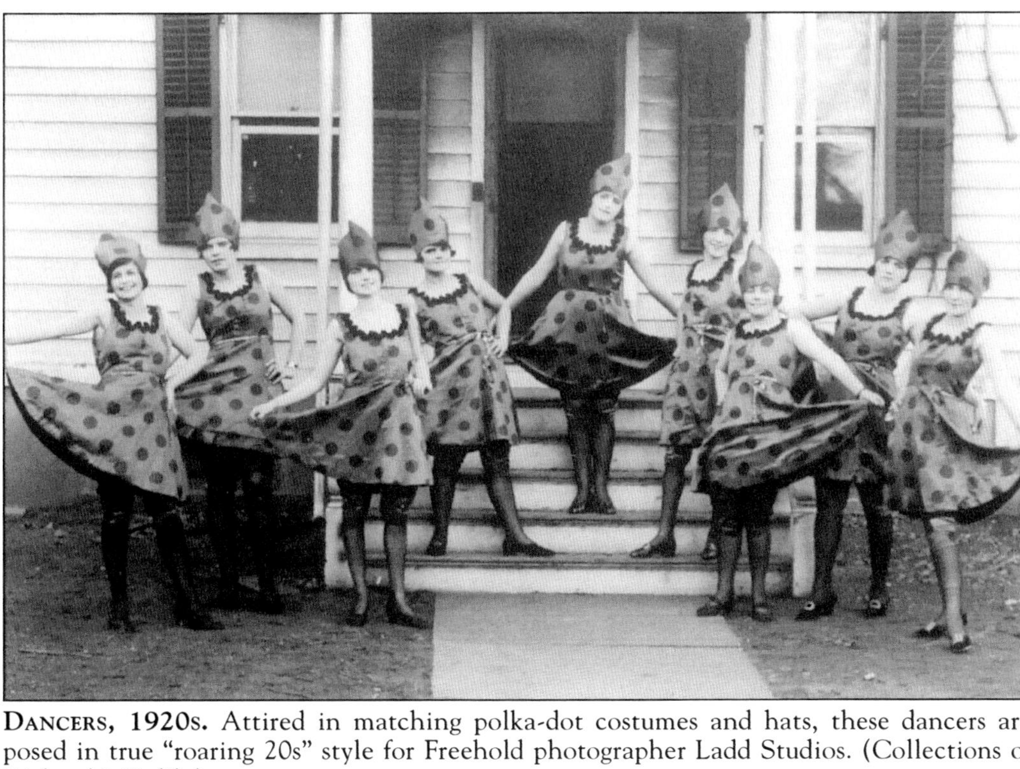

Dancers, 1920s. Attired in matching polka-dot costumes and hats, these dancers are posed in true "roaring 20s" style for Freehold photographer Ladd Studios. (Collections of Richard J. Dalik.)

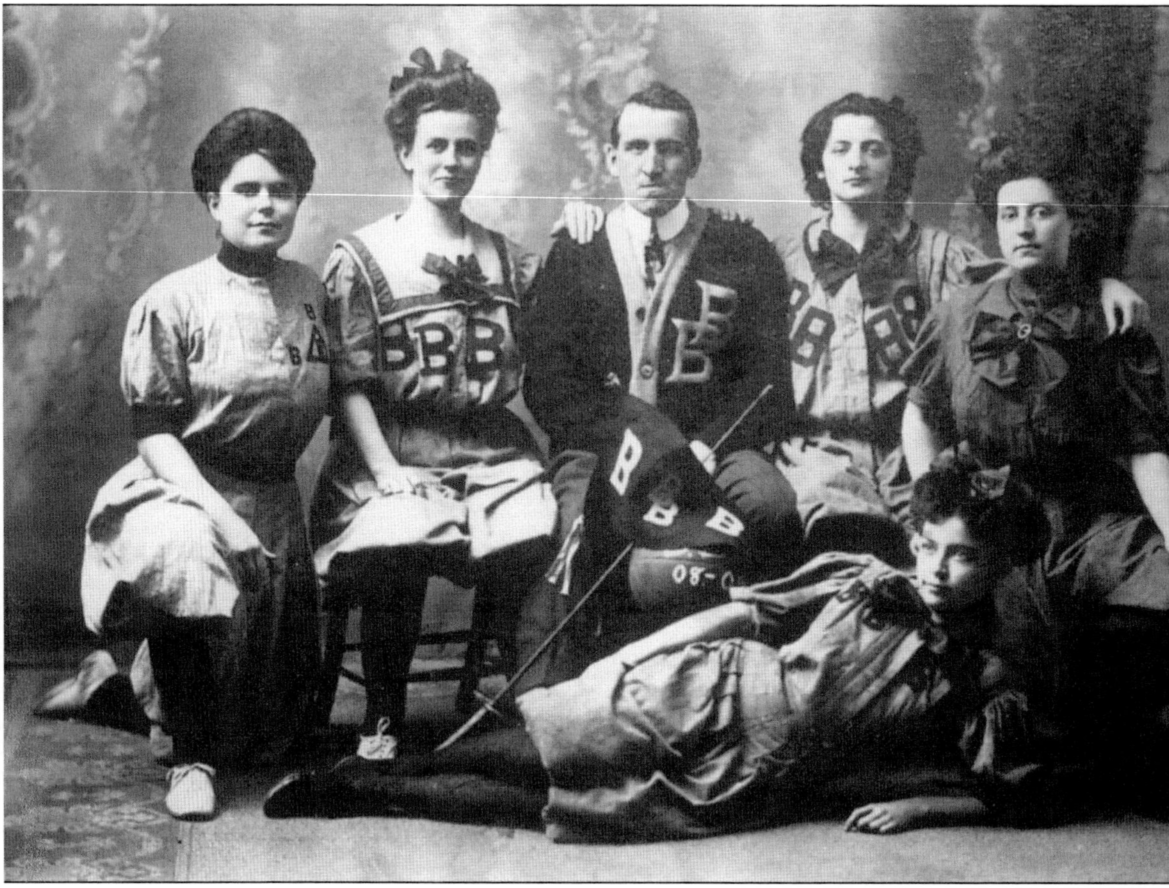

Women's Basketball Team, 1908. With their coach are five members of the women's 1908 basketball team sponsored by Brakeley's Canning Factory (see pp. 54-57). In the early years of the 20th century, women's team sports grew in popularity and like men's local sports teams, were sponsored by businesses, clubs, or other community organizations. (Photograph by Hall Studio, Freehold. Collection of Carl N. Steinberg.)

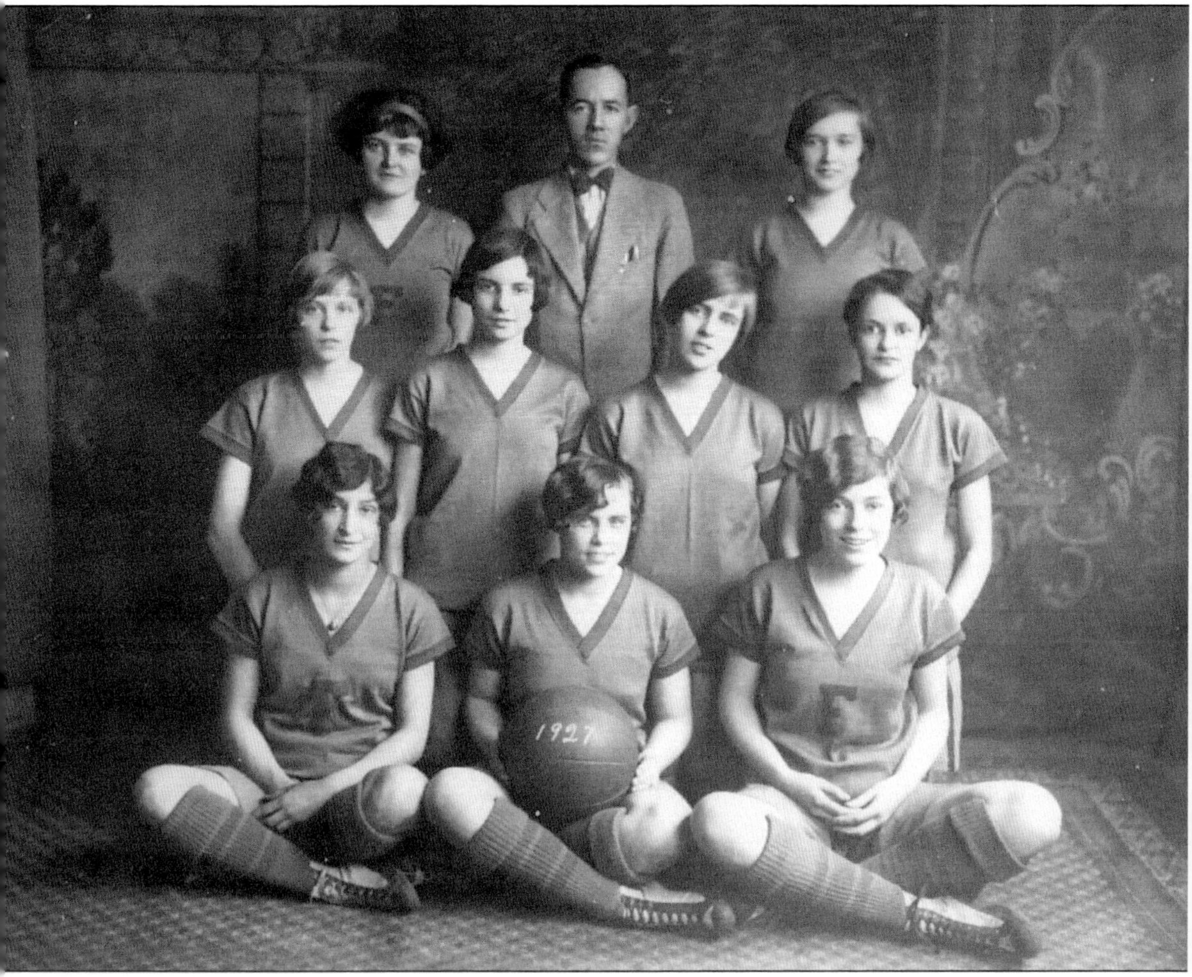

WOMEN'S BASKETBALL TEAM, 1927. This is a particularly engaging photograph of Coach William Eldridge and his Freehold High School players. Identified on the reverse are, Edna (Taft) Palmer, Dorothy Baird, Bea (Throckmorton) VanDerveer, Dot (Morris) Soden, Lucy Bell Dittmar, Ms. Deedmeyer, Lena (Reynolds) Benton, Ms. Lott, and Helen Ame—what a difference in uniforms from the photograph on the facing page! (Collection of Carl N. Steinberg.)

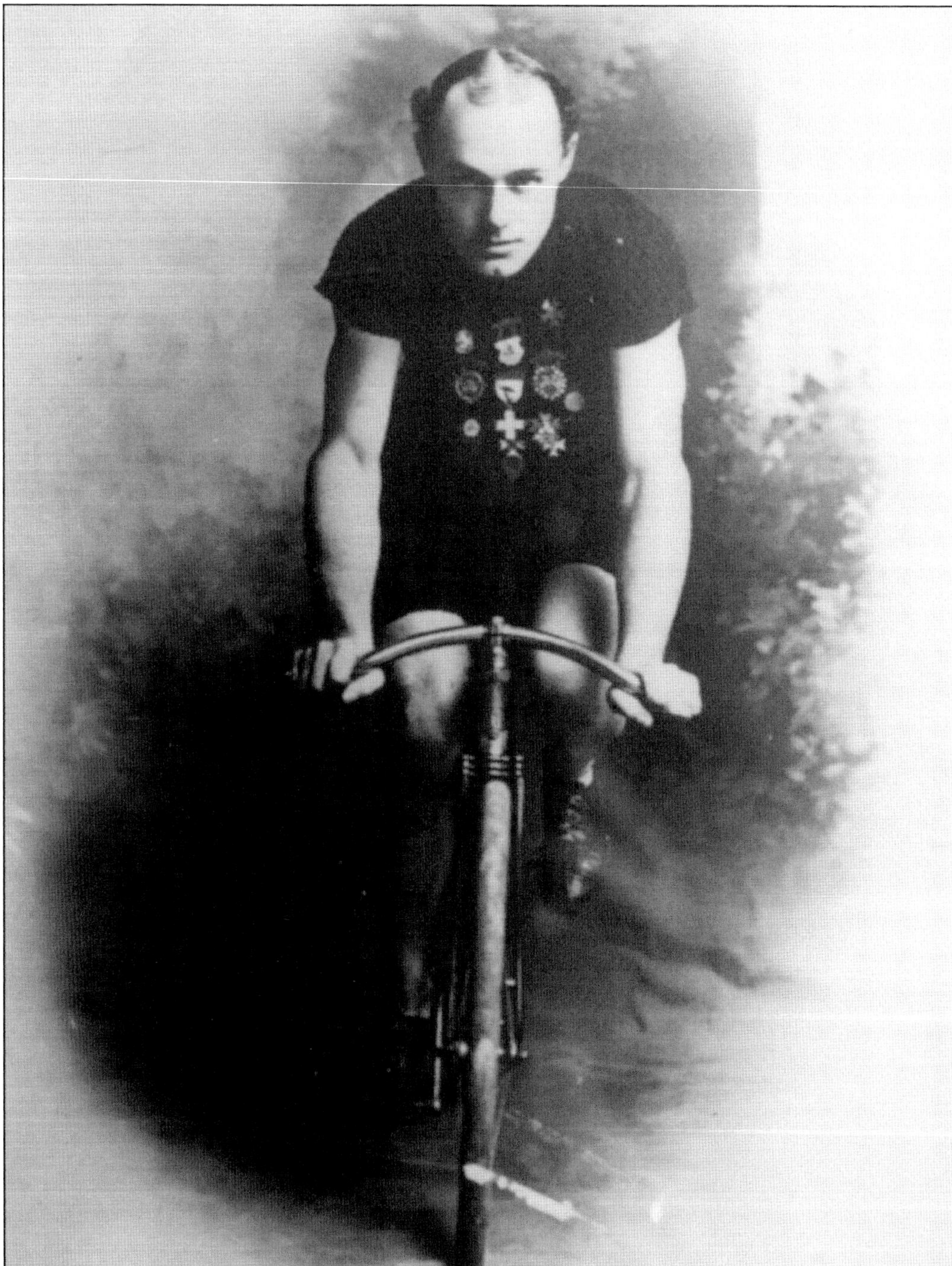

ARTHUR A. ZIMMERMAN, 1880s. Described by the press as one of the best athletes in the world, Freehold resident Zimmerman poses with some of his medals. In the year 1894, just before his retirement, he placed first in over 100 races in England, France, Germany, Ireland, and Belgium and can truly be considered an international superstar. (Collection of Carl N. Steinberg.)

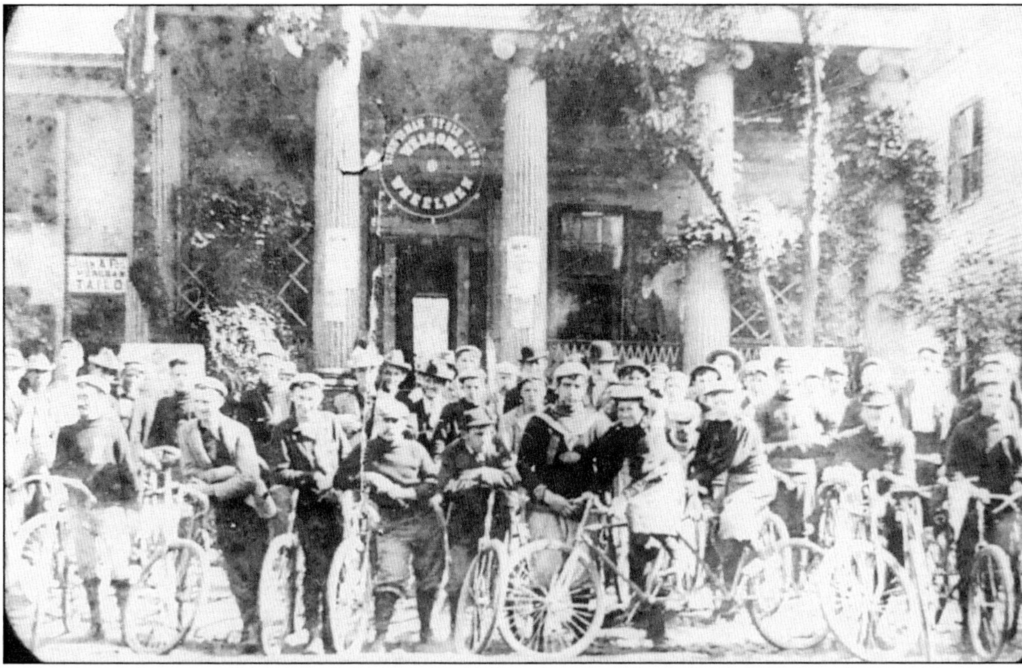

ZIMMERMAN CYCLE CLUB, C. 1900. The "Wheelers" were photographed on West Main Street before an outing. Arthur Zimmerman actively promoted his sport in this community, and numerous newspaper articles chronicle the adventures of the club that he sponsored. (MCHA Archives.)

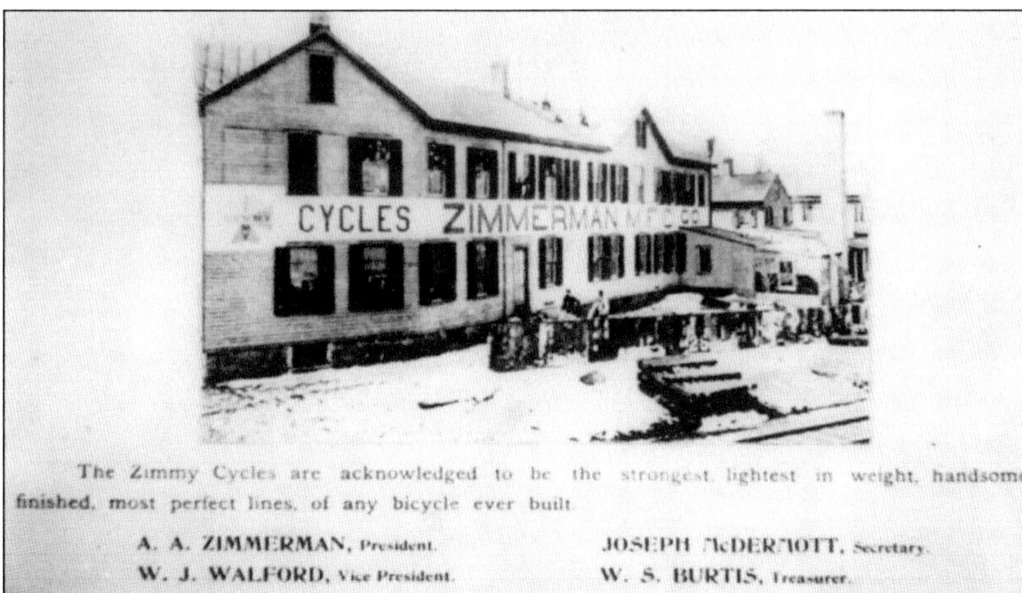

ZIMMERMAN MANUFACTURING COMPANY, C. 1895. Arthur Zimmerman opened his cycle factory on Elm Street in 1895 and manufactured several models of his "Zimmy" bicycle. A rare example can be seen at the Metz Bicycle Museum, recently opened behind 54 W. Main Street. (Collection of Carl N. Steinberg.)

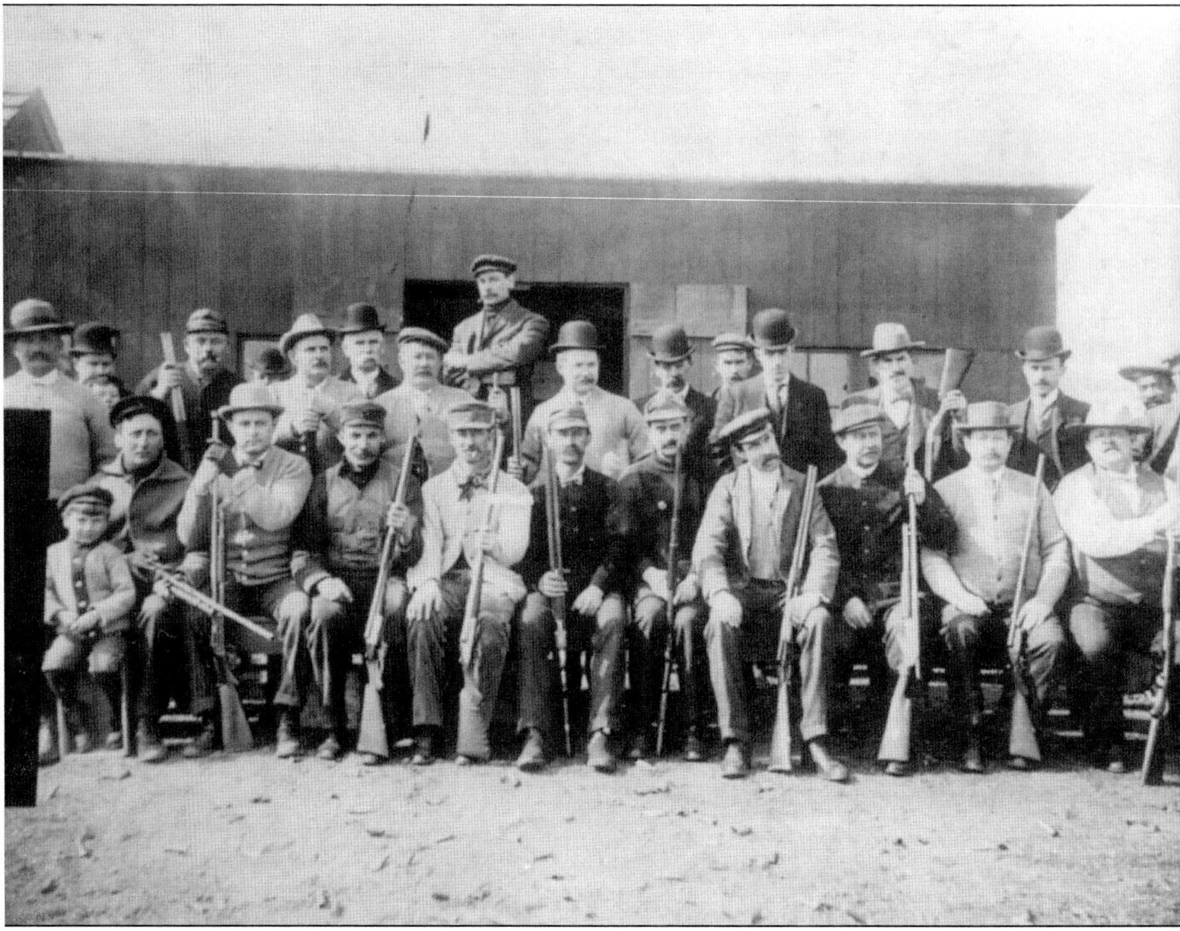

Freehold Gun Club, 1908. The Freehold Gun Club held the state championship from 1906 to 1913, and on March 5, 1908, when this photograph was taken, Edgar VanDerveer won the straight-run prize by breaking 57 clay pigeons in a row. (Collection of Carl N. Steinberg.)

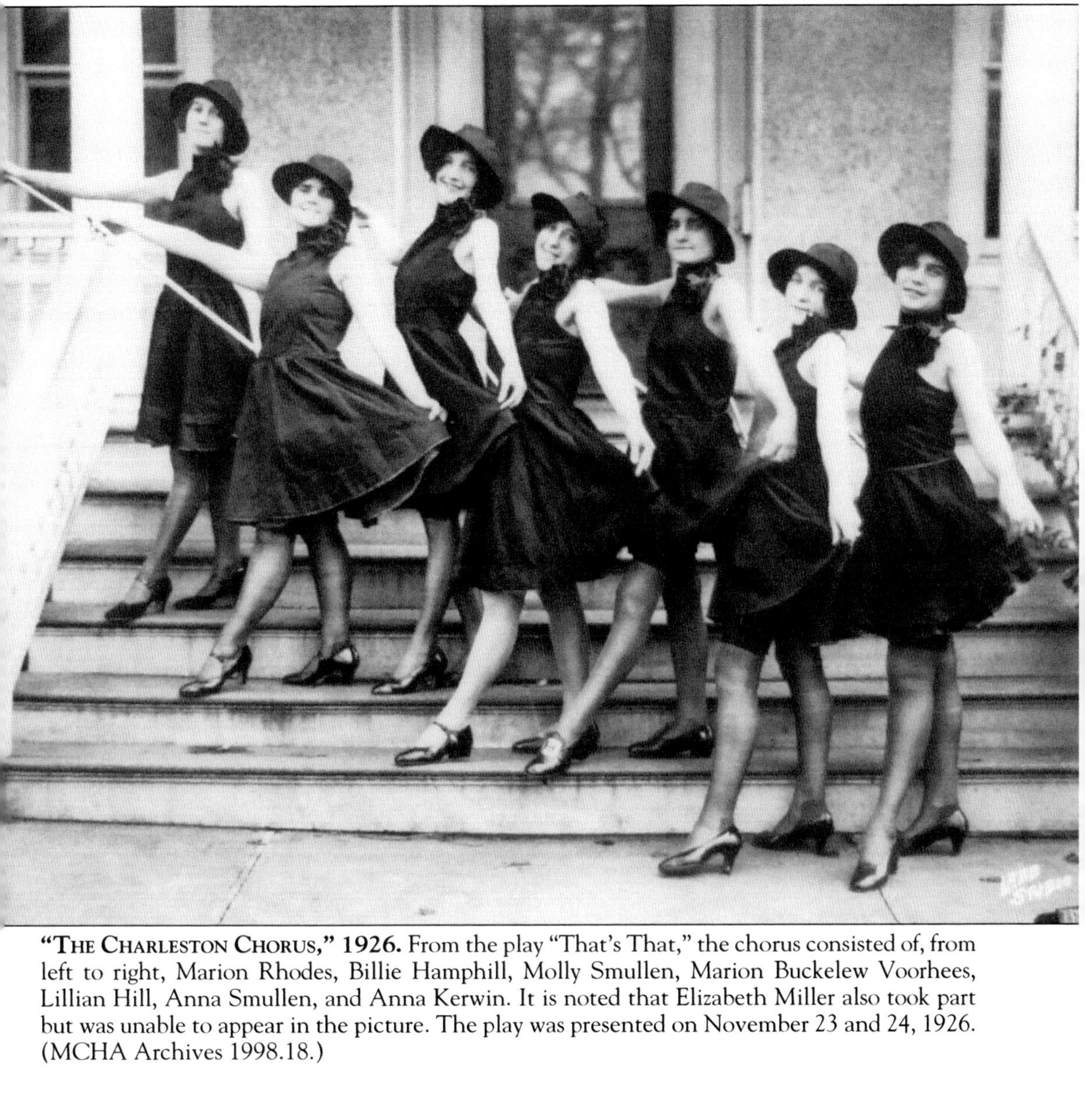

"THE CHARLESTON CHORUS," 1926. From the play "That's That," the chorus consisted of, from left to right, Marion Rhodes, Billie Hamphill, Molly Smullen, Marion Buckelew Voorhees, Lillian Hill, Anna Smullen, and Anna Kerwin. It is noted that Elizabeth Miller also took part but was unable to appear in the picture. The play was presented on November 23 and 24, 1926. (MCHA Archives 1998.18.)

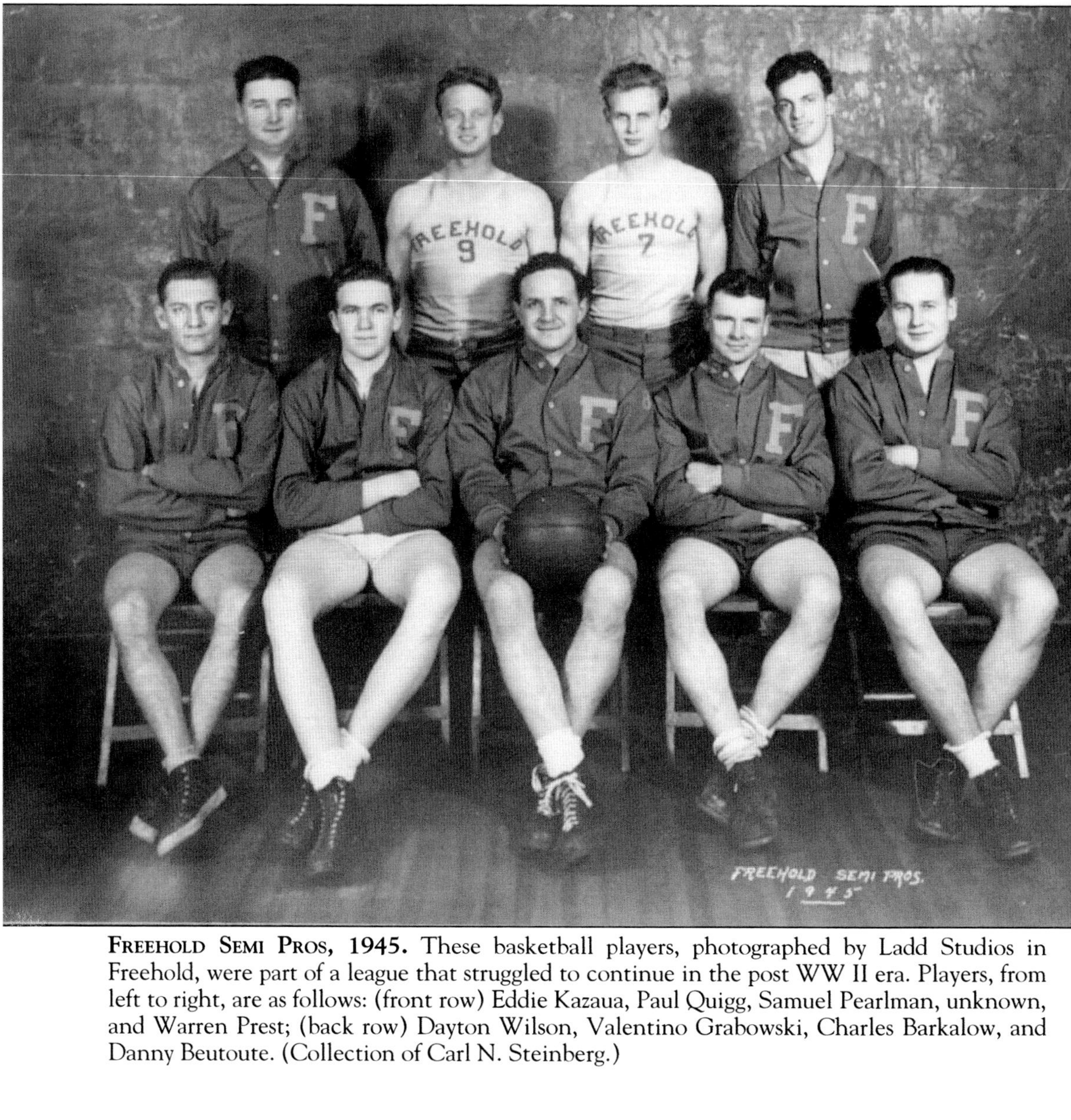

FREEHOLD SEMI PROS, 1945. These basketball players, photographed by Ladd Studios in Freehold, were part of a league that struggled to continue in the post WW II era. Players, from left to right, are as follows: (front row) Eddie Kazaua, Paul Quigg, Samuel Pearlman, unknown, and Warren Prest; (back row) Dayton Wilson, Valentino Grabowski, Charles Barkalow, and Danny Beutoute. (Collection of Carl N. Steinberg.)

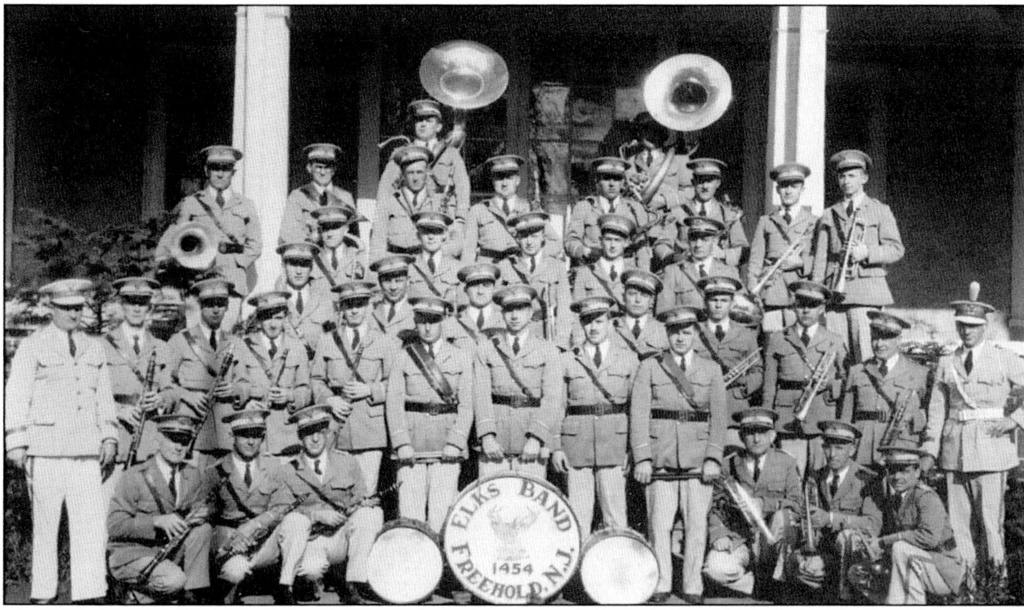

ELKS BAND, C. 1950S. The sizable Elks Marching Band provided a mainstay in the many parades down Main Street for which Freehold was well known. (Collection of Carl N. Steinberg.)

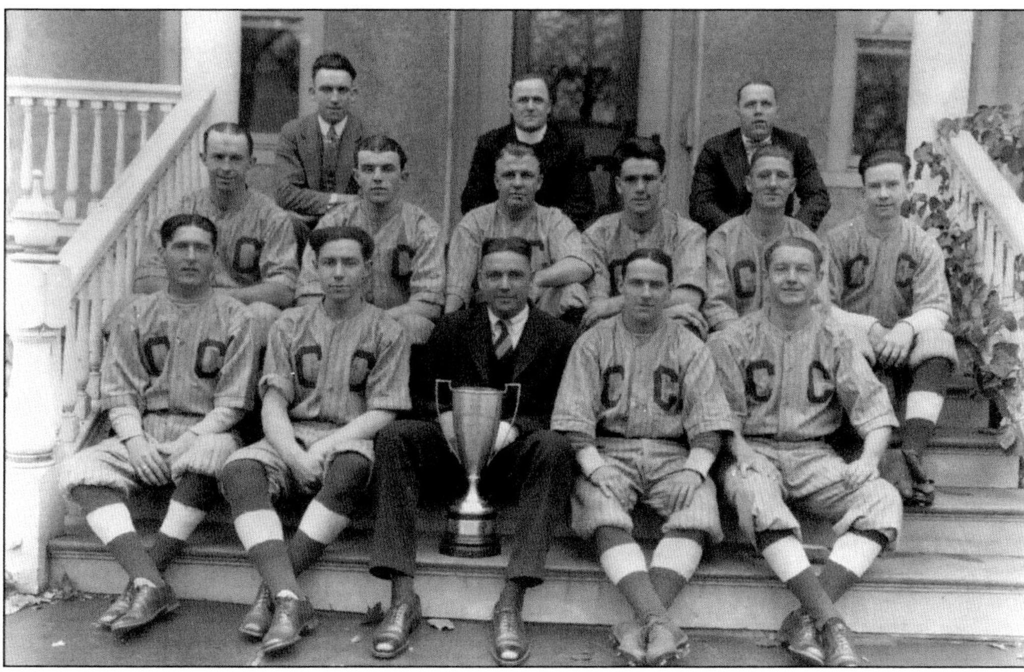

KNIGHTS OF COLUMBUS BASEBALL TEAM, LATE 1920S. During the early years of the 20th century, local sports teams provided the community with a primary source of entertainment. The players' jerseys bear the letters "CC" for Columbian Club. A number of the players have been identified, including Gilday Freeman, Bill Rhoades, Hank Coyne, Con Clancy, Jack Queeney, Slats Carey, Raymond Sheehan, Vince Fox, Joseph Kennedy, and Father E.J. Heil of St. Rose. (Collection of Kevin Coyne.)

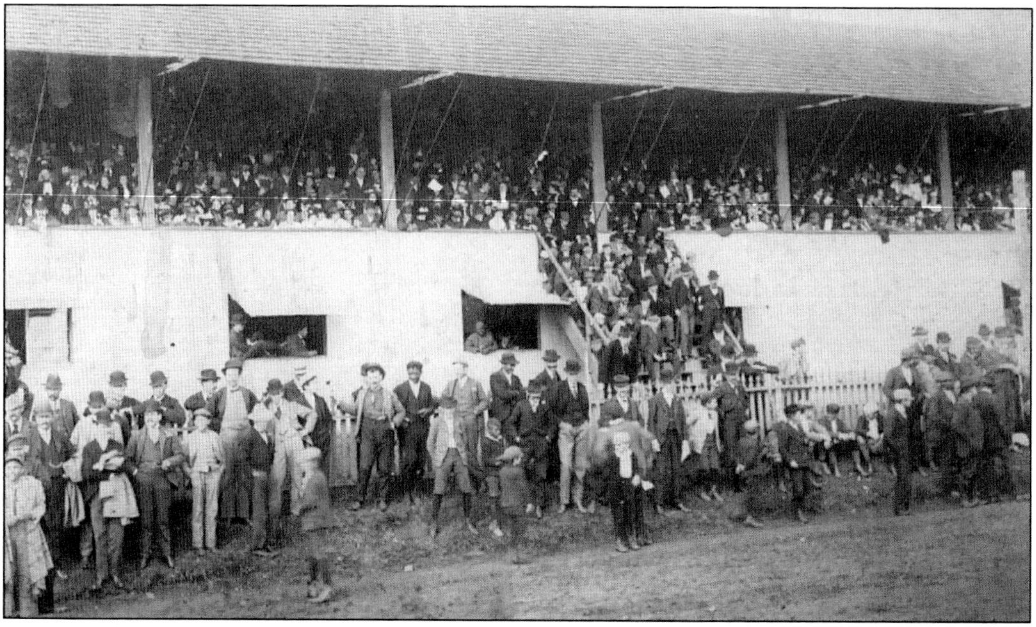

Grand Stand at the Fair Grounds, c. 1920s. Spectators watch as the horses approach the grand stand on Decoration Day (Memorial Day) at the Monmouth County Fairgrounds, which were located off Brinkerhoff Street. (Collection of Carl N. Steinberg.)

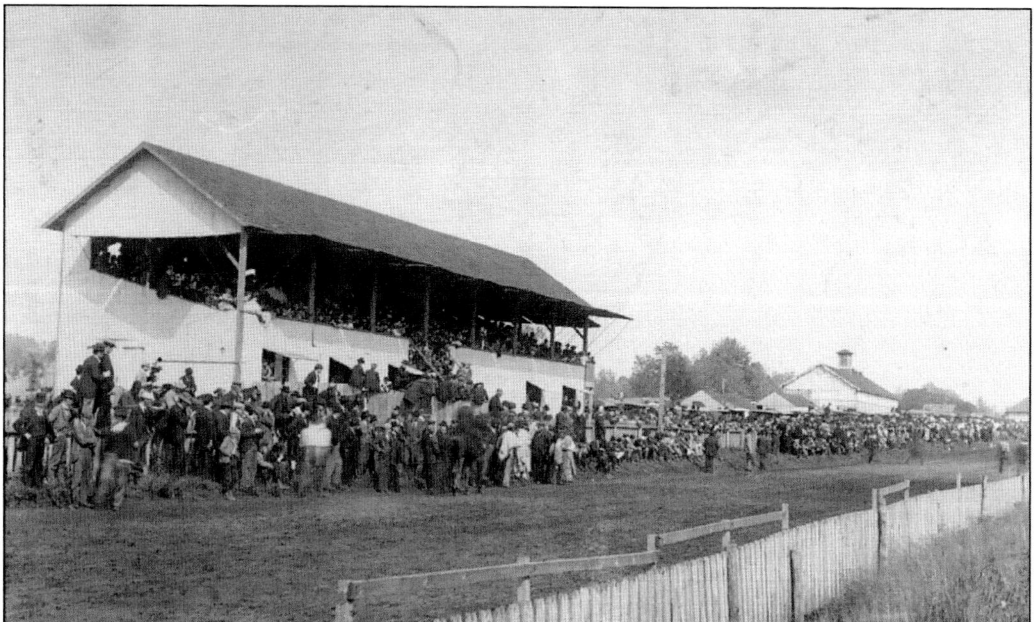

Grand Stand at the Fair Grounds, c. 1920s. The large wooden framed grandstand at the county fairgrounds offered under-cover seating for hundreds and also accommodated vendors in space below. (Collection of Carl N. Steinberg.)

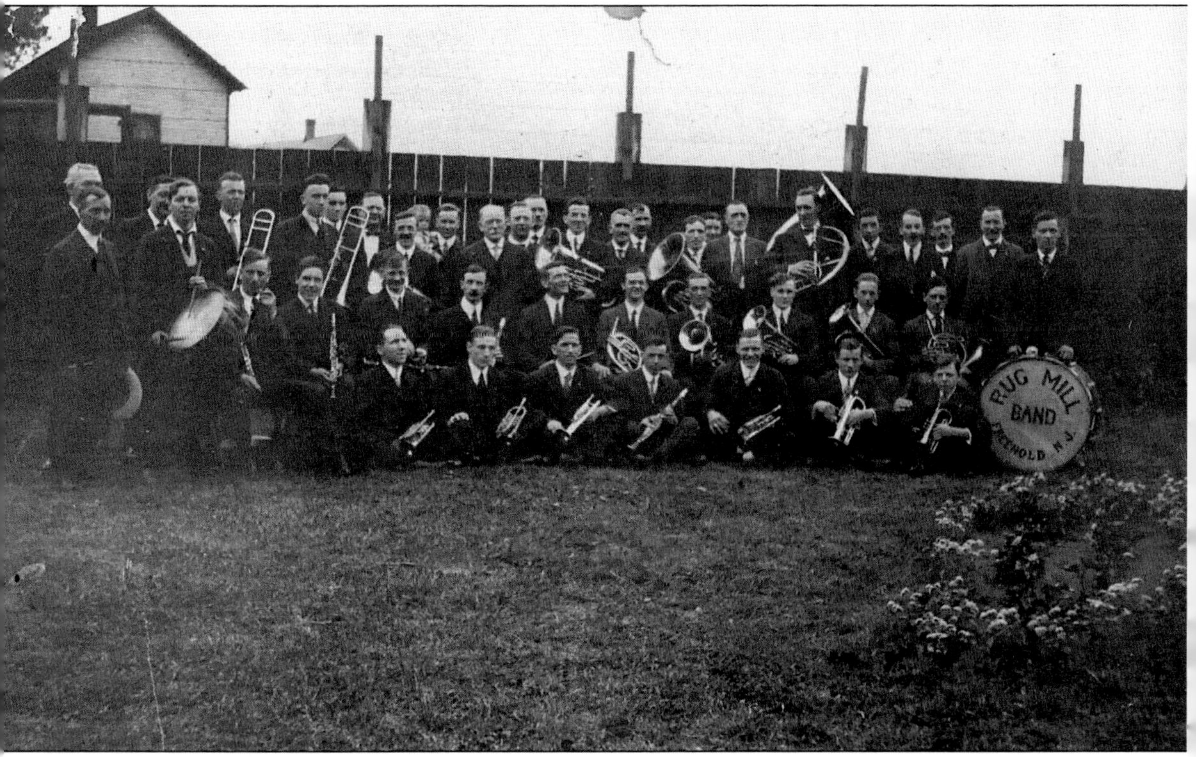

RUG MILL BAND, C. 1930S. The economic heart of Freehold, the A & M Karagheusian Rug Mill operated from 1905 to 1965 and employed nearly half of the work force of the town at one time. Employee organizations such as this one (see also p. 39) reinforced the strong sense of community that Rug Mill workers enjoyed. (Collection of Kevin Coyne.)

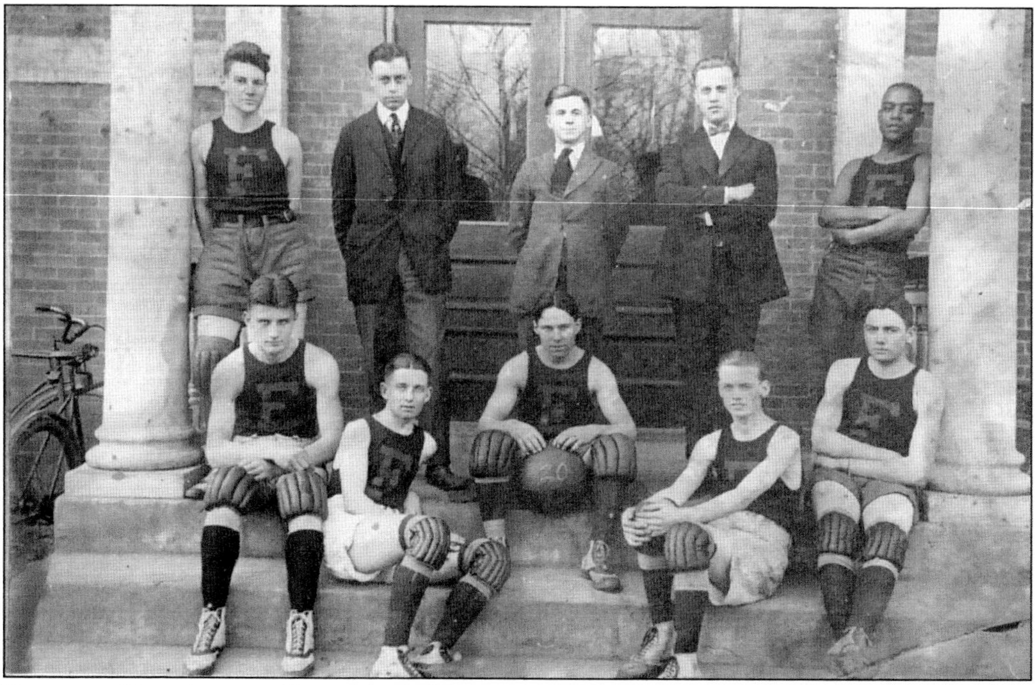

Freehold High School Basketball Team, 1920. Lounging on the front steps of the high school on Hudson Street, team members, wearing their kneepads, look ready for a game. (Collection of Carl N. Steinberg.)

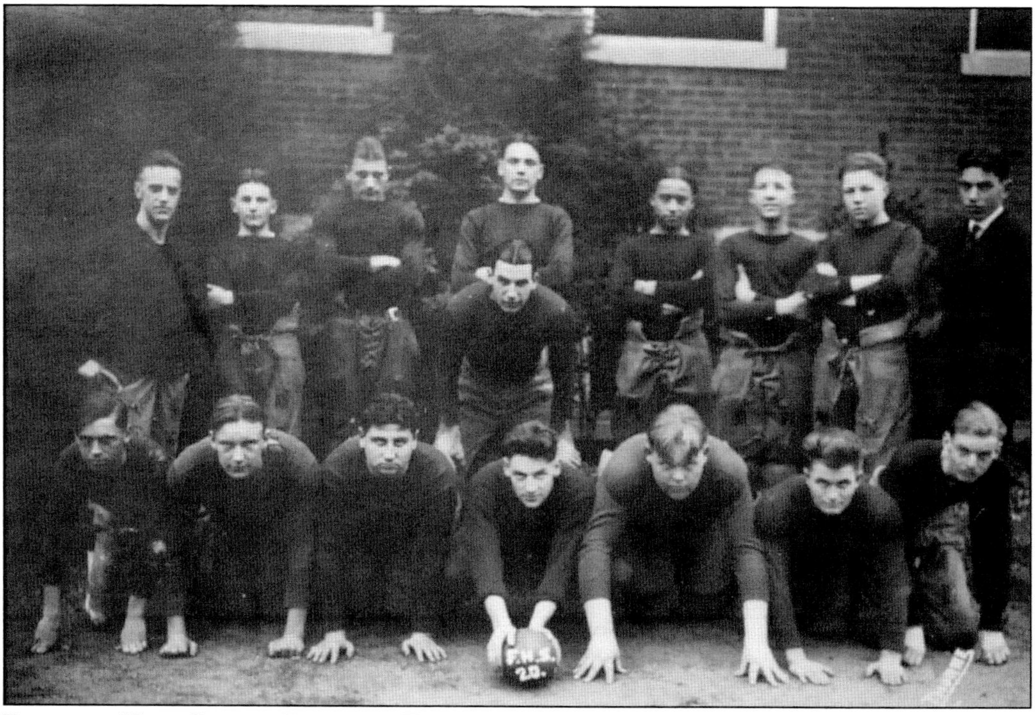

Freehold High School Football Team, 1920. Members of the high school football team look equally ready for play. (Collection of Carl N. Steinberg.)

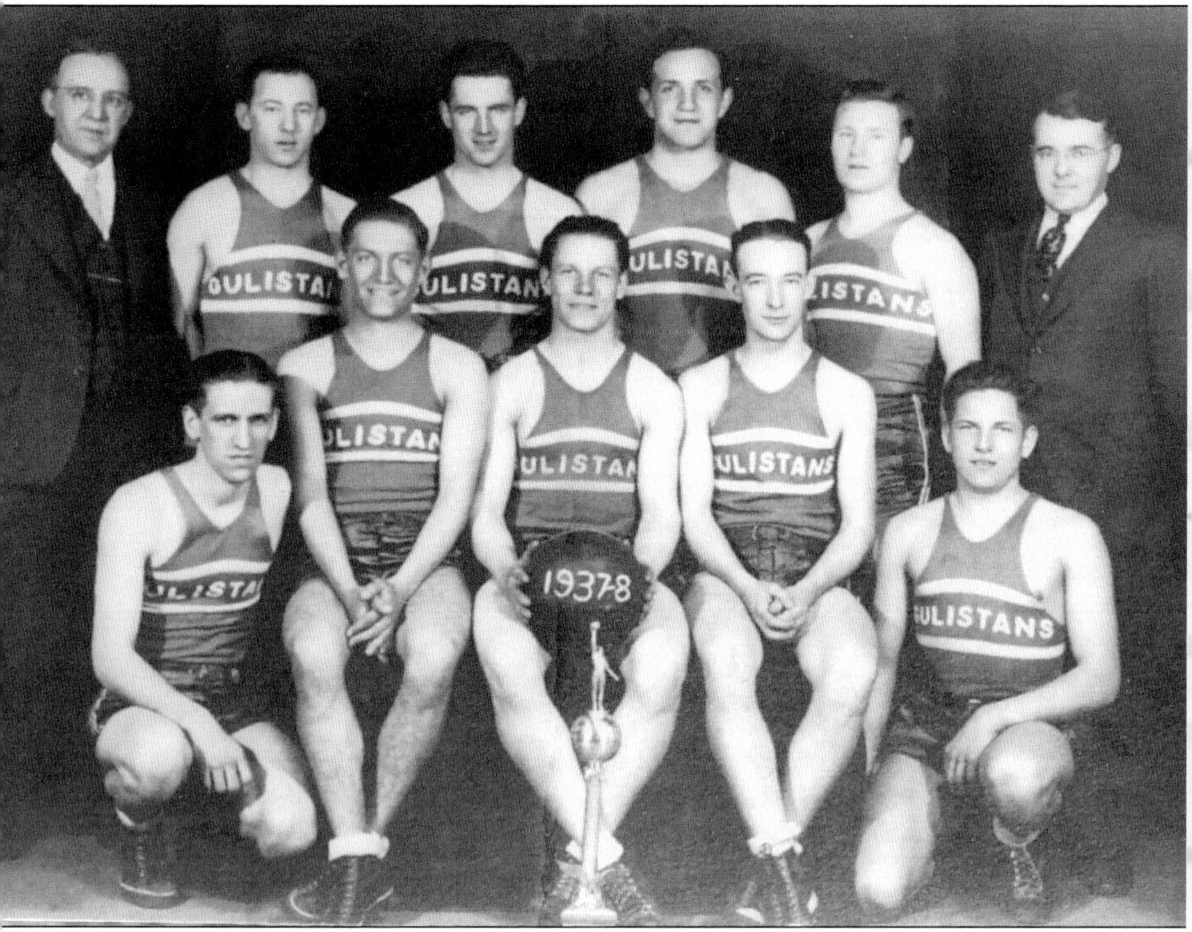

Rug Mill Basketball Team, 1937–8. In their championship year, the members of the Karagheusian Rug Mill's basketball team, the "Gulistans," pose with their trophy. The name Gulistans referred to one of the types of rugs made at the mill. (Photograph by Ladd Studios. Collection of Carl N. Steinberg.)

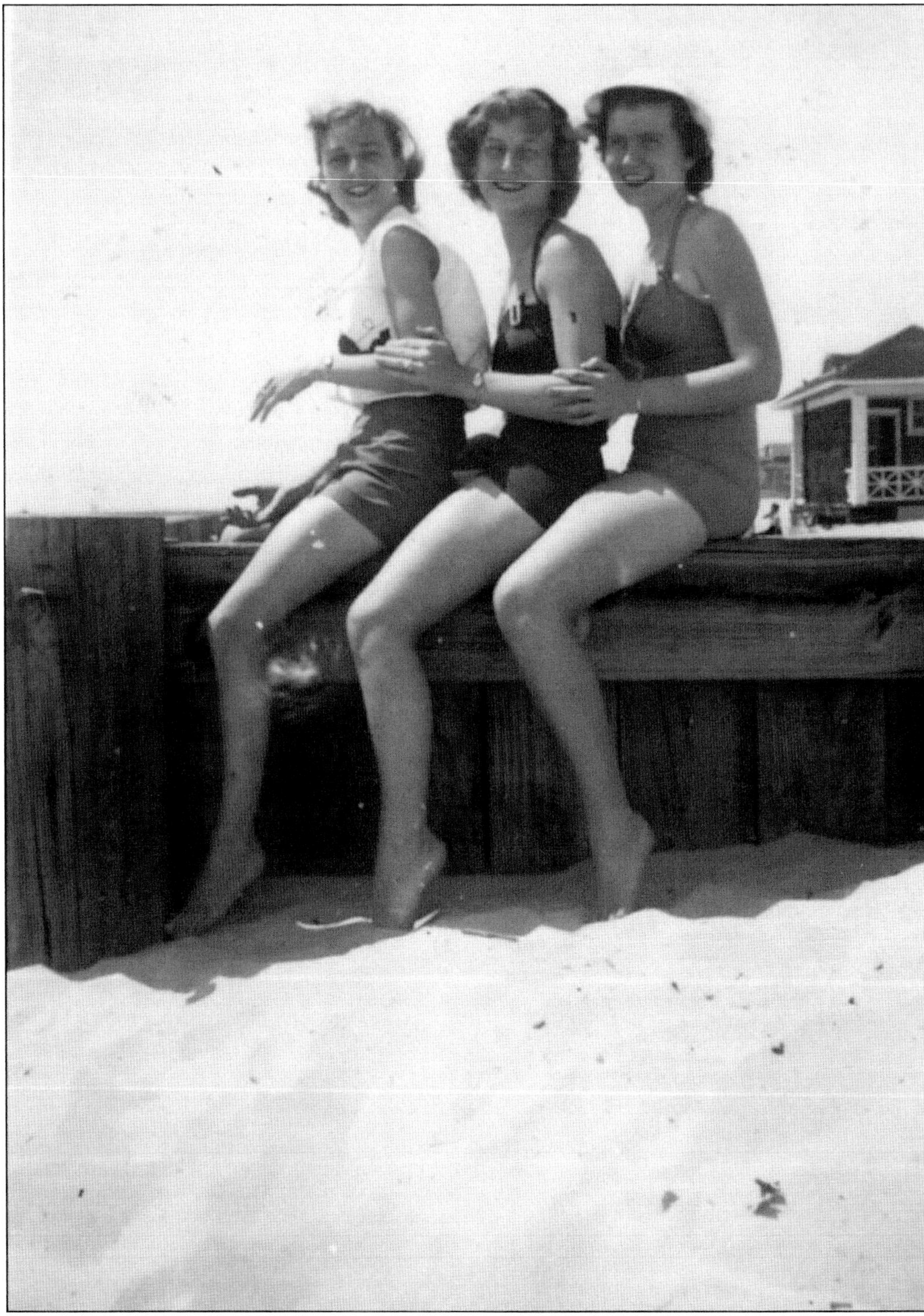

Freehold Bathing Beauties, c. 1950. Going to the shore was always a popular activity for Freehold families. These ladies enjoying a day at Manasquan Beach are, from left to right, Betty Cook, Mary Jane Anderson, and Mary Barber. (Collection of Mary Jane Whalen.)

Three

Colonial Villages

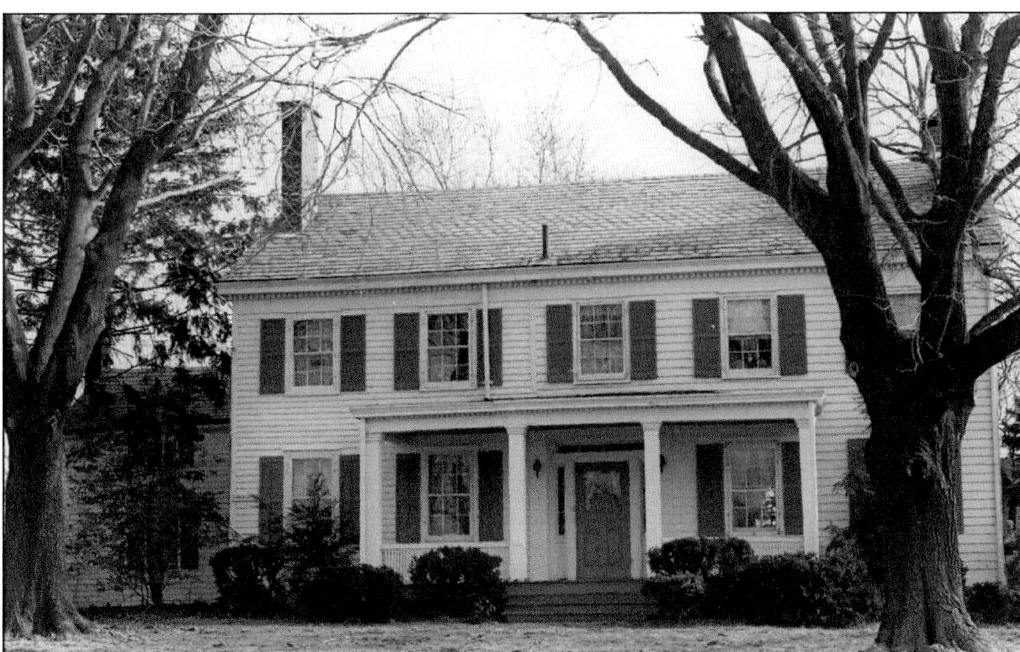

Forman Farm, built mid- to late 18th century with 19th-century additions. One of a number of Forman family farms built in the eastern part of Freehold Township, this may be the original family farmstead. It exists as a working farm and is currently home to the Los Alamos Dressage Center. (Monmouth County Historic Sites Inventory.)

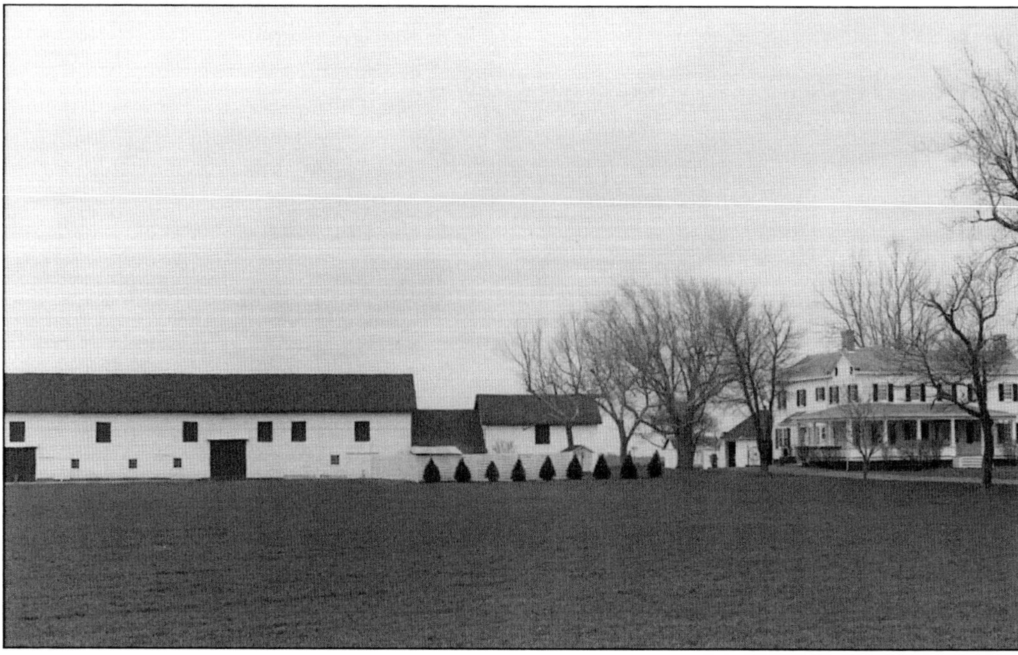

RUSSELL CLAYTON FARM, C. 1835. This farmhouse, with its large barn and outbuildings, mirrors another Clayton farm complex across the road to create one of the most striking vistas in the county's vanishing agricultural landscape. (Monmouth County Historic Sites Inventory.)

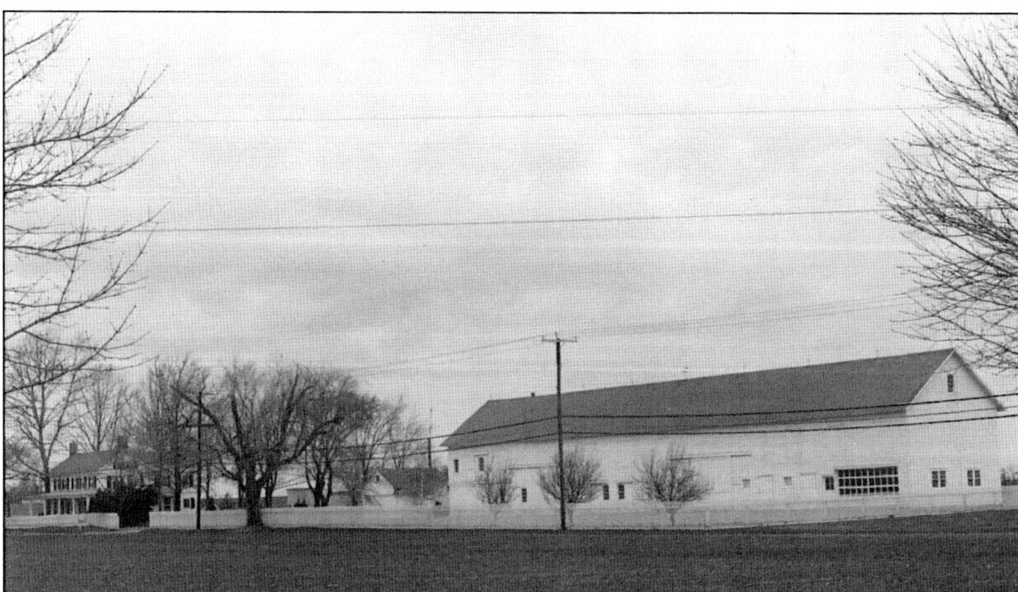

WILLIAM CLAYTON FARM, C. 1840–50. Both of these farms located on Route 537 were originally owned by the Parker family, but since the turn of the 20th century they have been owned by Clayton family members. (Monmouth County Historic Sites Inventory.)

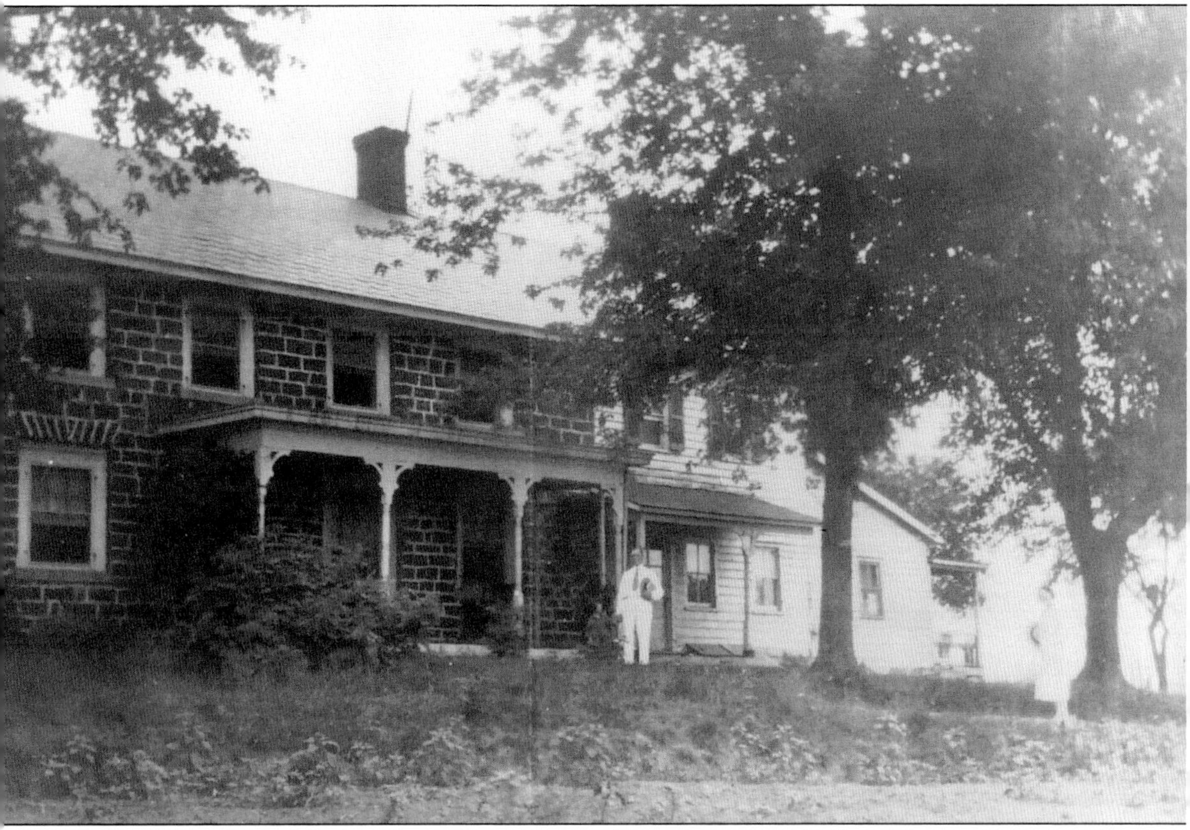

THOMPSON STONE HOUSE, BUILT 1702. Cornelius Thompson built this extraordinary house for himself and his wife, Elizabeth, on a 3,000-acre tract west of Freehold in what is now Manalapan. The house was used as one of the British headquarters before the Battle of Monmouth. In spite of its sturdy construction—the walls were two feet thick—the house, one of Monmouth County's architectural treasures, burned in the 1970s. (MCHA Archives FR207.)

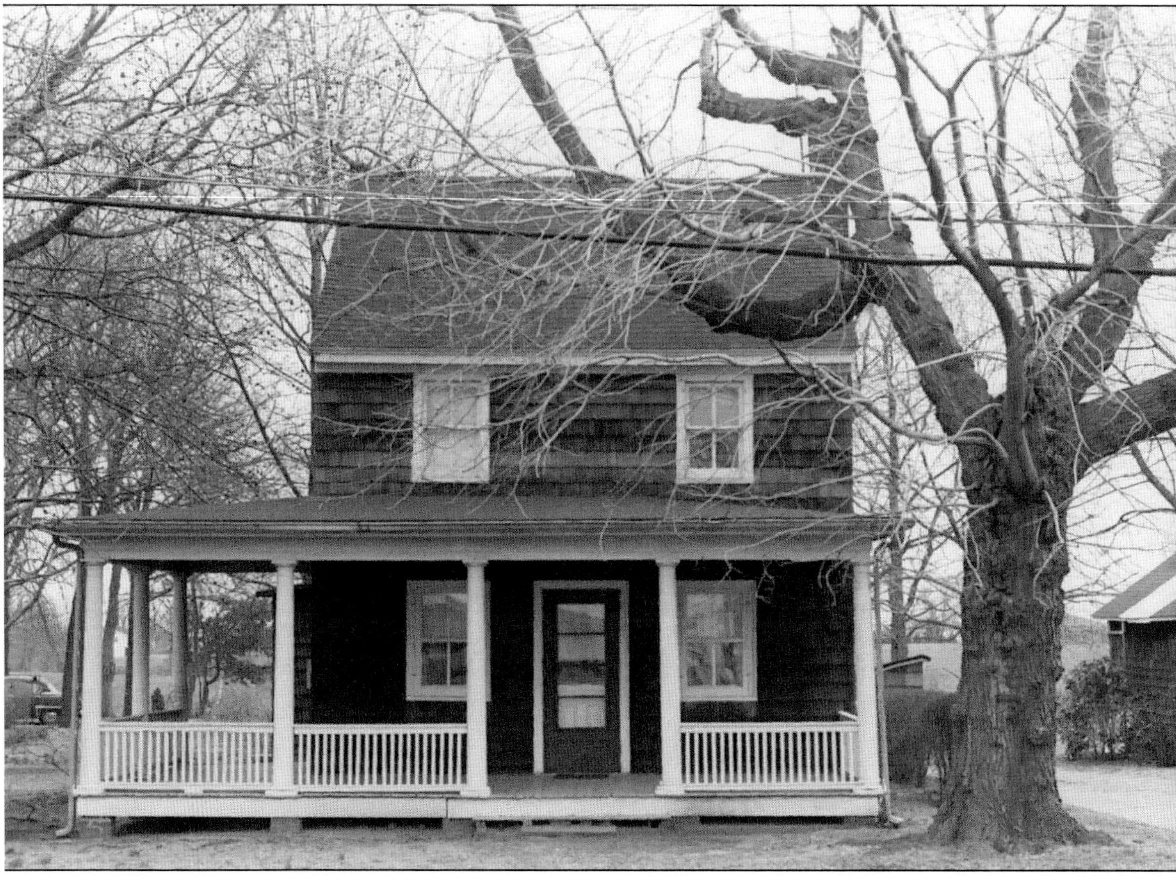

West Freehold House, built c. 1900–1950. The 10-15 small houses that made up the village of West Freehold were of this type, square and plain. The village provided the local farm community with a blacksmith, tavern, and schoolhouse among other services. (Monmouth County Historic Sites Inventory.)

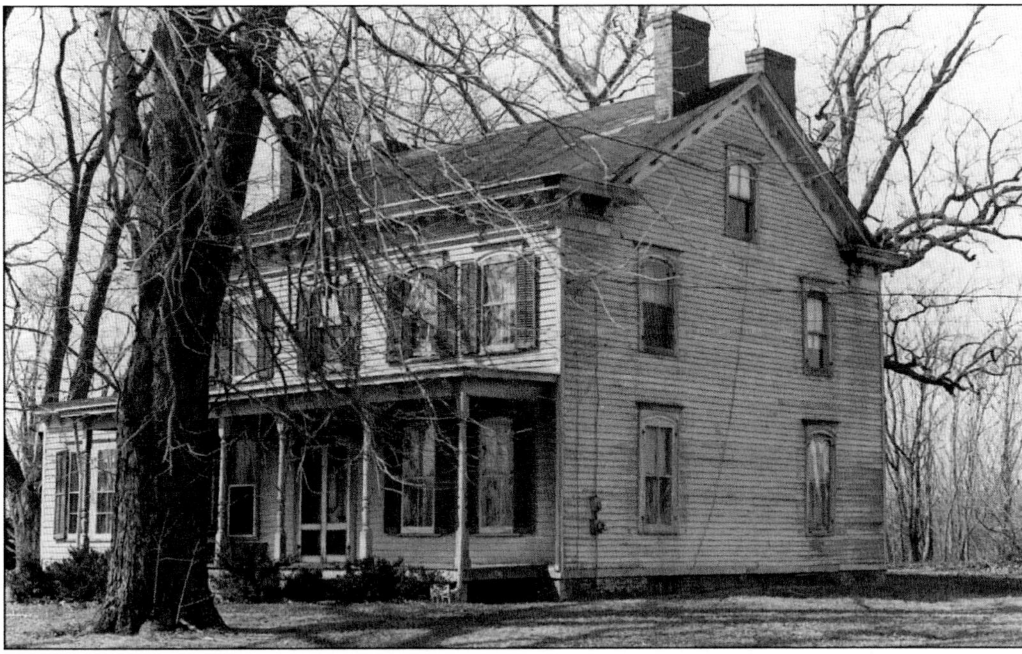

BOND HOUSE, 1860–70. A fine example of the Italianate-style farm house that was so popular in the Freehold area, this house is on the outskirts of the West Freehold Village opposite the Oakley Farm. The owner maintains an organic produce stand today, keeping the property in agricultural use. (Monmouth County Historic Sites Inventory.)

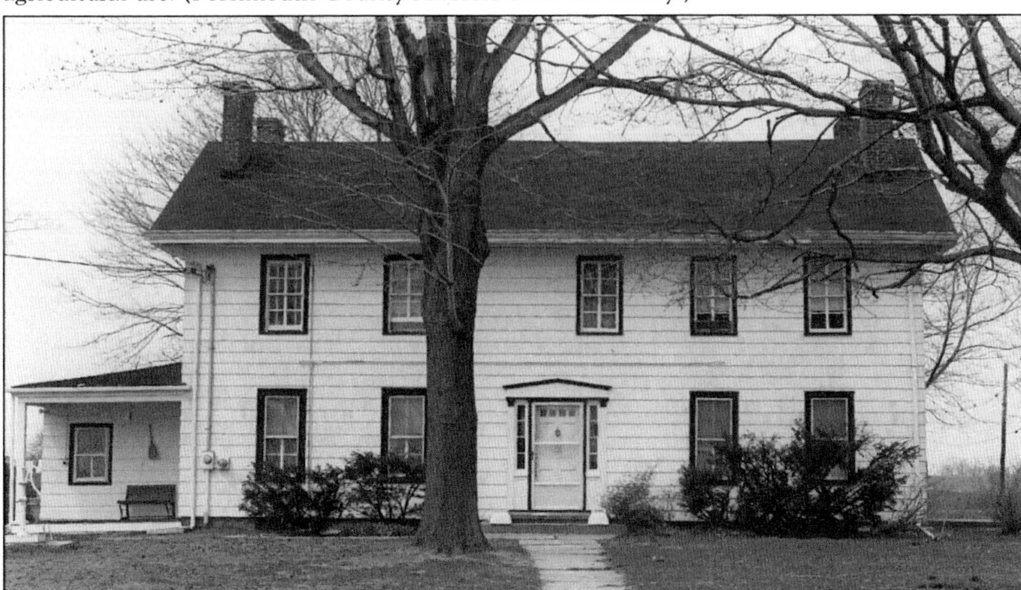

SOLOMON FARM, LATE 18TH TO EARLY 19TH CENTURY. A substantial portion, if not all, of this house was damaged by fire as the British moved through after the Battle of Monmouth in 1778. From appearances inside and out, none of the 18th-century structure remains, yet this early farm house is an integral part of what remains of the village of West Freehold. (Monmouth County Historic Sites Inventory.)

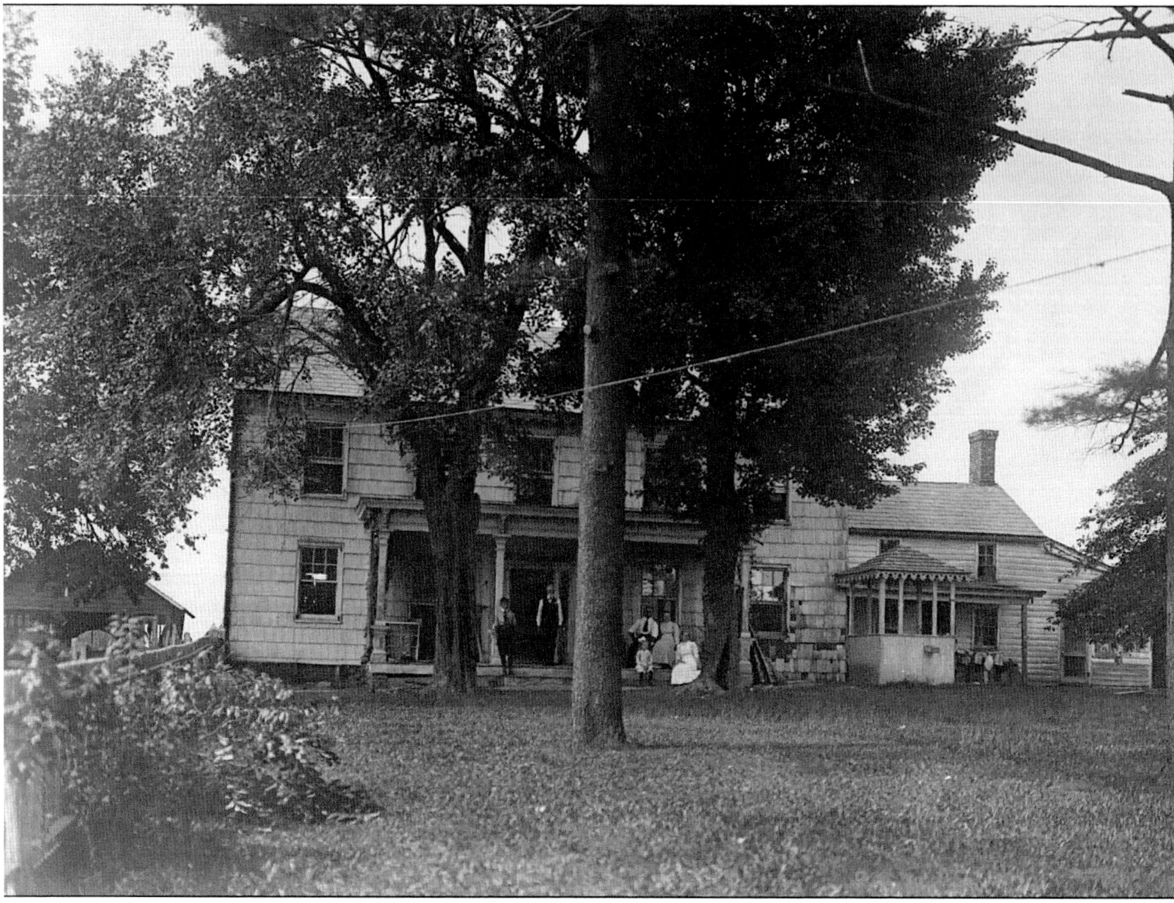

OAKLEY FARMSTEAD WITH THE OAKLEY FAMILY, PHOTOGRAPH C. 1914. Built *c.* 1720 with later 18th- and 19th-century additions, this is the only structure in Freehold Township listed on the National Register of Historic Places. Successive owners have kept this an active working farm beginning with the probable first builder of the house, George Walker. Later owners were Elijah Combs, Richard Hartshorne, and Charles Oakley Jr., who purchased the farm in 1911. By that time, 23 outbuildings supported the farming operation. The Oakley Farmstead has recently been acquired by the Township of Freehold and will be used as a historical and cultural resource for the community. (Courtesy Freehold Township Historic Preservation Commission.)

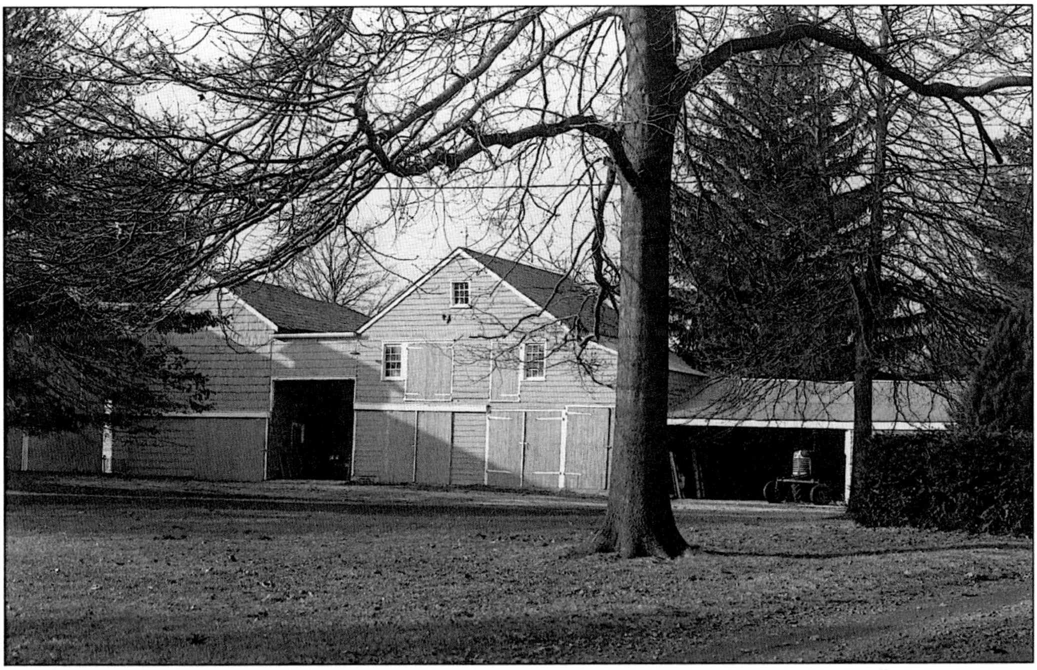

Oakley Farmstead Sheds, built 19th century. Part of the extensive complex of the Oakley farm, these sheds housed farm equipment like the old tractor visible in one section. (Courtesy Freehold Township Historic Preservation Commission.)

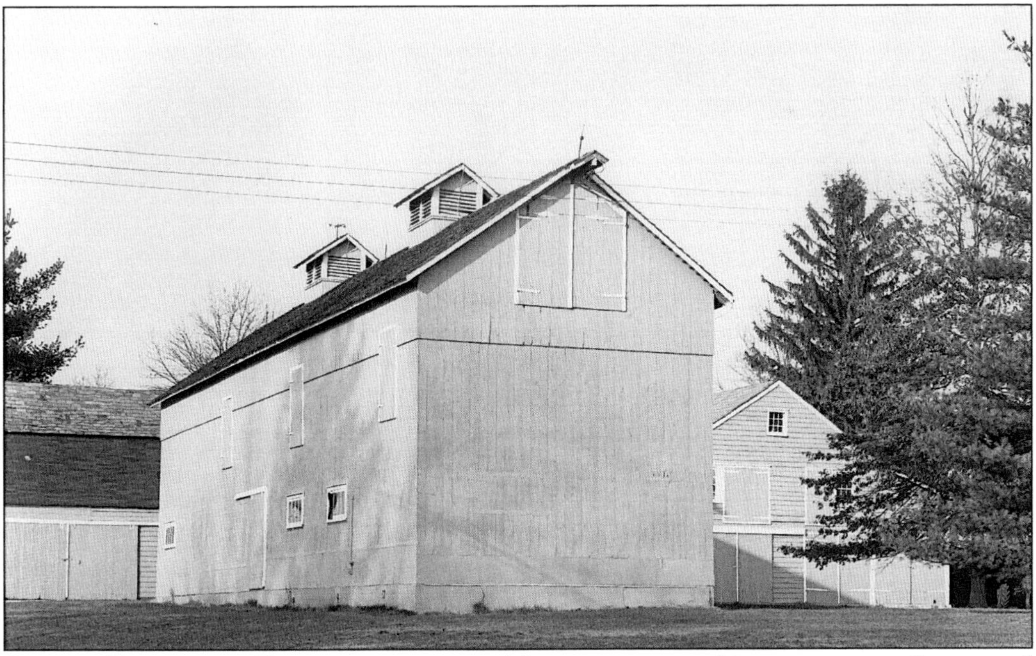

Oakley Farmstead Barn, built late 19th or early 20th century. Large and spacious barns like this one were common in the western part of Monmouth County and reflected the prosperous agricultural environment. (Courtesy Freehold Township Historic Preservation Commission.)

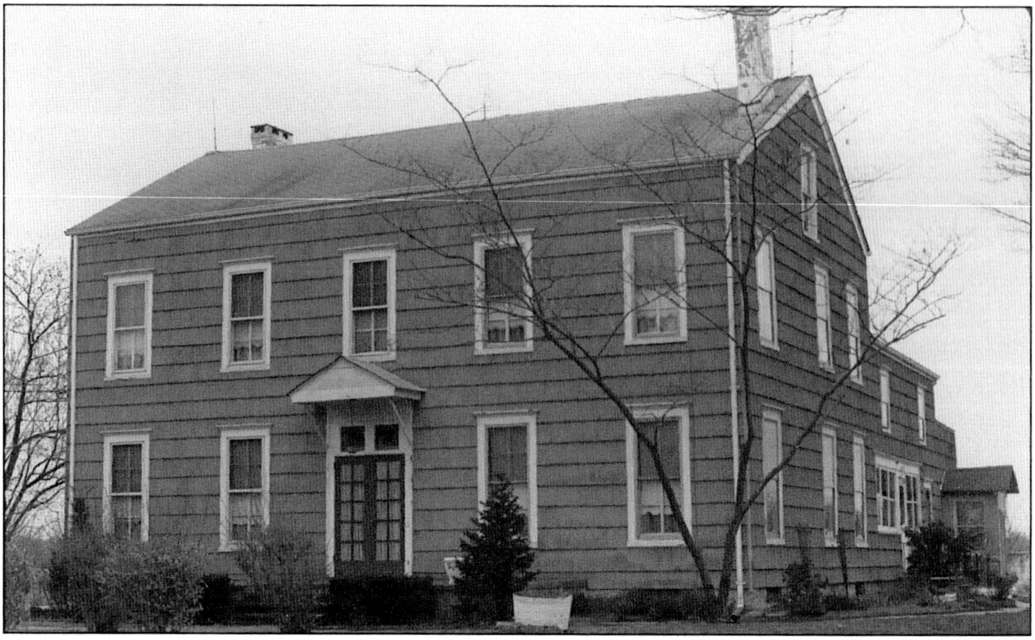

William M. Smith House, built c. 1860. At the center of Smithburg, which is at the crossroads of Route 537 and Siloam Road, this house was built by the son of Asher Smith, for whom the village was named. Asher owned and operated an inn on the opposite corner of the intersection. (Monmouth County Historic Sites Inventory.)

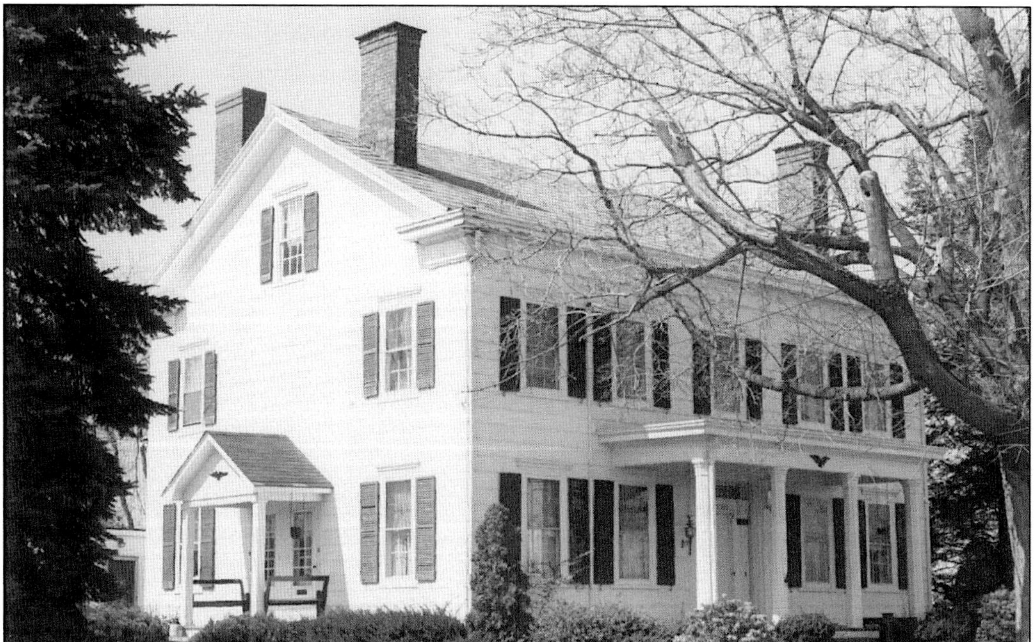

J. DuBois House, built 1840–1850. The Greek Revival style was also popular for Freehold farmhouses as exemplified by this house, which is located on Pond Road. John DuBois was part of a large family that settled in Monmouth County. He raised potatoes and corn as did so many area farmers. (Monmouth County Historic Sites Inventory.)

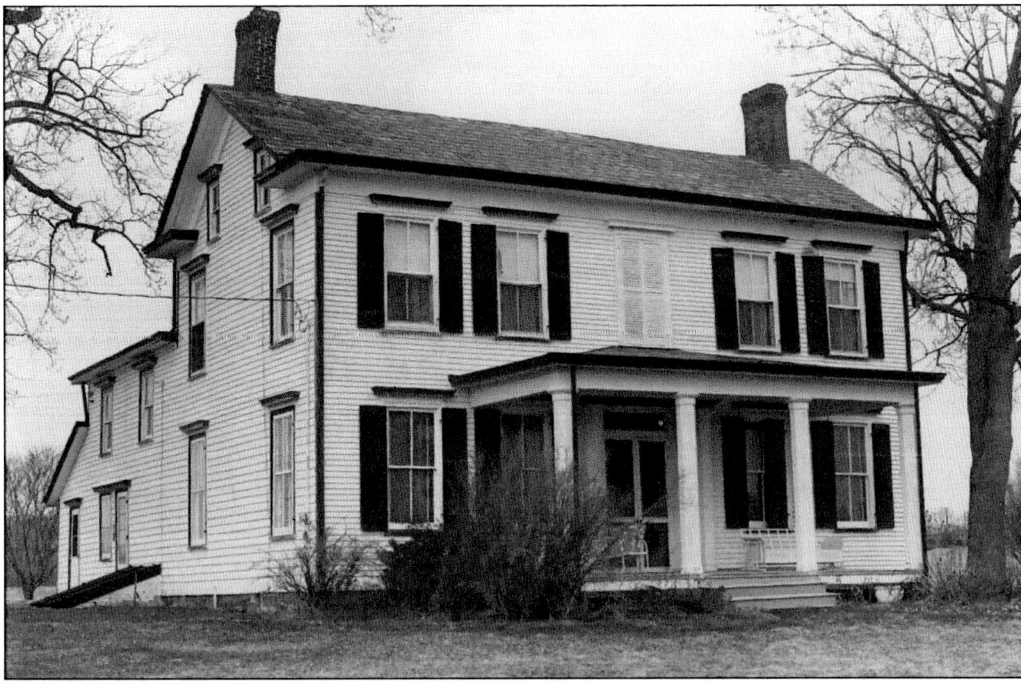

J.F.T. Forman House, built 1860–1870. Part of the extensive "Forman neighborhood" in the eastern part of the township, this farmhouse is near the boundary of the borough. It has survived the subdivision of the farm for a housing development and, through the intervention of Freehold Township, will be restored as a residence. (Monmouth County Historic Sites Inventory.)

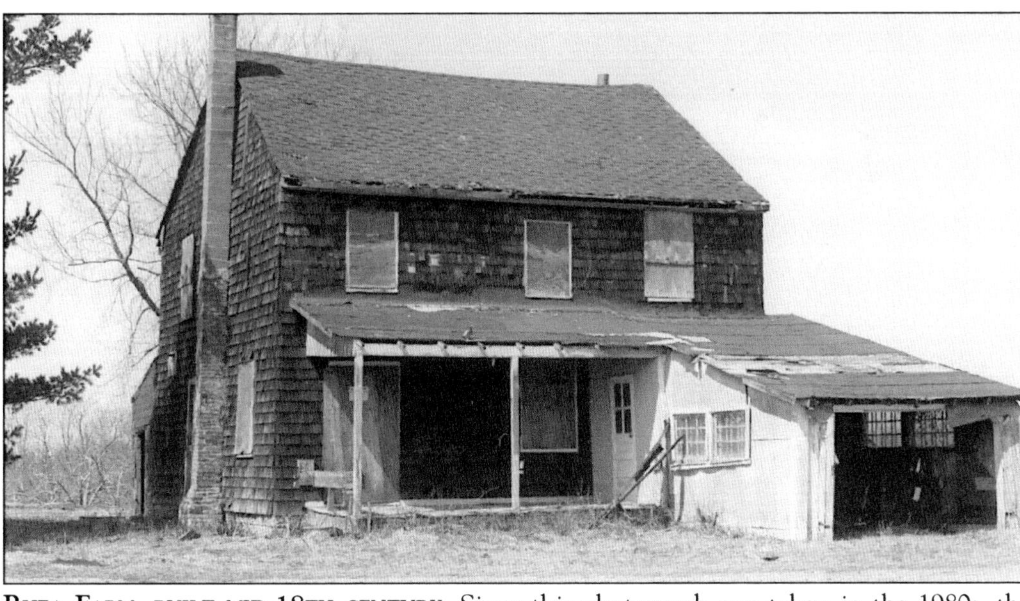

Rhea Farm, built mid-18th century. Since this photograph was taken in the 1980s, the house, which is part of the Monmouth Battlefield State Park, has been painstakingly restored to its 18th-century appearance, funded in part by the New Jersey Historic Trust. (Monmouth County Historic Sites Inventory.)

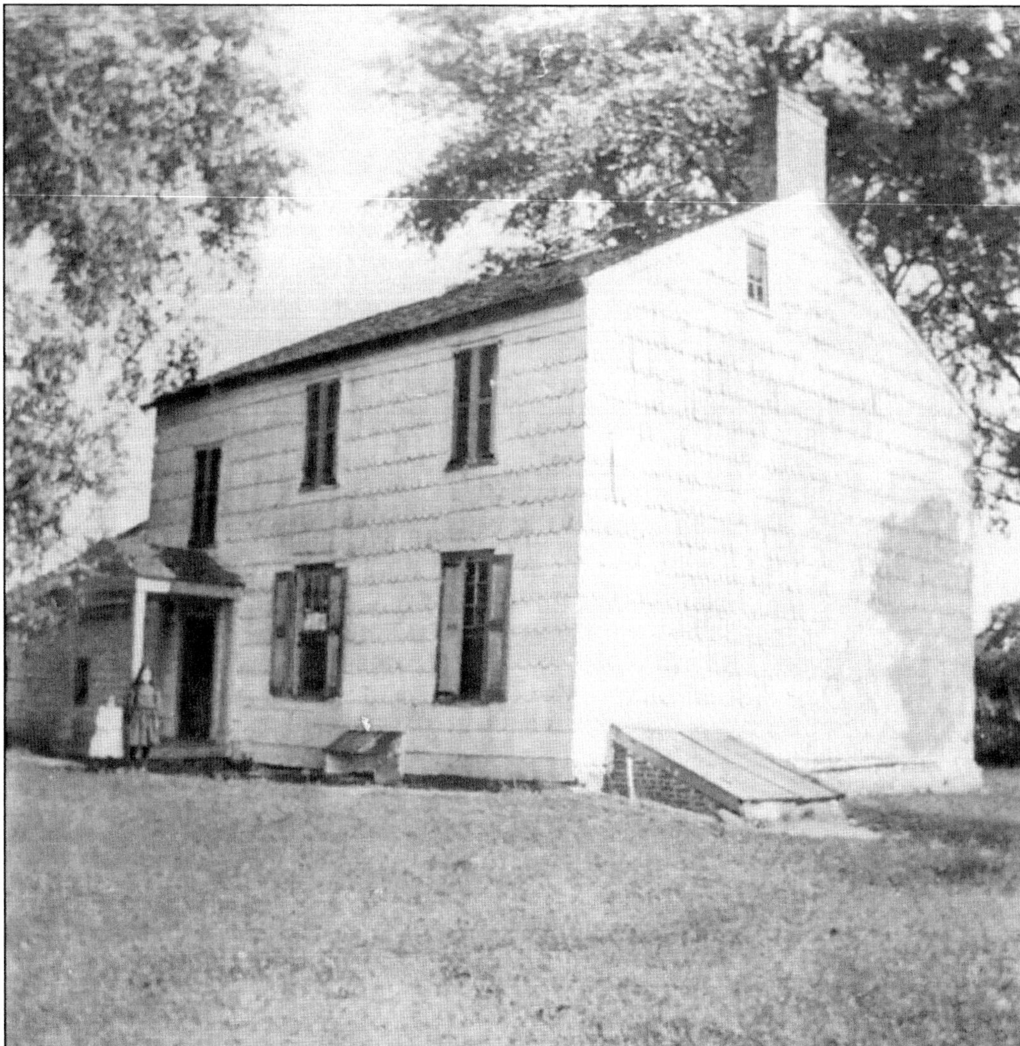

The John Craig House, built c. 1747. Photographed in 1899 by W. Ryall Burtis, this view of the Craig House, which also stands on the Battlefield, shows it in essentially unaltered condition, as an inscription on the reverse notes, "almost exactly as it was at that date [1778]." (MCHA Archives T19.)

Four

Farming

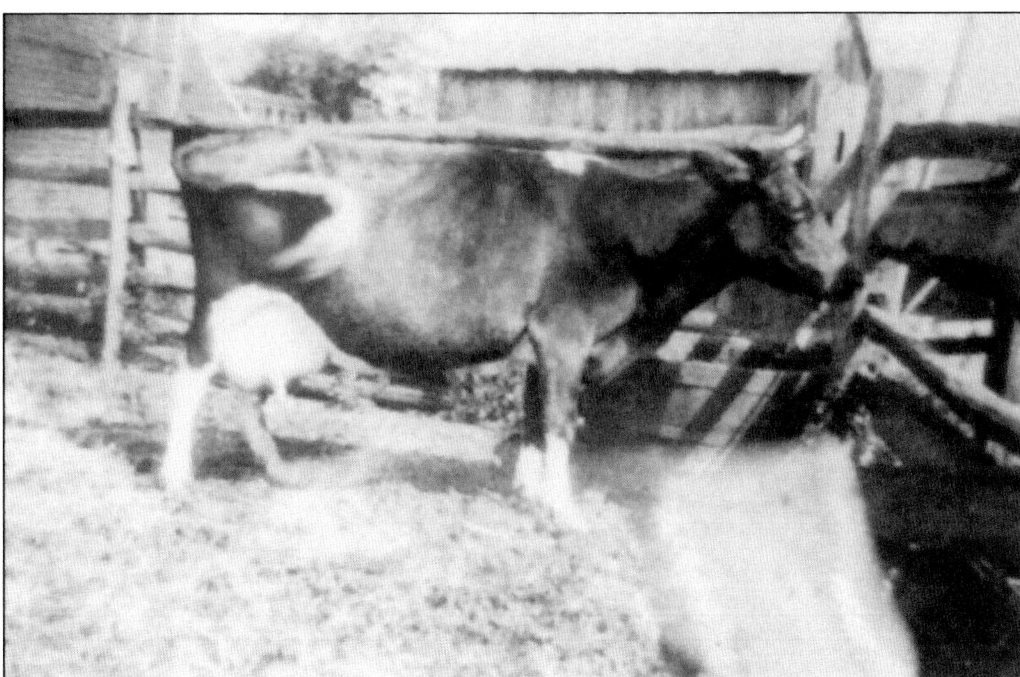

Barnyard Resident, c. 1920s. Livestock was kept at the Moreau farm, also known as Clinton's Headquarters or the Covenhoven House, in Freehold Borough. This snapshot is entitled, "The Old Watering Place." (MCHA Archives FR306.)

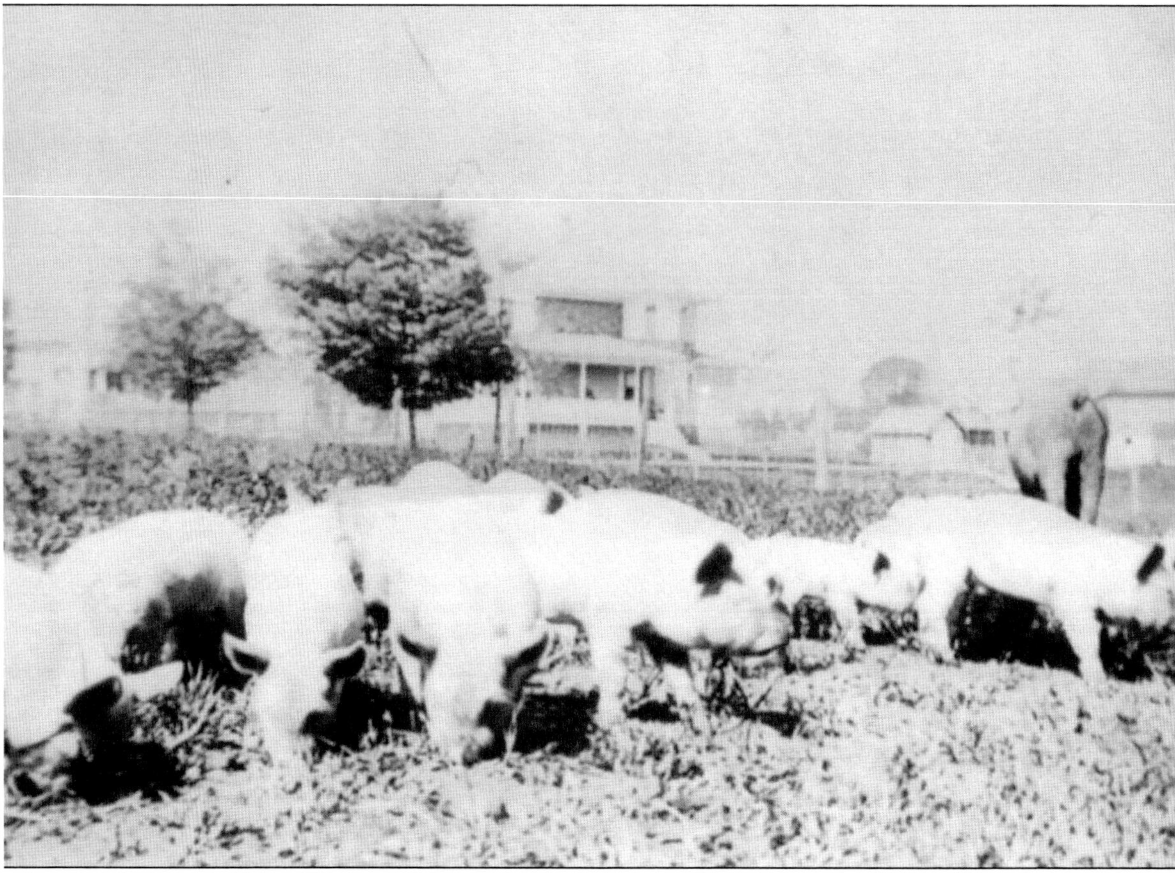

Pigs, c. 1920s. Pigs were also kept at the Moreau's farm in Freehold. (MCHA archives FR222.)

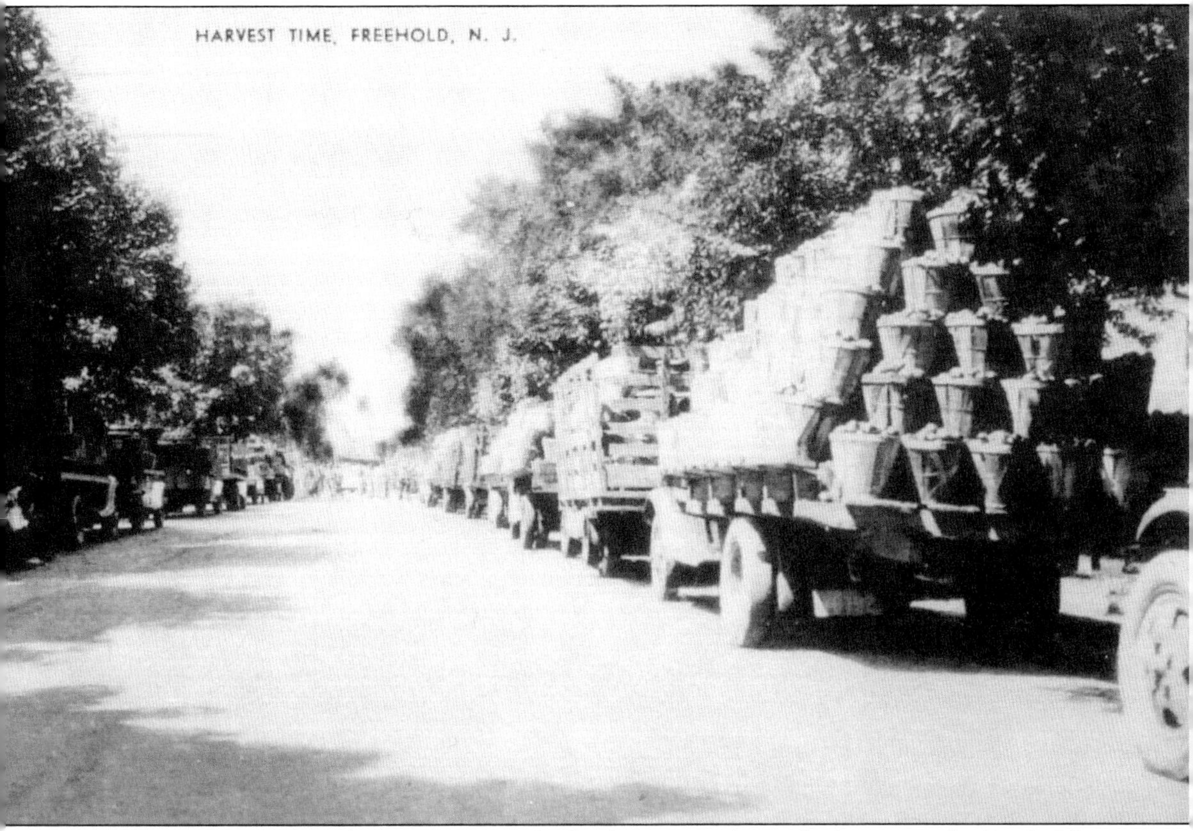

HARVEST TIME, c. 1930s. The potatoes were by far the principal crop for farmers in the Freehold area. Truckloads of potatoes stacked in baskets were lined up to be loaded onto the train to go to market. Many of the potatoes from Freehold went to Pennsylvania to be processed into chips. (Collection of Richard J. Dalik.)

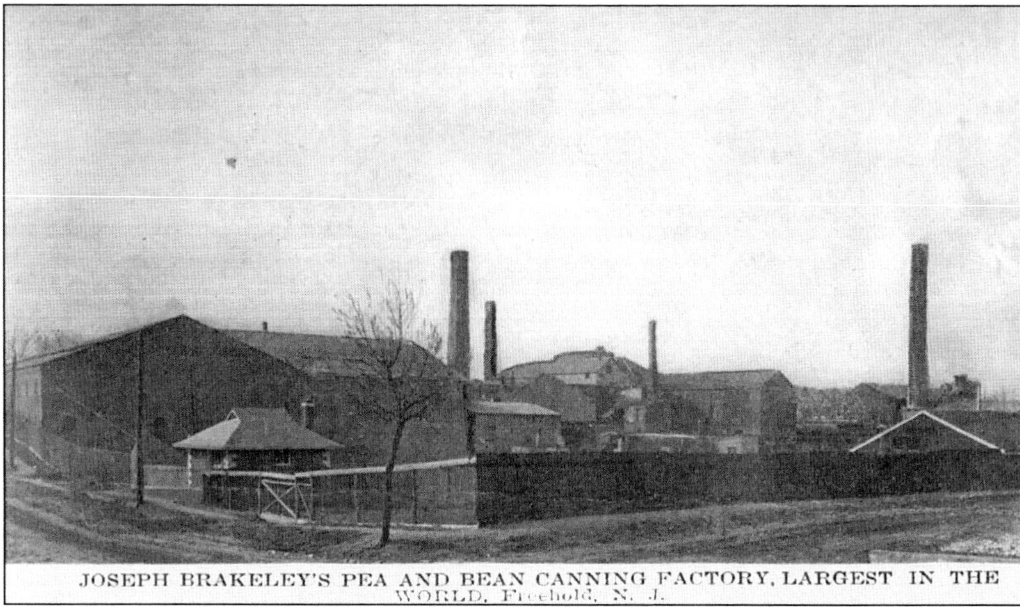

BRAKELEY'S CANNING FACTORY, C. 1920. Joseph Brakeley's pea and bean canning factory, established in 1882, is credited with being the "largest in the world" on this postcard view. In 1902, it was turning out up to 177,000 cans of peas and beans each day. Located at the intersection of Bowne and Manalapan Avenues, the complex of buildings stood until recently. The canning factory closed in 1927. (Collection of Richard J. Dalik.)

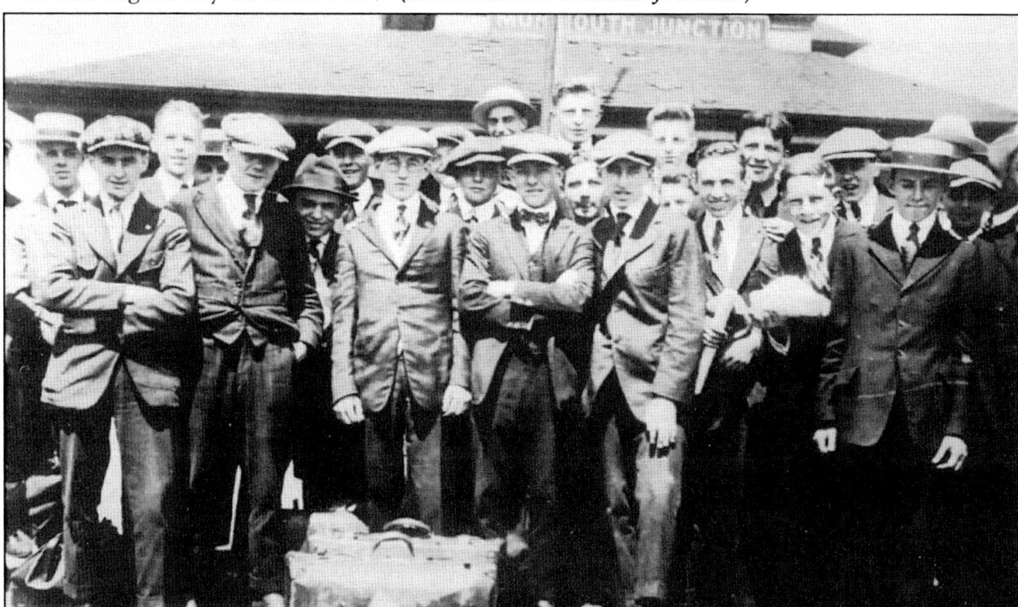

FARM WORKERS, 1915. Seasonal labor for Brakeley's consisted of high school boys from urban areas—Newark, East Orange, Elizabeth, Rahway, Jersey City, and Trenton. These young men were just arriving to spend their summer at "Camp Brakeley." A scrapbook of photographs taken by one of these young men is in the collection of the Monmouth County Historical Association. (MCHA Archives 1997.16.)

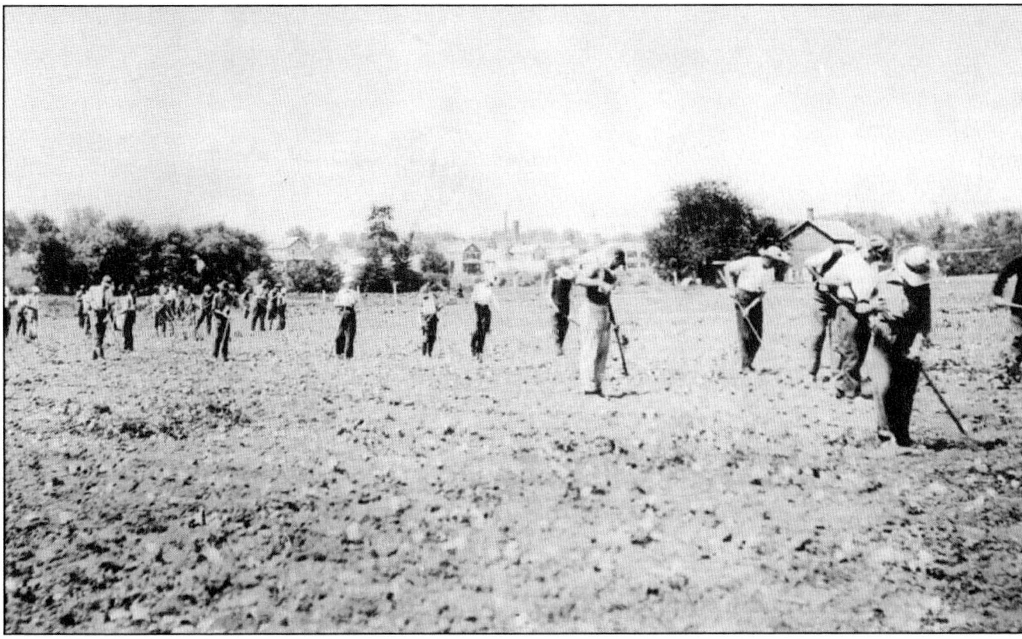

Field Work, 1915. The summer workers tended the vegetable crops that Brakeley raised for processing on the 3,000 acres of farmland that he owned or leased in Freehold and Colts Neck. (MCHA Archives 1997.16.)

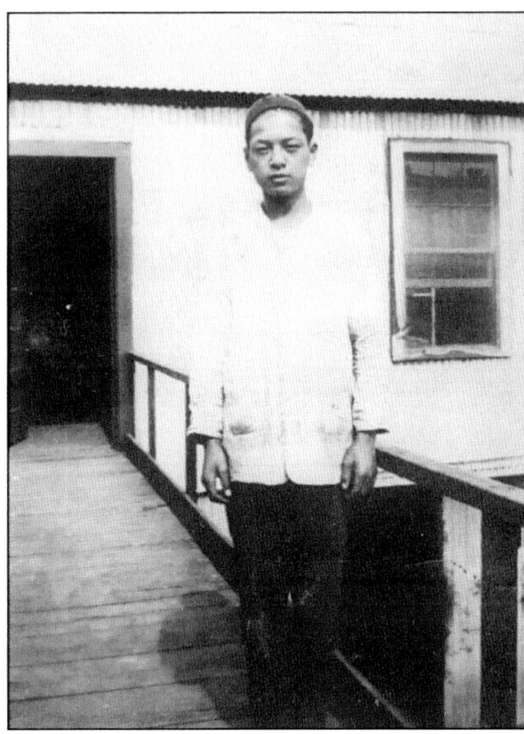

Louie Sing, 1915. The Brakeley factory complex included a barracks and dining hall. On the reverse of this snapshot is written, "Louie Sing, a friend and assistant bellhop in the kitchen and a good sport." (MCHA Archives 1997.16.)

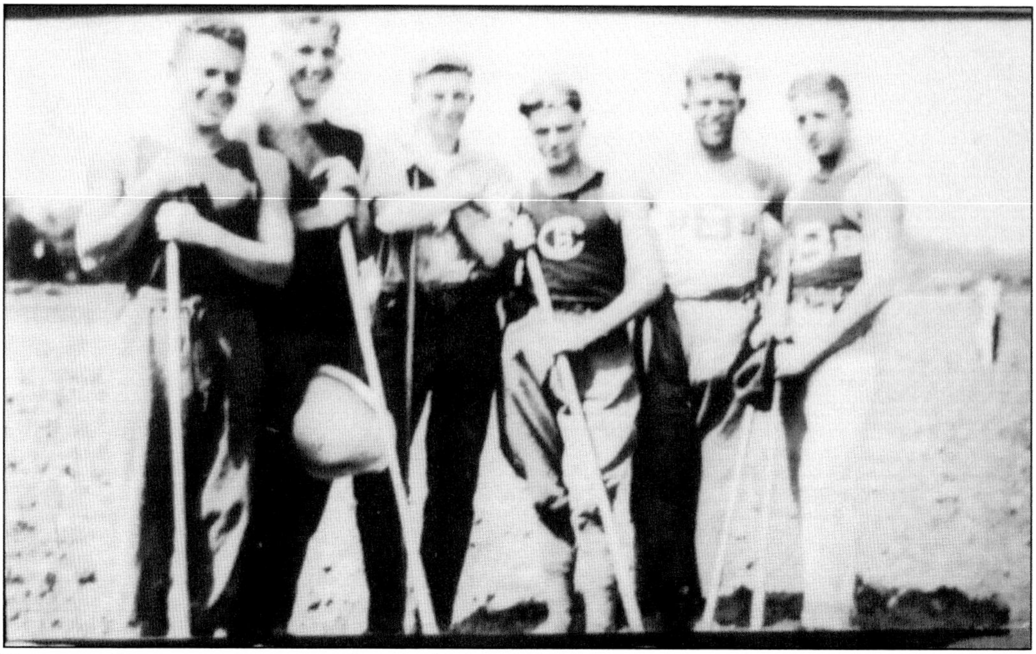

BRAKELEY BOYS, 1915. An unidentified group of young men sport shirts emblazoned with the letters "B" or CB" for Camp Brakeley. They appear to be older than the group on p. 54 and may have been the crew leaders. (MCHA Archives 1997.16.)

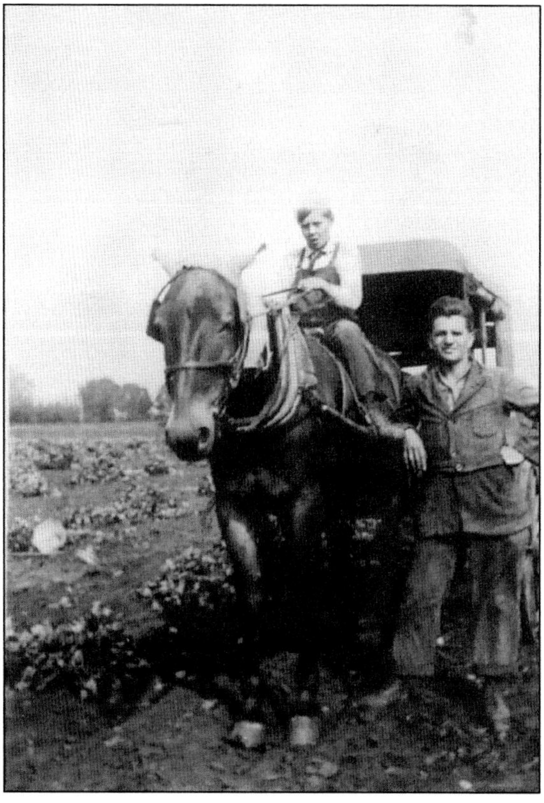

WATER WAGON, 1915. A water wagon provided relief to the field workers. This is identified as "Louie Roskin, my partner and Elmer the waterboy beside the water wagon." (MCHA Archives 1997.16.)

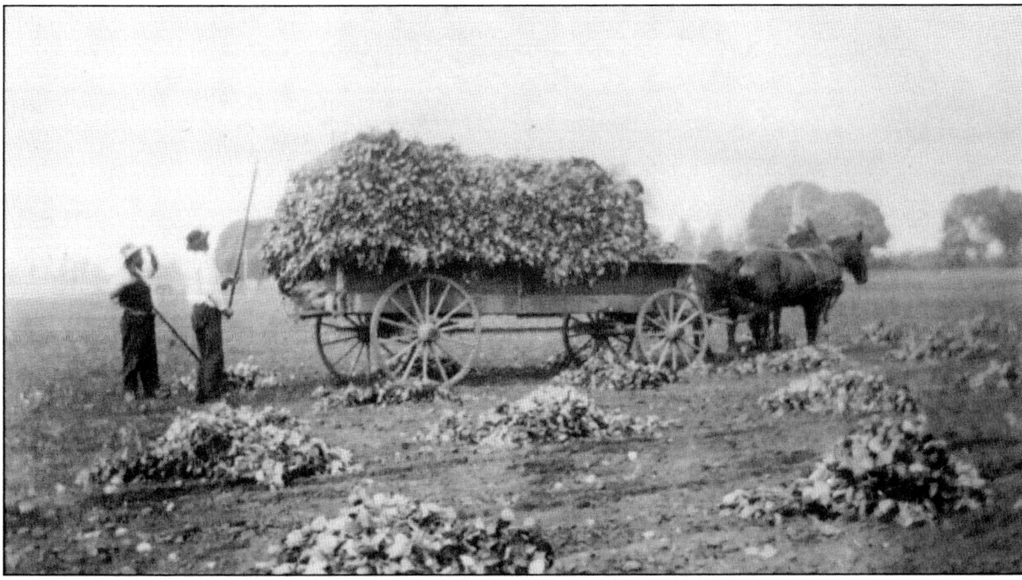

BEAN WAGON, 1915. Harvest time in the bean field meant piling the wagon high, vines and all. Joseph Brakeley is credited with inventing pea and bean shellers and sorters to facilitate processing his crops. After this process, the stripped vines were returned to the fields to be disked into the soil. (MCHA Archives 1997.16.)

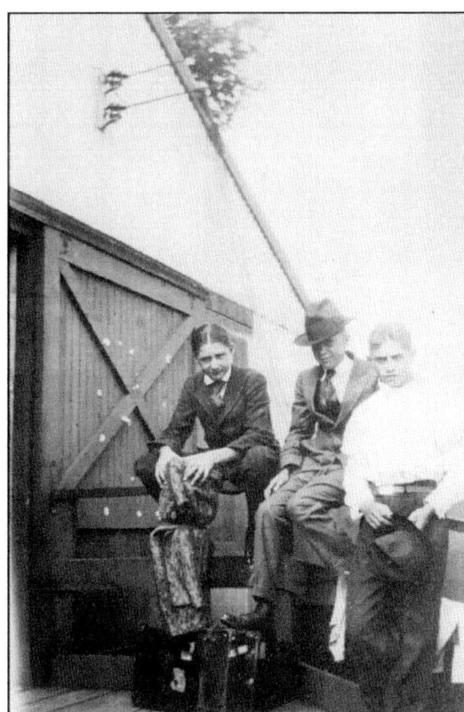

BUDDIES, 1915. The unknown Brakeley boy who kept this scrapbook of photographs to document his summer in Freehold photographed these friends and wrote their names on the back of the picture. They are MacInery (Mac), Bill Warr, and I. Yanowsky (Yanow). (MCHA Archives 1997.16.)

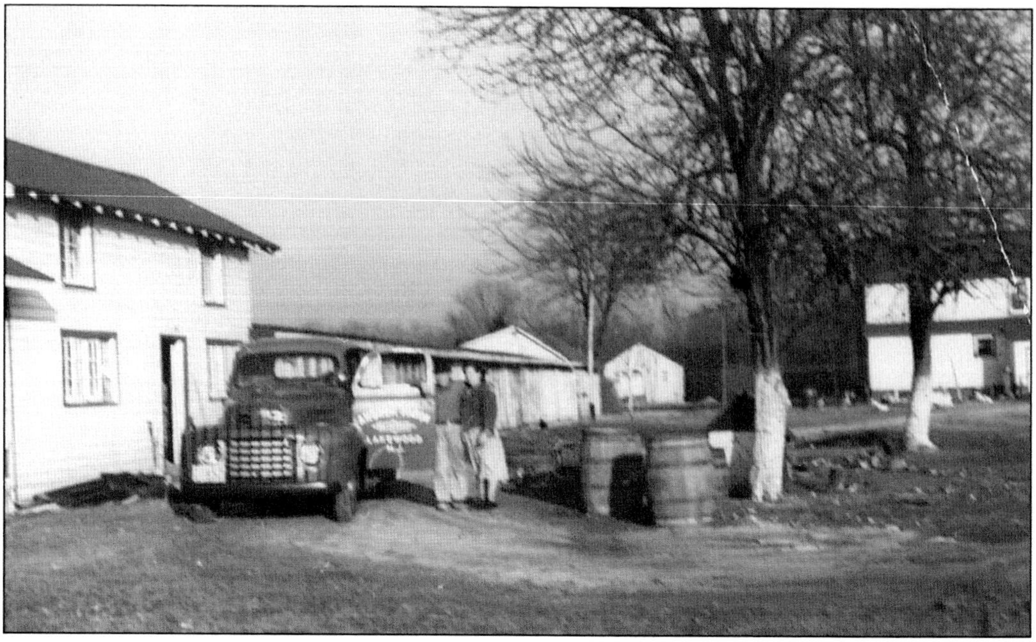

LAZINGER EGG FARM, C. 1940. A number of Jewish families settled in the Freehold, Howell, and Lakewood areas in this period to set up egg farms. The land was reasonably priced and these family ventures offered an opportunity to escape the urban environment. (Collection of Dr. Zeff Lazinger.)

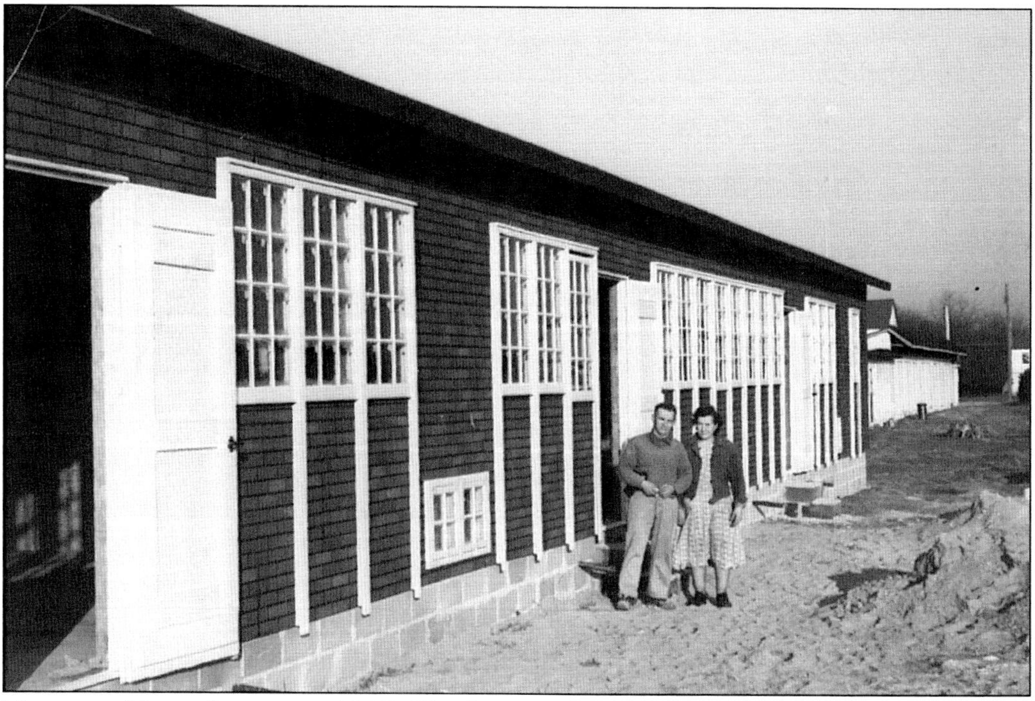

MAX AND MIRLA LAZINGER, 1946. The Lazingers prospered in their egg farming business located in Freehold on Route 9. They proudly stood in front of a new building in their complex. (Collection of Dr. Zeff Lazinger.)

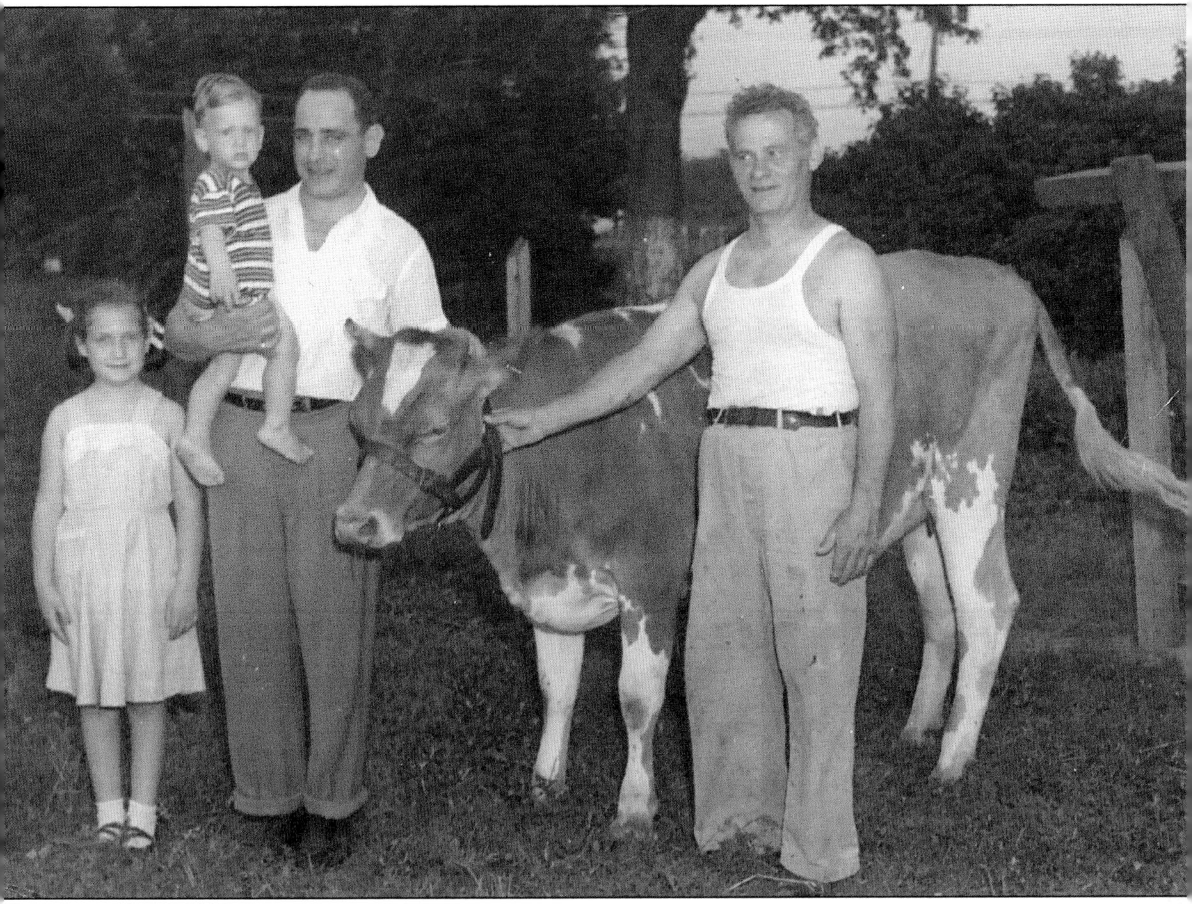

FAMILY PORTRAIT WITH COW, C. 1947. Max Lazinger holds one of his cows to pose with son-in-law Joe Thaler and grandchildren Miles and Wendy. (Collection of Dr. Zeff Lazinger.)

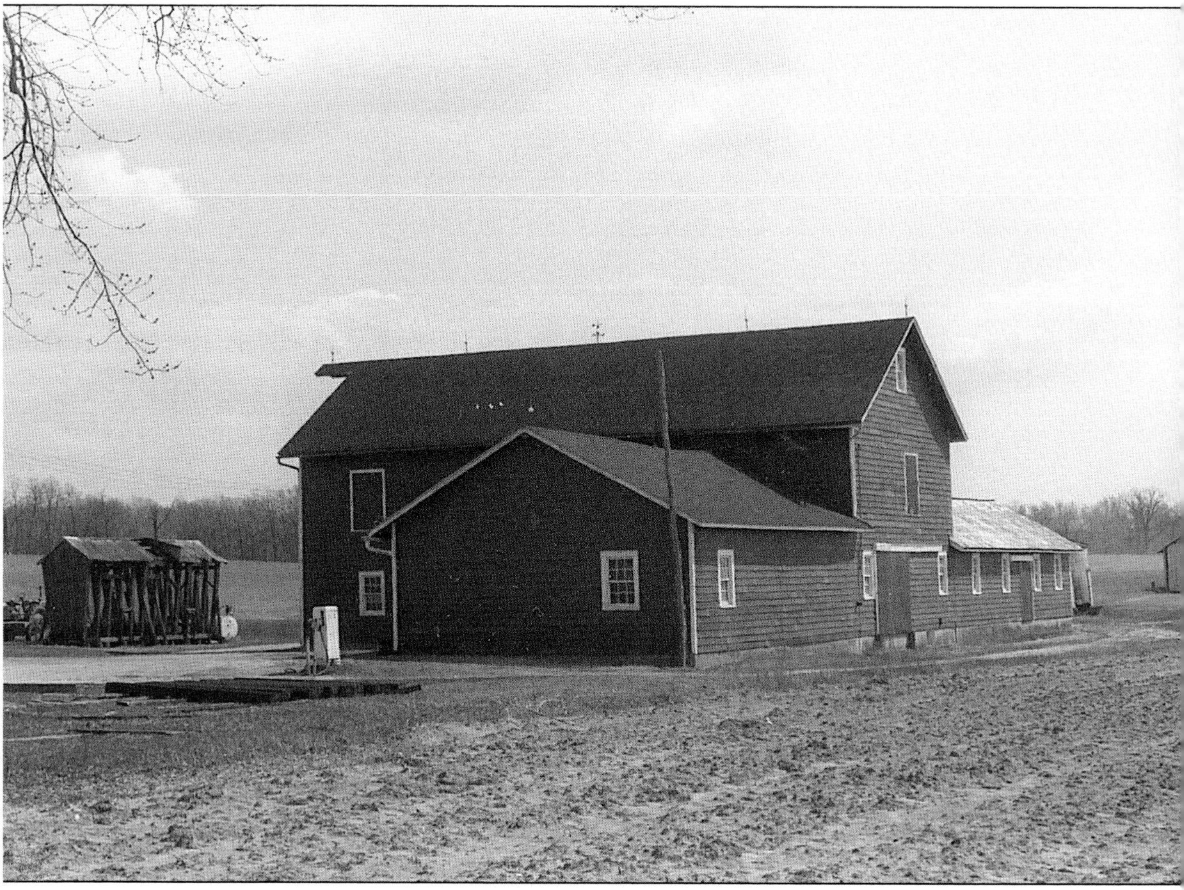

BARN, LATE 19TH CENTURY. This barn is part of a surviving farm complex in the northeastern part of Freehold Township on Burlington Road. Groups of barns and outbuildings like these were once plentiful and characterized Freehold's rural environment. (Monmouth County Historic Sites Inventory.)

Five

SCHOOL DAYS

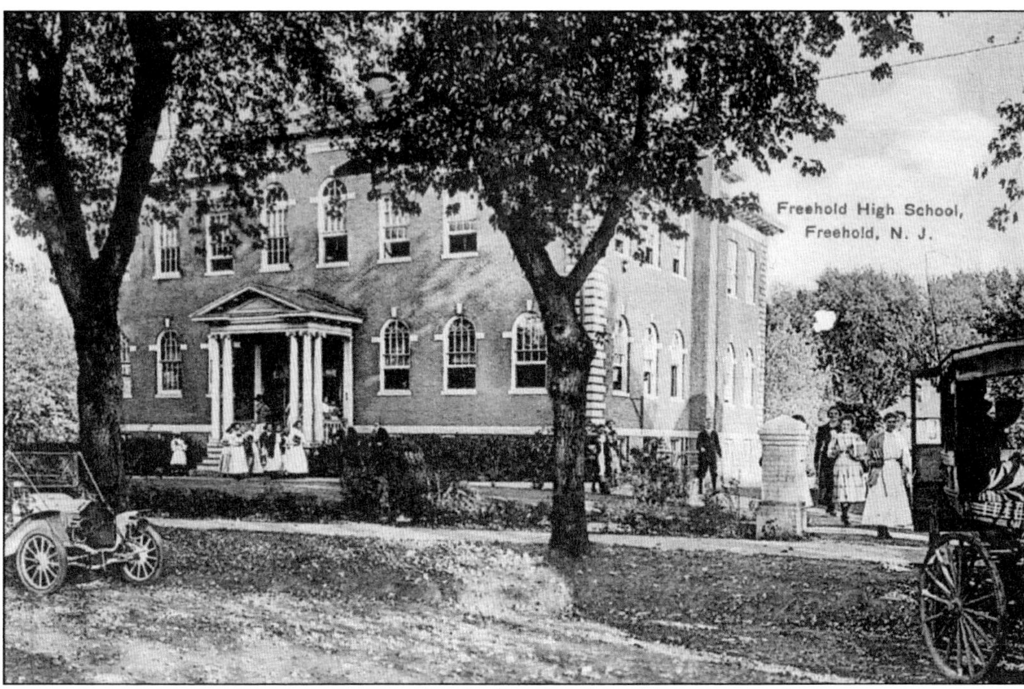

FREEHOLD HIGH SCHOOL, C. 1910. The high school building on Hudson Street now serves as the borough police department. In its day, it served a growing and prosperous population including these stylishly dressed young ladies and gentlemen. (Collection of Richard J. Dalik.)

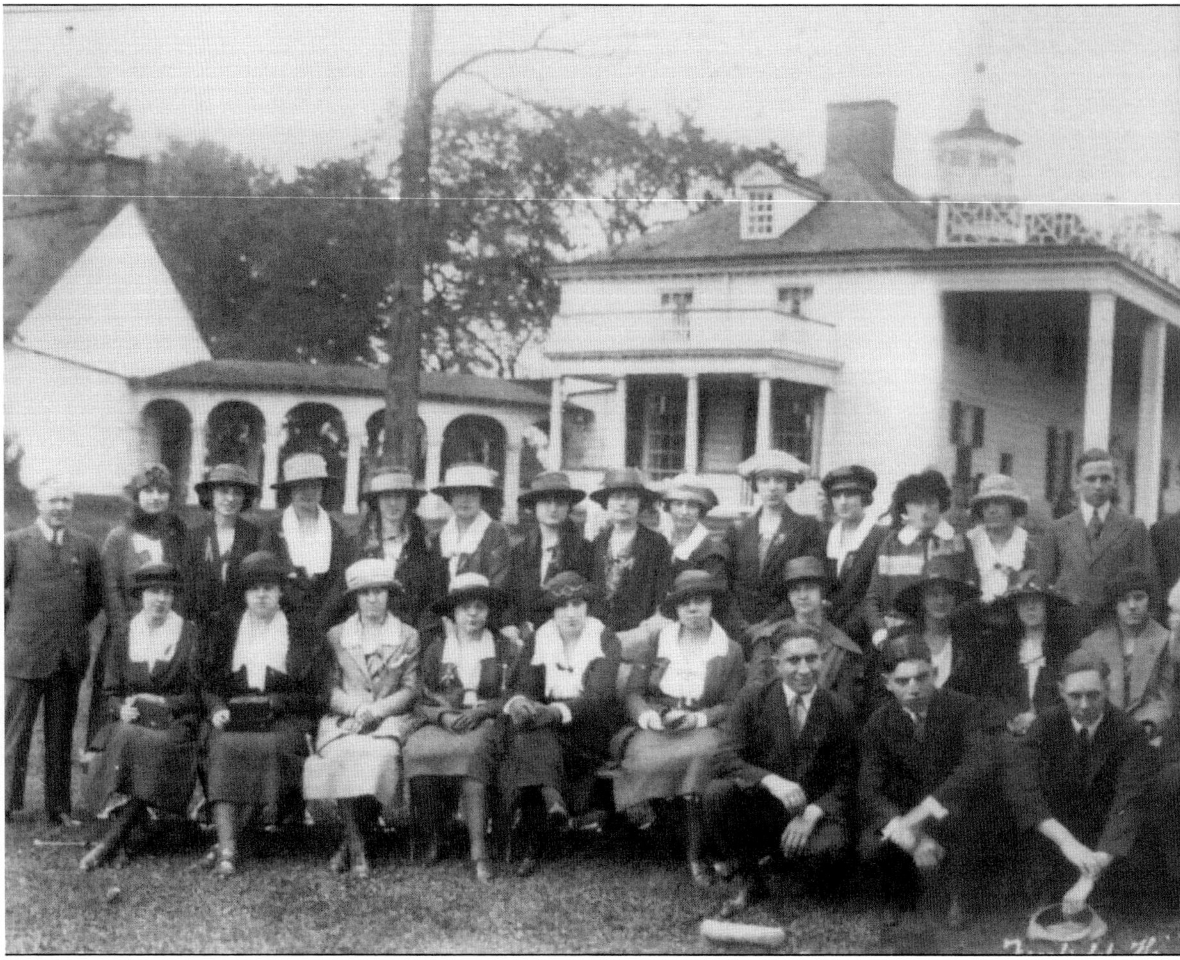

Trip to Mount Vernon, 1921. Freehold High School students made a class trip to Mount Vernon in May 1921. Photographer J.M. Naiman of Washington, D.C., made this panoramic view of the entire class, as he probably did for hundreds of other high school classes from other

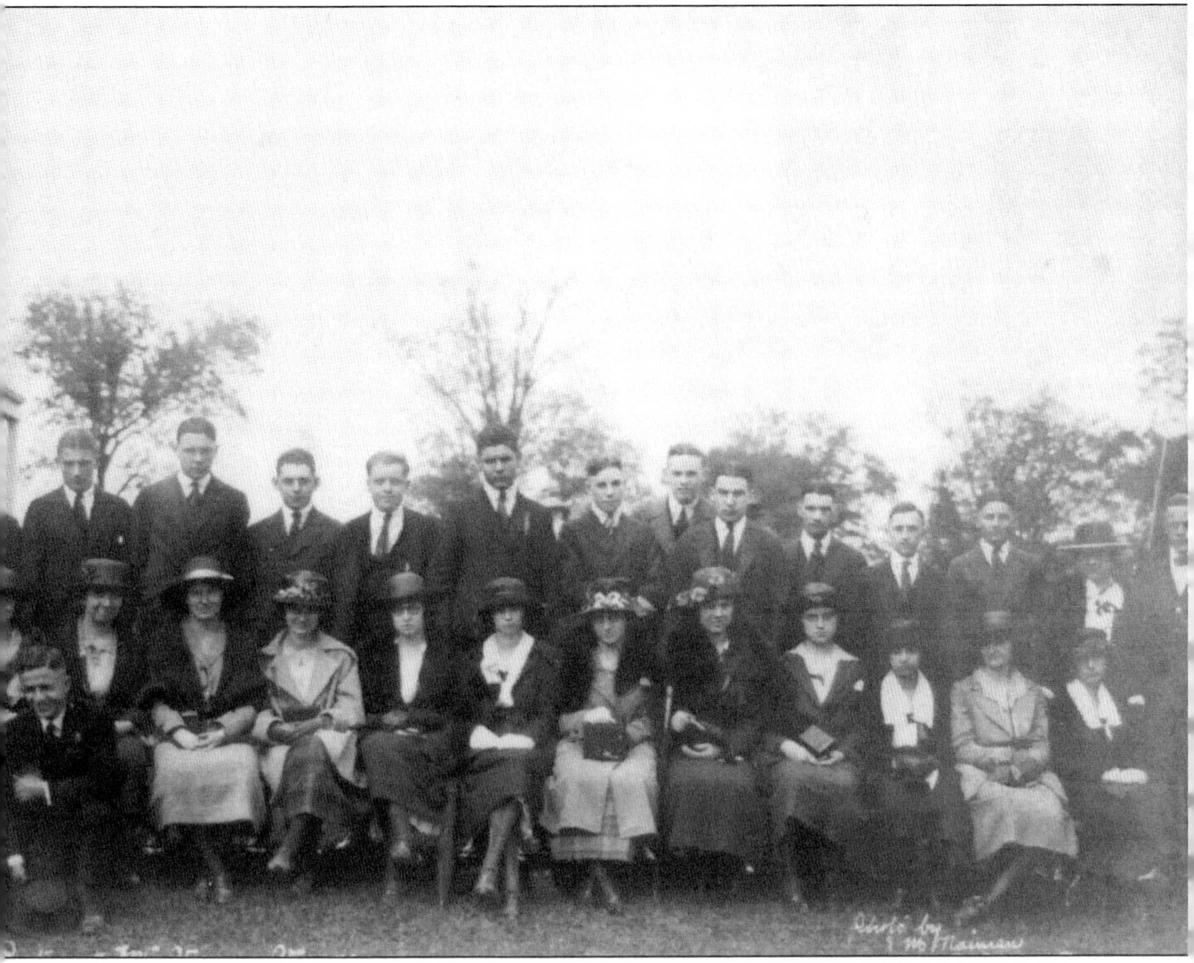

parts of the country. On the reverse is a list of the subjects' names, including Mr. McSherry, the railroad representative who presumably took charge of the group's transportation arrangements. (MCHA Archives FR484.)

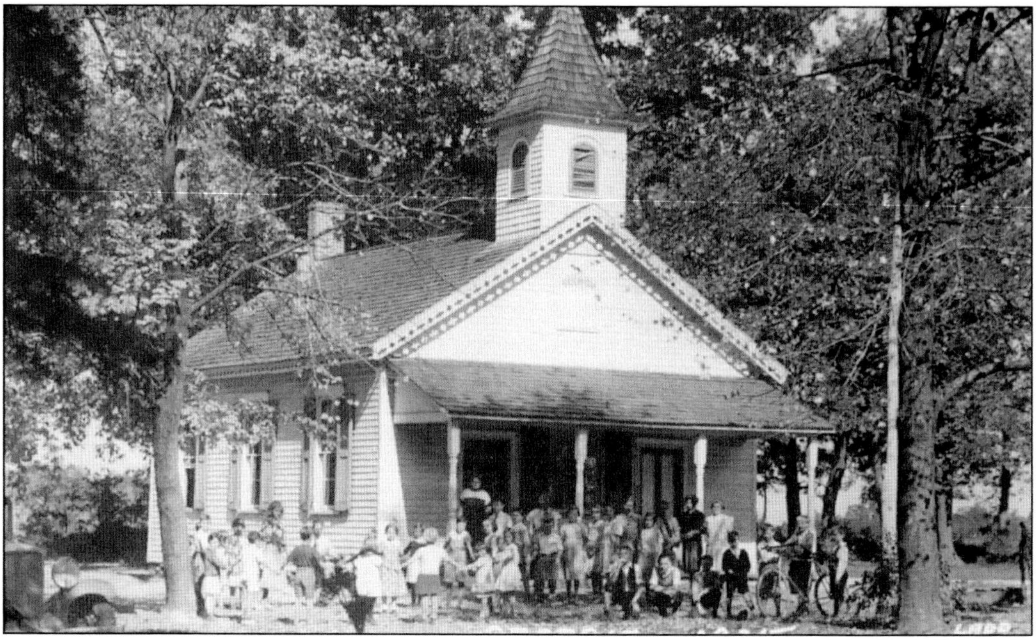

Georgia School, 1920s. A number of one-room schoolhouses served rural Freehold Township. This one, built in 1862, and the West Freehold School still stand as reminders of a simpler past. Each year, the class picture was taken with the students gathered on the porch. The younger ones joined hands in a circle, perhaps for ring-around-the-rosy. (Collection of Carl N. Steinberg.)

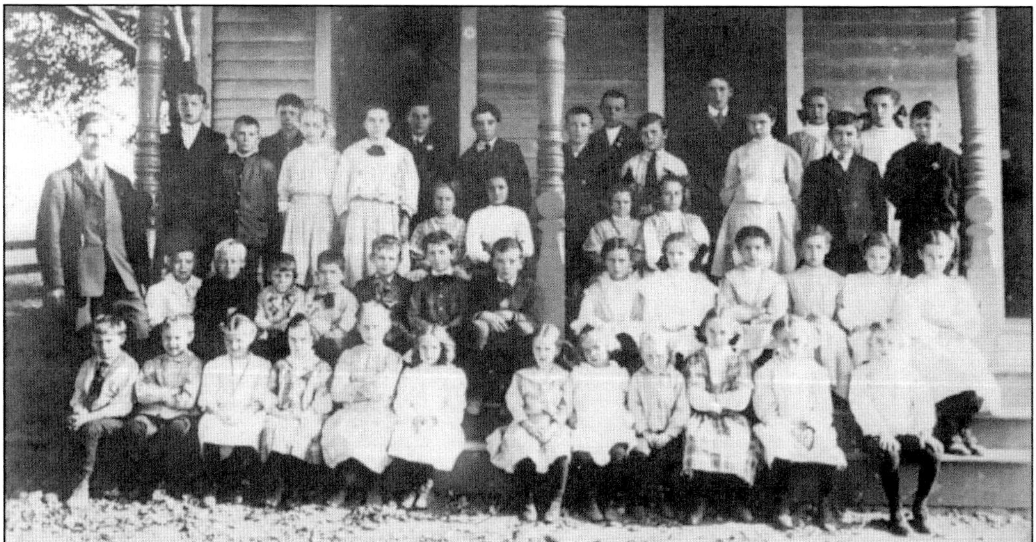

West Freehold School, 1909. A more somber and disciplined group picture was taken of West Freehold in 1909. Among the surnames identified on the reverse are Conovers, VanDerveers, Claytons, Thompsons, and Schancks. The teacher is Andrew J. Conover. Records of the West Freehold School in the MCHA Archives show that over the years, both men and women were hired to teach, but the women were paid far less. (Collection of Carl N. Steinberg.)

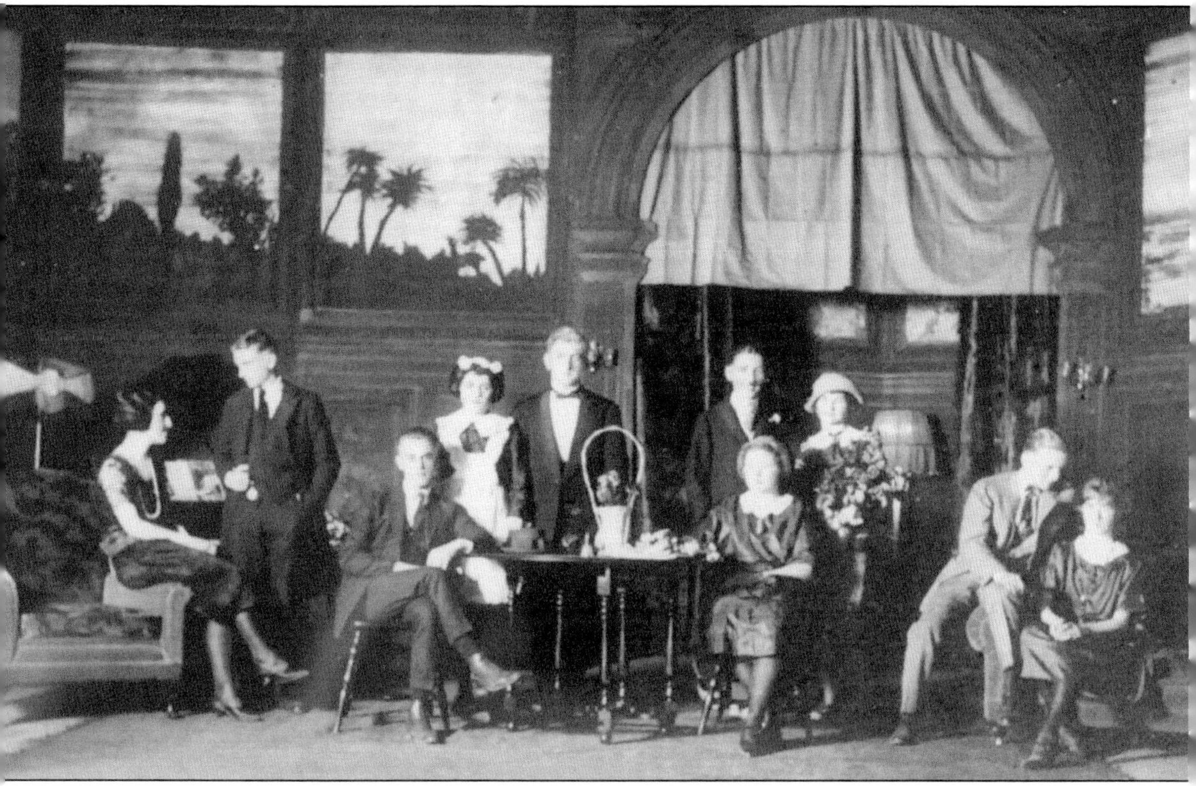

"The Prince of Liars," 1922. The Freehold High School presented this play on March 17, 1922. The stars of the production were, from left to right, as follows: (standing) Helen Miller, Edward Fountain, John Witman, Helen Robinson, Clifford Van Kirk, Henry Carr, and Margaret Murphy; (seated in front) Ruth Palmer, Jack MacMurtrie, and Elizabeth Allaire. (Collection of Carl N. Steinberg.)

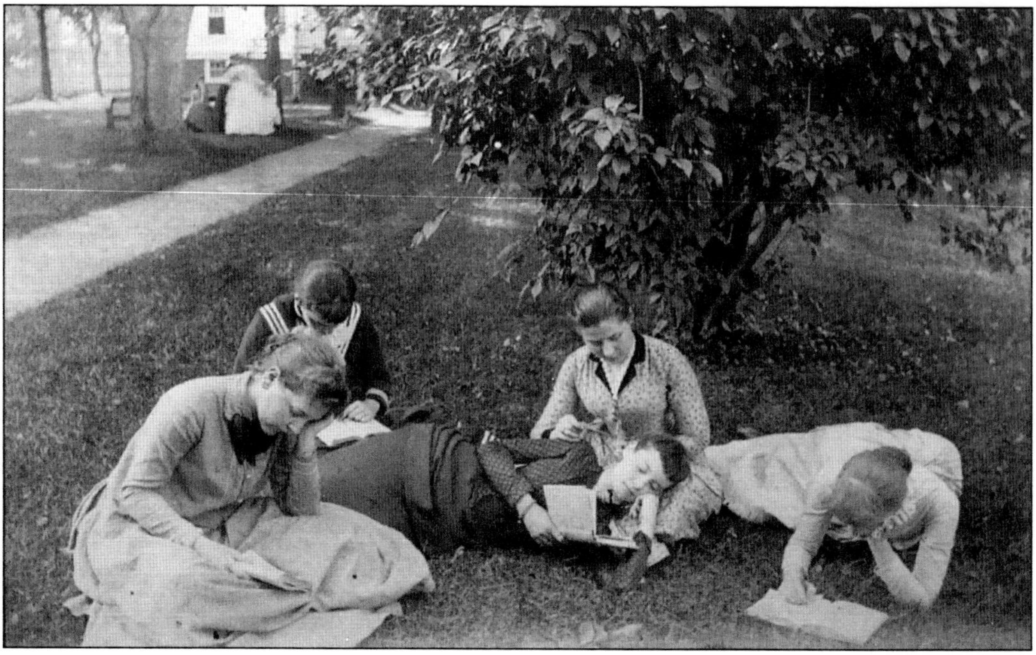

READING IN THE SHADE, 1880s. Five students from the Freehold Young Ladies' Seminary (FYLS), which was founded in 1844, lounged in the shade to read their lessons together. The school consisted of several buildings located on a block between Broad and Main Streets. (MCHA Archives FR525.)

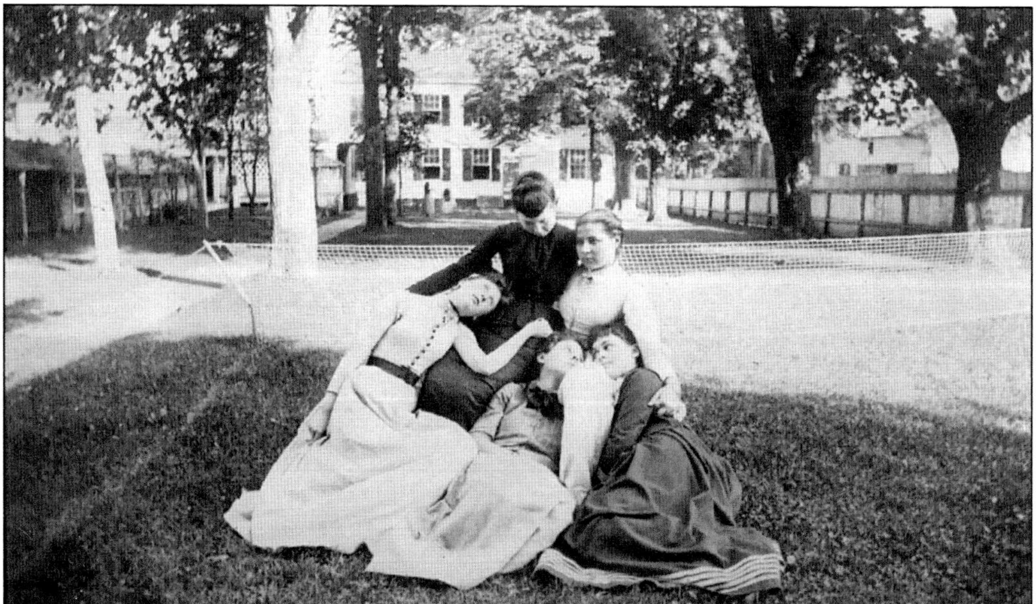

POSING FOR THE CAMERA, 1880s. This series of photographs seems to have been taken on the last day of school. These dear friends huddled together before being separated for the summer—or perhaps they are playing Art History charades and the answer is Pieta? (MCHA Archives FR529.)

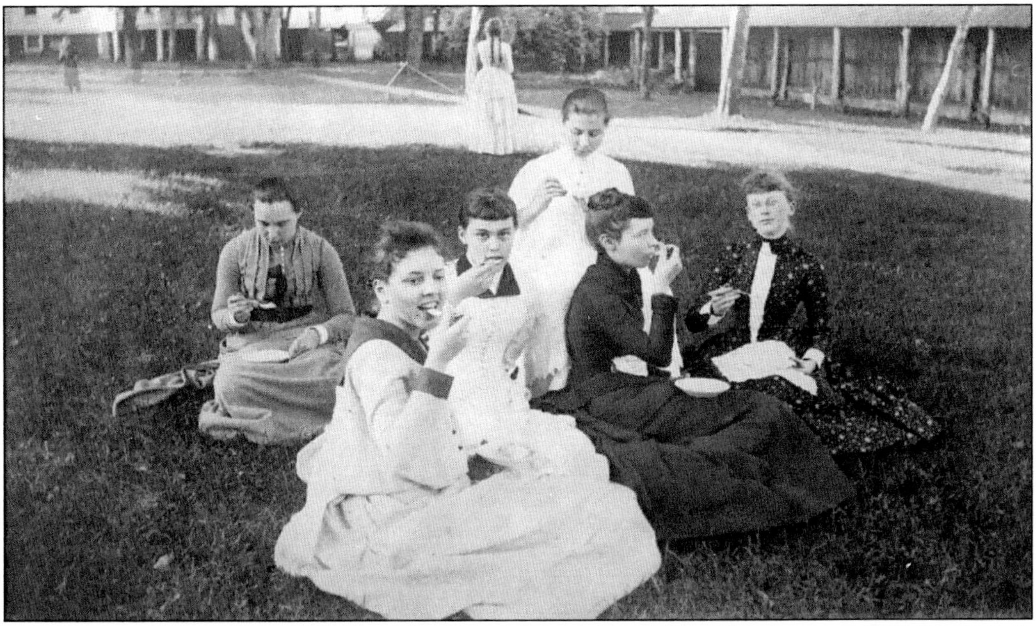

LUNCH *AL FRESCO*, 1880s. FYLS students are, from left to right, Floss Layton, Effie Underhill, Bess Smith, Ted Newton, Marguerite Lowe, Grace Cook, and Ada Smith (in the background playing tennis). (MCHA Archives FR528.)

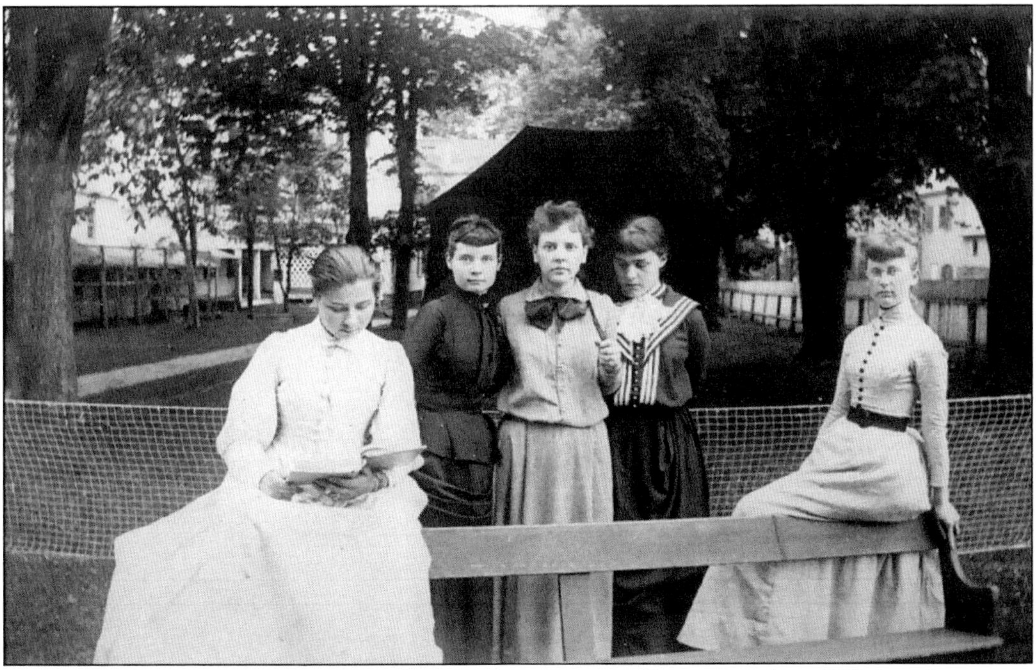

AT THE TENNIS COURT, 1880s. Looking uncharacteristically serious, these FYLS students pose in front of the tennis net. Tennis was a part of the physical education curriculum, and, in keeping with the times, the girls played in long skirts. (MCHA Archives FR527.)

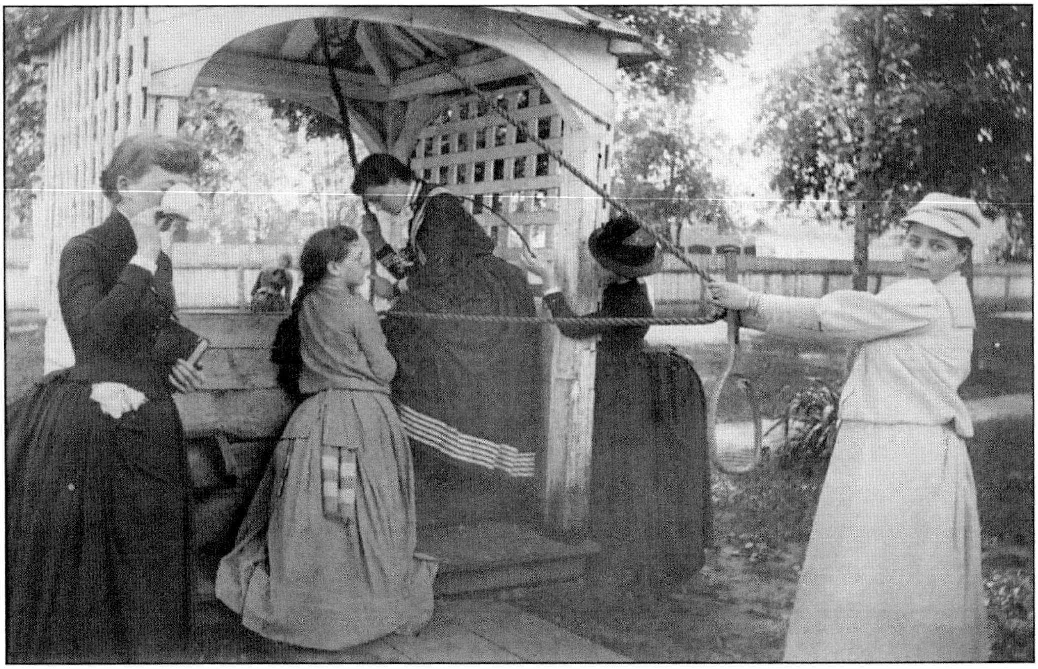

At the Well, 1880s. An old well was used on the grounds of the FYLS for drinking water. The girl drawing water was being tickled by a friend, peeking from around the side of the well house. (MCHA Archives FR526.)

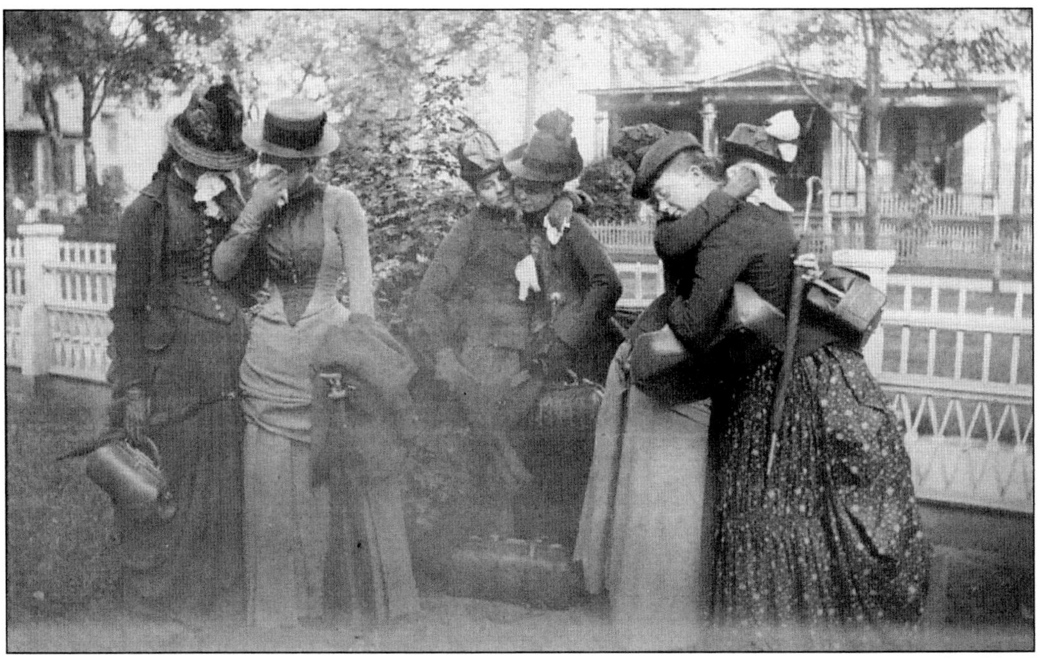

Close of School Year, 1880s. Dressed for travel, seminary students embraced and sobbed for the camera before parting for the summer. Lasting friendships developed among the young ladies who attended school together, and often, as documented by remaining letters, they corresponded with each other long after their school days. (MCHA Archives FR531.)

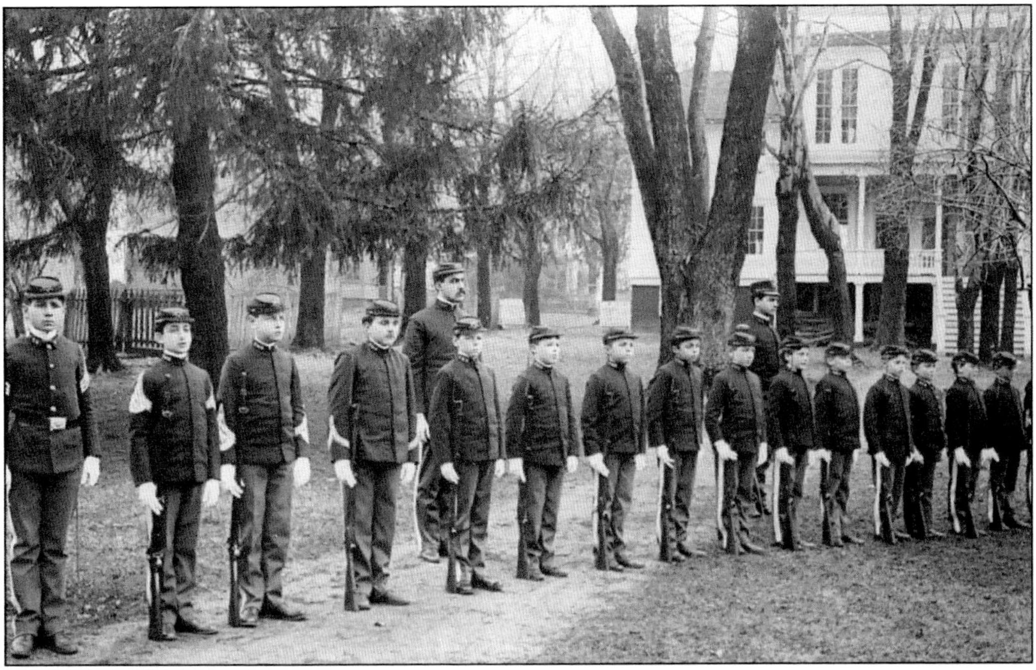

FREEHOLD MILITARY SCHOOL, C. 1910. The Freehold Military School began in 1900 on the grounds of the FYLS, which had recently closed—what a change in the deportment of the students on this campus! (Collection of Richard J. Dalik.)

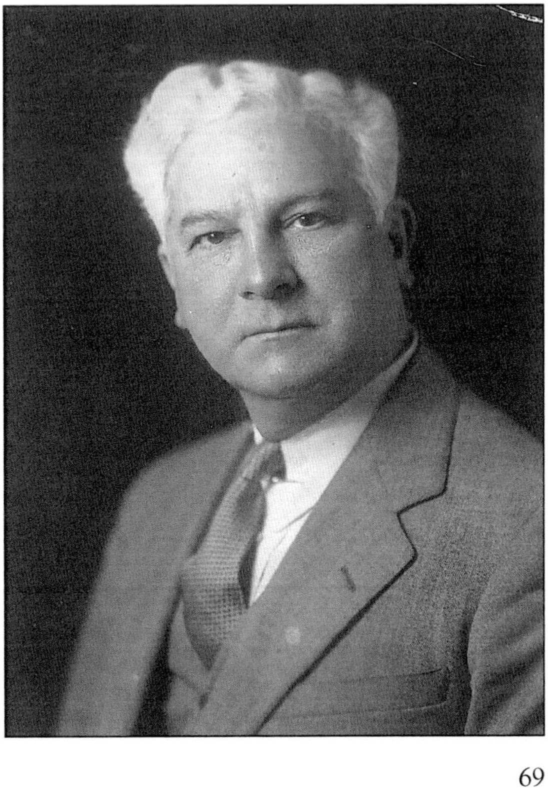

MAJOR CHARLES M. DUNCAN, C. 1920. Major Duncan served as headmaster at the Freehold Military School, which was owned by Colonel Charles Jefferson Wright. Colonel Wright also owned the New Jersey Military Academy (the successor to the Freehold Military Academy) and the two merged in 1916 under Duncan's leadership. (Collection of Nancy DuBois Wood.)

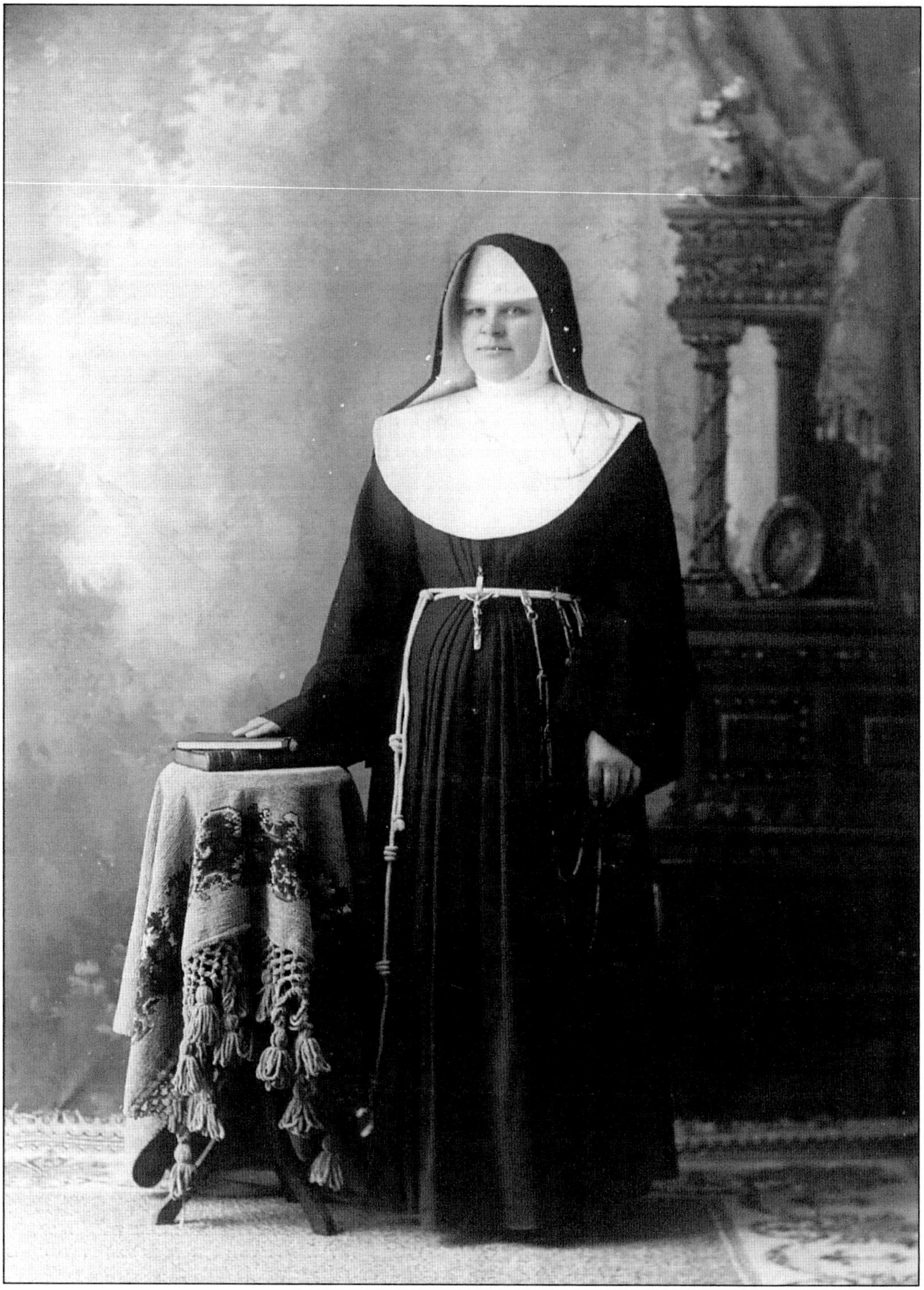

Unidentified Sister, c. 1880s. In 1875, St. Rose Parish in Freehold opened the first parochial school in the county. Several years later, it expanded and engaged three sisters from the Third Order of St. Francis in Philadelphia to come teach the students. This is most likely one of those three. (Photograph by Hall Studio, Freehold. Collection of Kevin Coyne.)

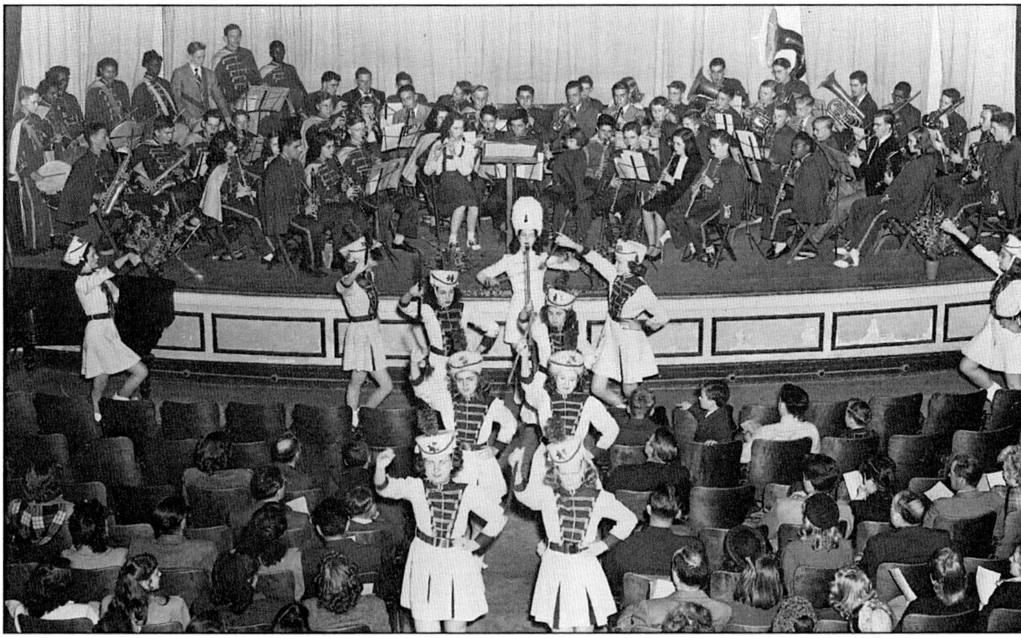

MAJORETTES, 1948. The Majorette squad marched for the audience at the Freehold High School's Spring Band Concert. (Collection of Mary Jane Whalen.)

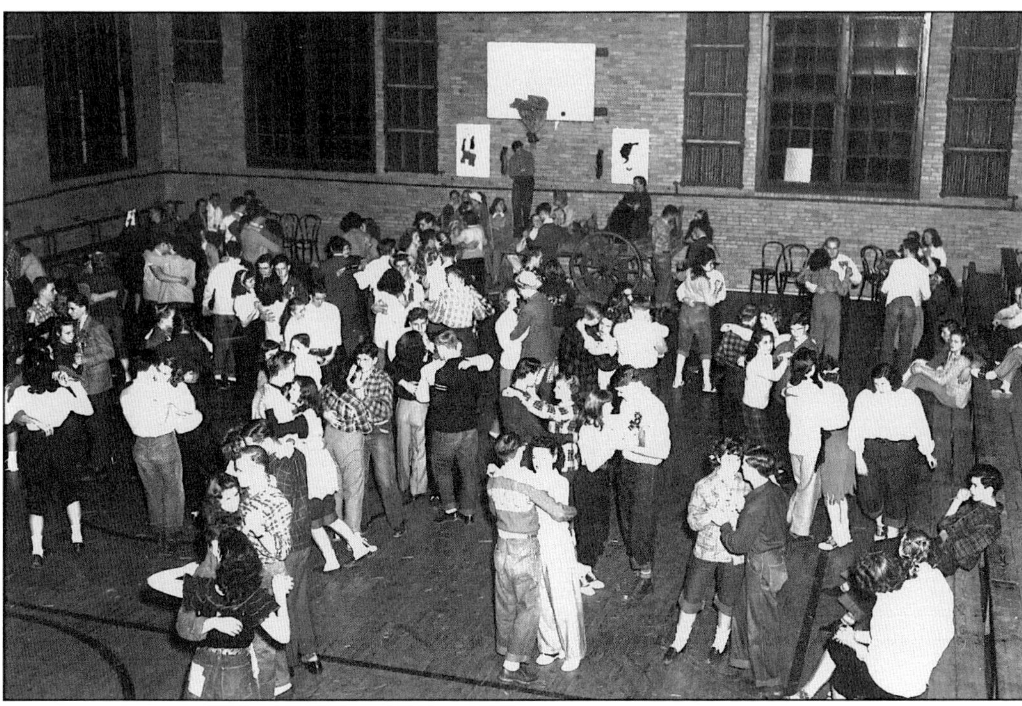

SADIE HAWKINS DANCE, 1948. Freehold High School held a sock hop in February to celebrate Sadie Hawkins Day. According to one attendee, it was a very enjoyable evening. (Collection of Mary Jane Whalen.)

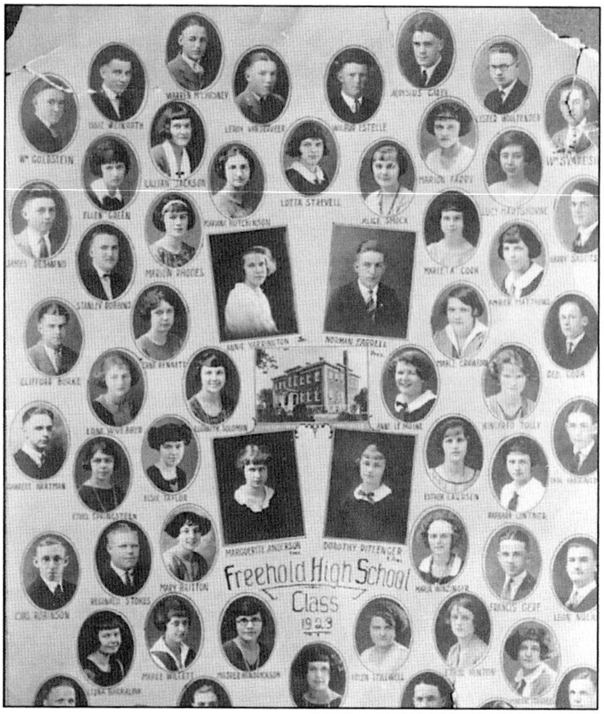

CLASS PICTURE, 1923. Freehold High School's class of 1923 is shown in this popular portrait format. The hairstyles and attire show the students to be a very fashion conscious and sophisticated group indeed. (MCHA Archives.)

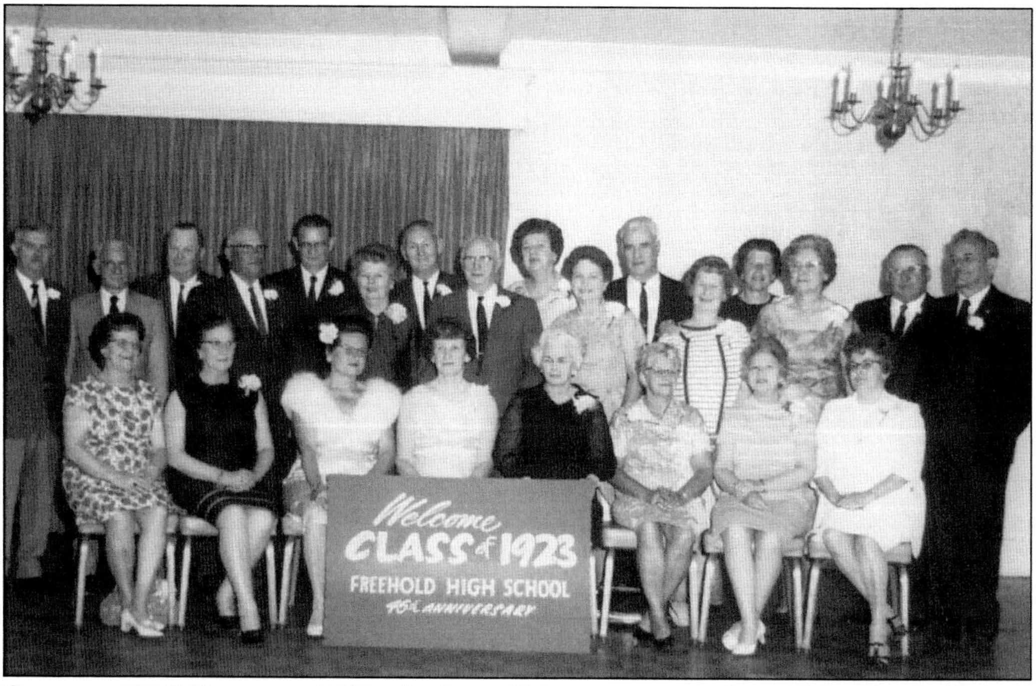

CLASS OF 1923 REUNION, 1968. At their 45th reunion, members of the Freehold High School's class of 1923 were as stylish as ever. (Photography by Bernard Studio. MCHA Archives 1998.18.)

Six

Commerce and Industry

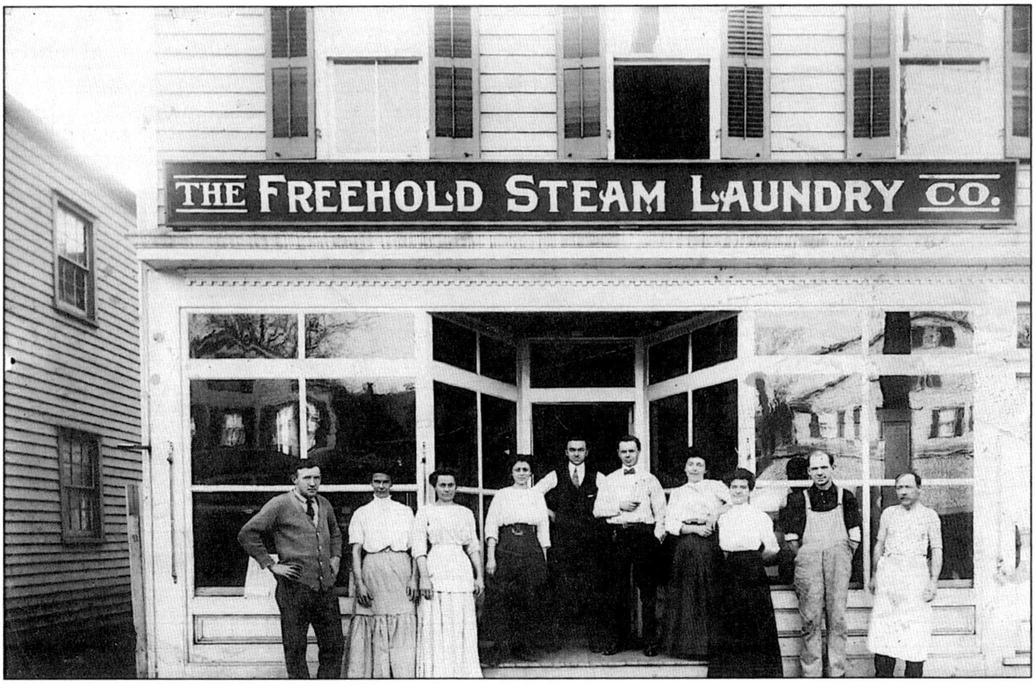

Freehold Steam Laundry, c. 1880s. Several laundry businesses thrived in 19th-century Freehold to serve the growing community's needs. Before the age of permanent press, commercial steam laundries provided a strong and thorough cleaning process that was not possible to perform at home. (Collection of Carl N. Steinberg.)

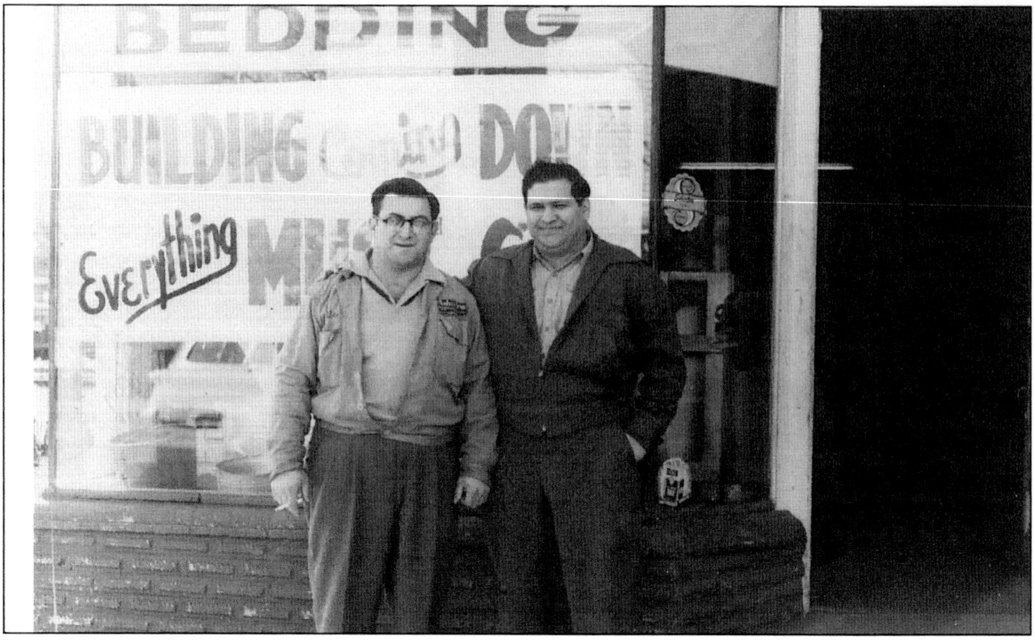

JACK AND ABE STEINBERG, 1953. Freehold Furniture Exchange, then located at 46-50 Throckmorton Street, was founded in the 1920s by Sarah Steinberg and later run by her sons, Jack and Abe Steinberg. It provided all general household needs from appliances to rugs to baby carriages. The business is carried on by the third generation today. (Collection of Carl N. Steinberg.)

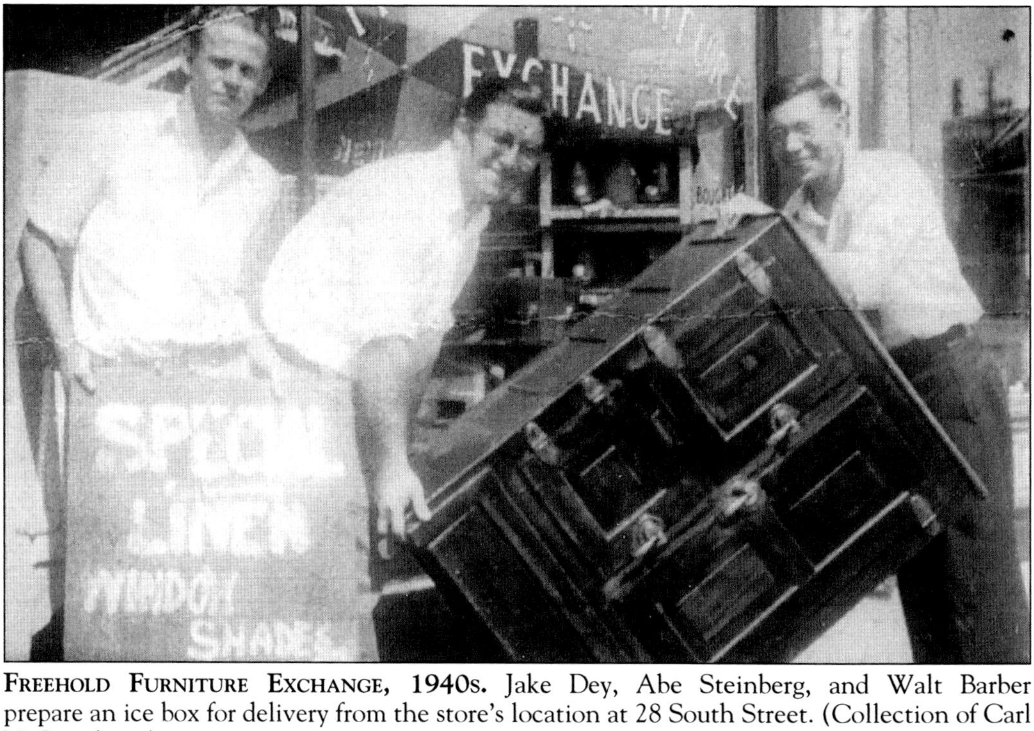

FREEHOLD FURNITURE EXCHANGE, 1940s. Jake Dey, Abe Steinberg, and Walt Barber prepare an ice box for delivery from the store's location at 28 South Street. (Collection of Carl N. Steinberg.)

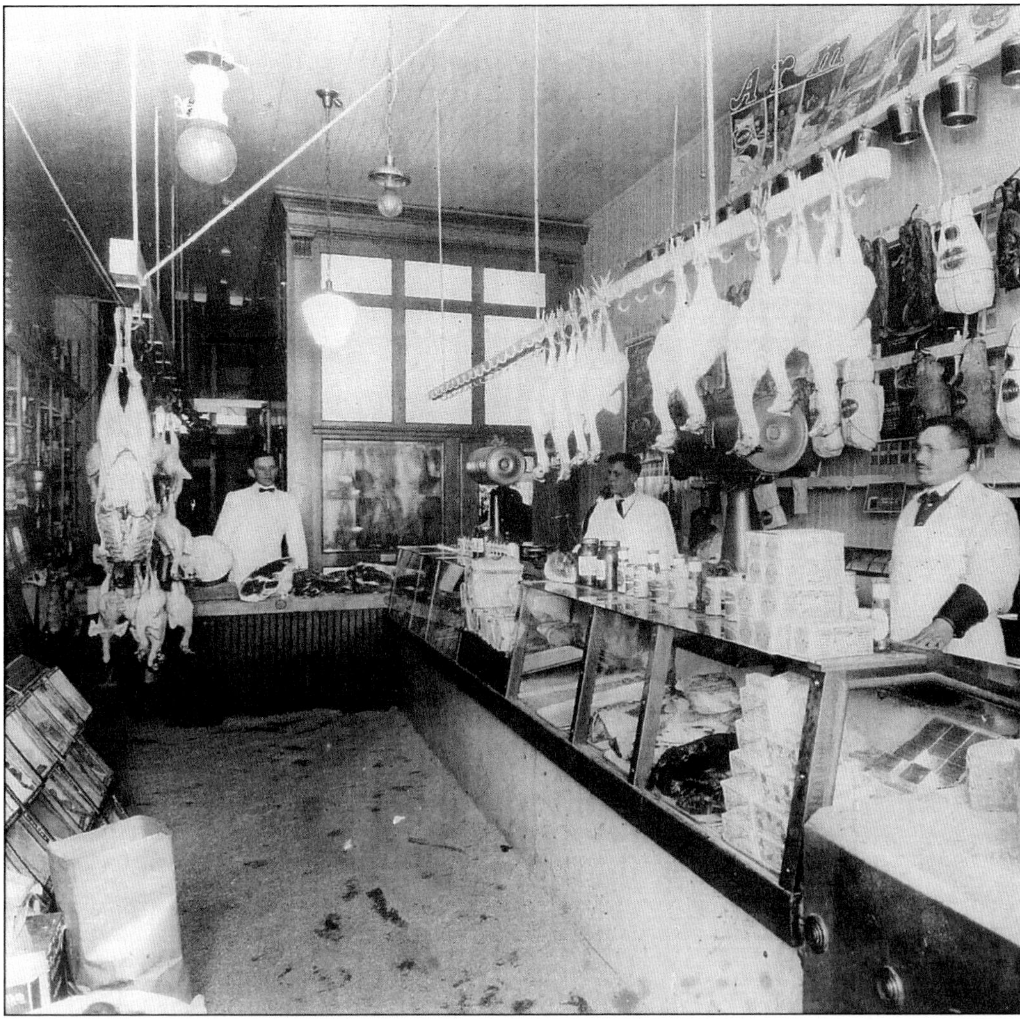

SAGOTSKY'S BUTCHER SHOP, C. 1925. The interior of the butcher shop on Main Street shows meats and poultry ready for purchase, as well as canned goods. Israel Sagotsky ran the shop at 44 West Main Street with his sons, Max and Morris. From left to right, are Max, Morris, and Israel. See a photograph of their truck on p. 111. (Collection of Carl N. Steinberg.)

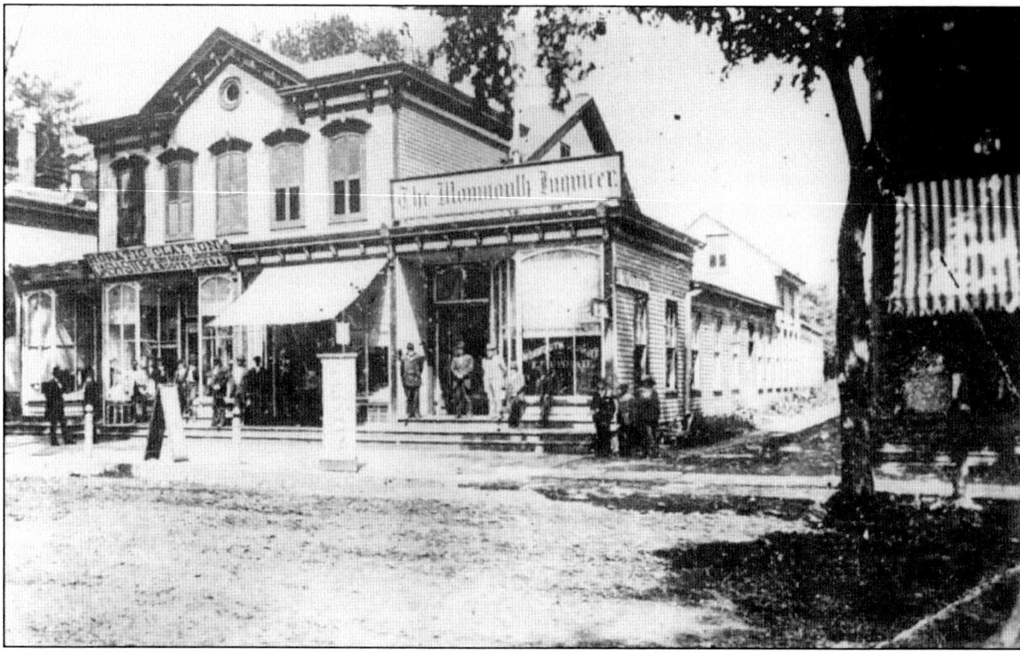

Clayton's Dry Goods, c. 1890. The mainstay of small town life was the dry goods store, which carried a variety of consumer needs from shoes to patent medicines to groceries. (Collection of Carl N. Steinberg.)

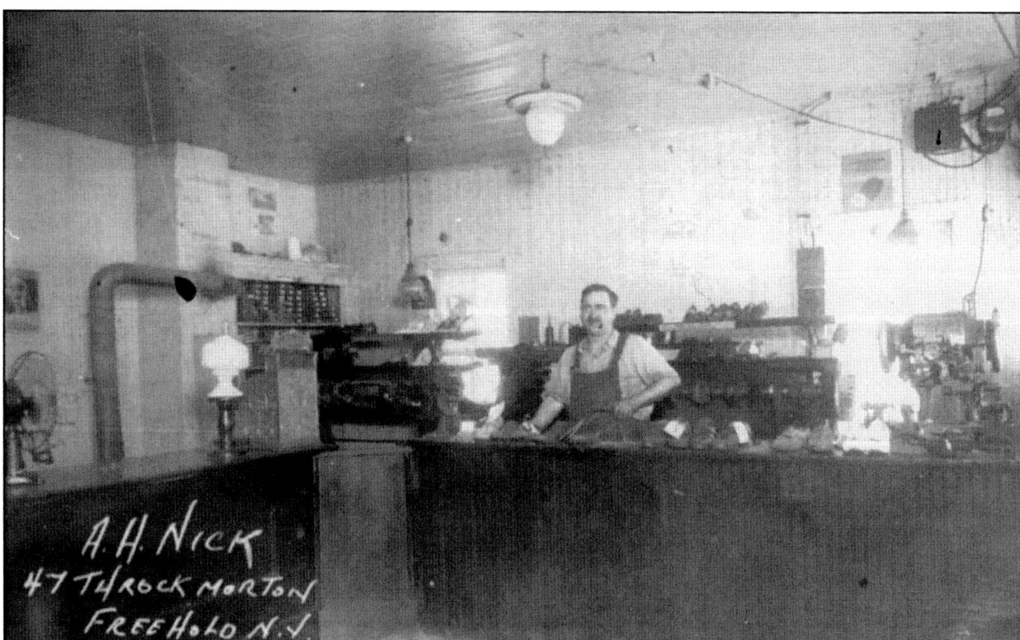

A.H. Nick, c. 1910. Shoemaker Nicholas Accasano operated out of a store that was located at 47 Throckmorton Street where a strip of 1960s storefronts now house Thrift Shops and the Open Door. According to a descendant, a sign maker's error changed Mr. Accasano's business name to "A.H. Nick." (Collection of Carl N. Steinberg.)

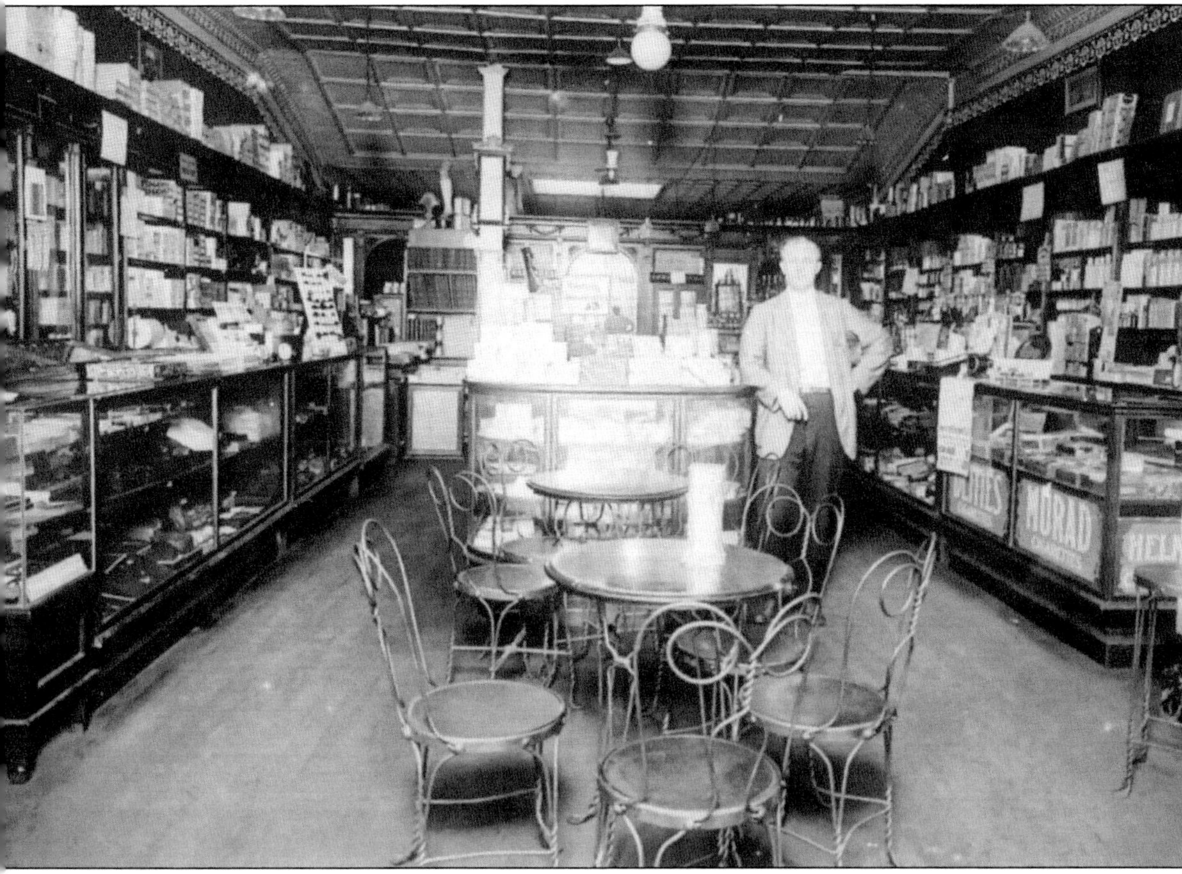

Bacon's Drug Store, c. 1920. The perfect interior details of E.G. Bacon's store—the tin ceiling, soda fountain, and wire ice cream chairs—create a vivid impression of small town life that Hollywood set designers would envy. (Collection of Richard J. Dalik.)

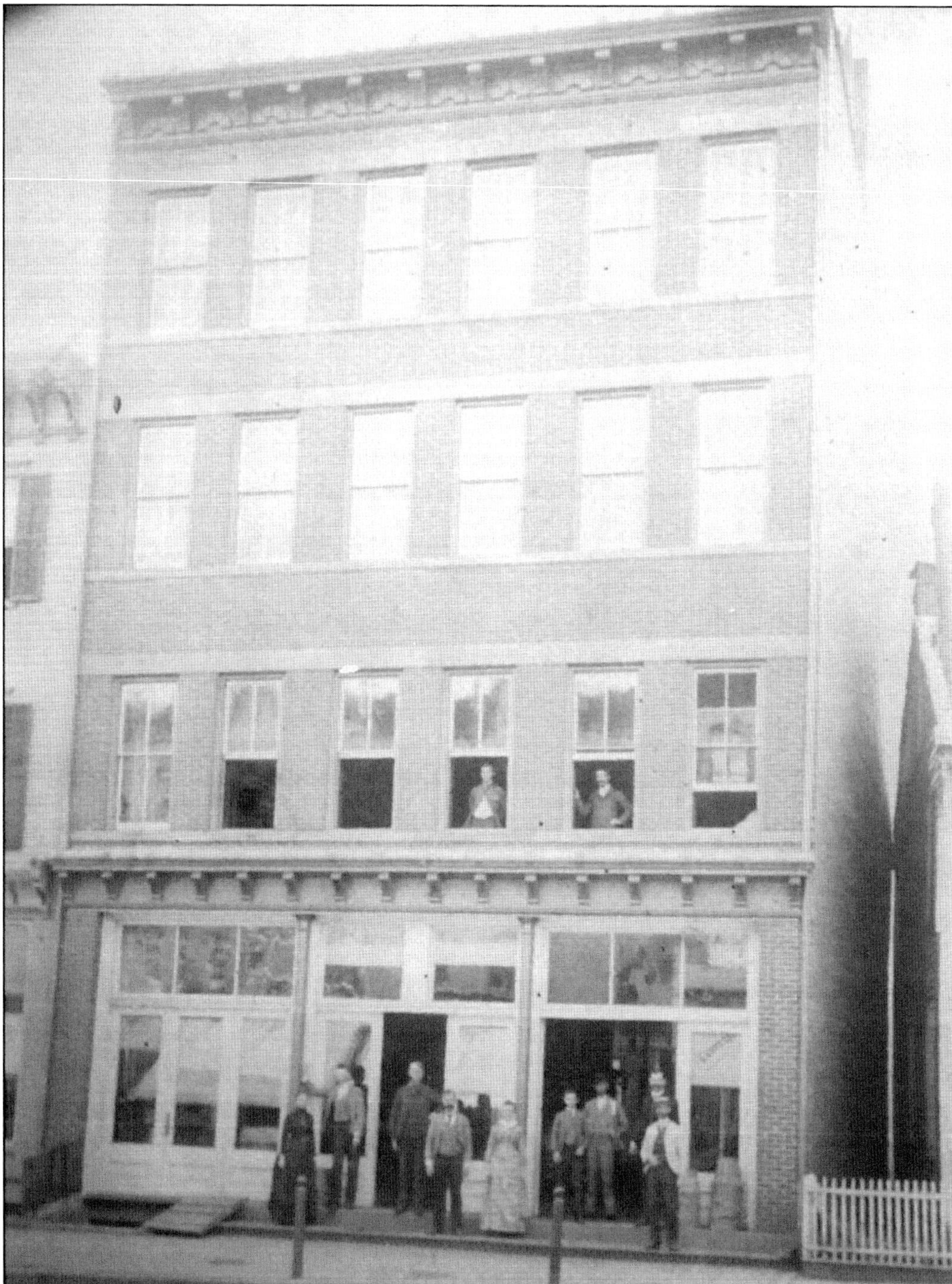

D.C. PERRINE'S, c. 1880s. The growth of Freehold's business center along Main Street and South Street produced some fine and substantial examples of commercial Victorian architecture. Perrine's store, built in the 1870s, sold "general merchandise" and was noted in the press as the largest and most successful business of its kind in the county. (Collection of Carl N. Steinberg.)

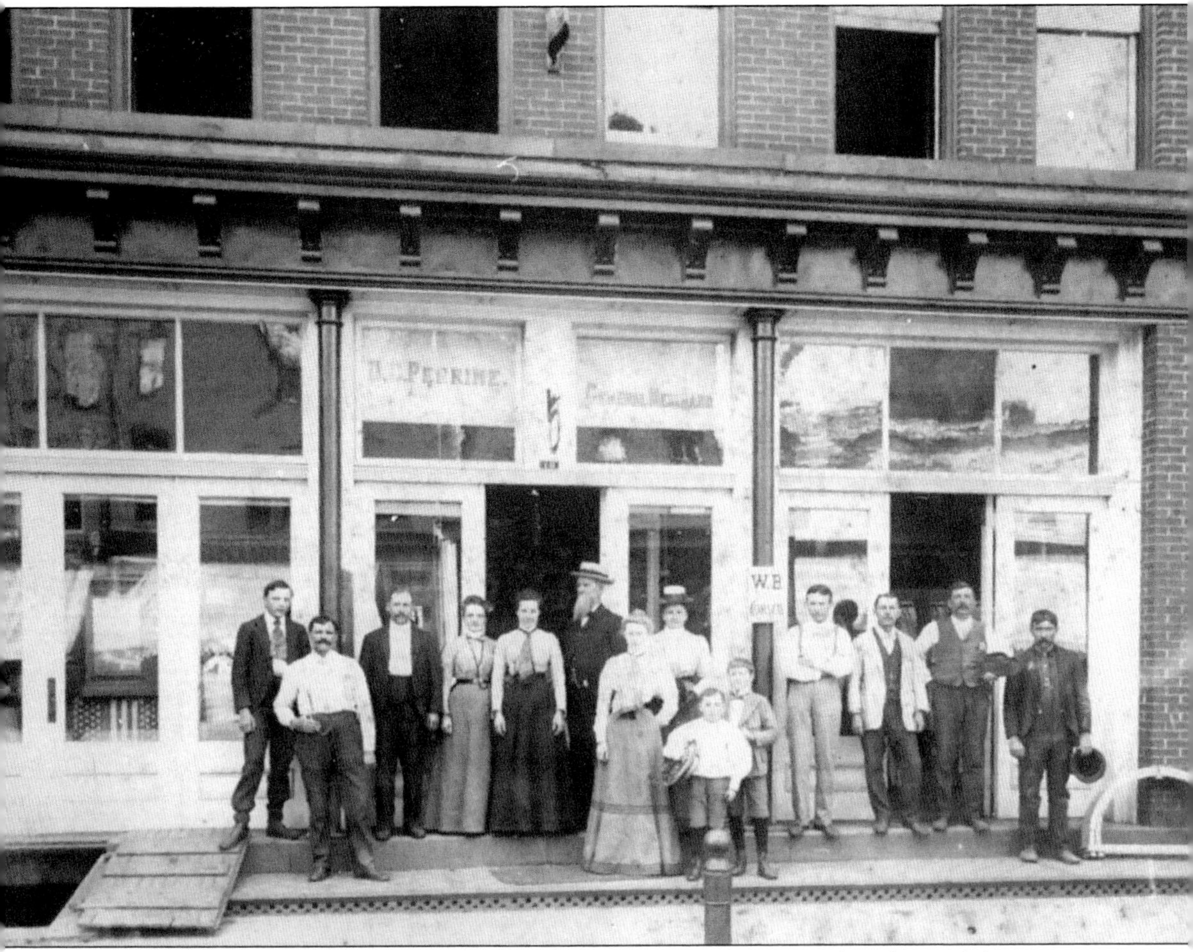

D.C. Perrine's c. 1880s. The owners and employees of Perrine's posed in front of the store. David Clark Perrine died in 1888 and his son, David VanDerveer Perrine, took over the business, keeping this location and building a new store on Main Street. (Photograph by Bergman & Freidin, Asbury Park and Ocean Grove. Collection of Carl N. Steinberg.)

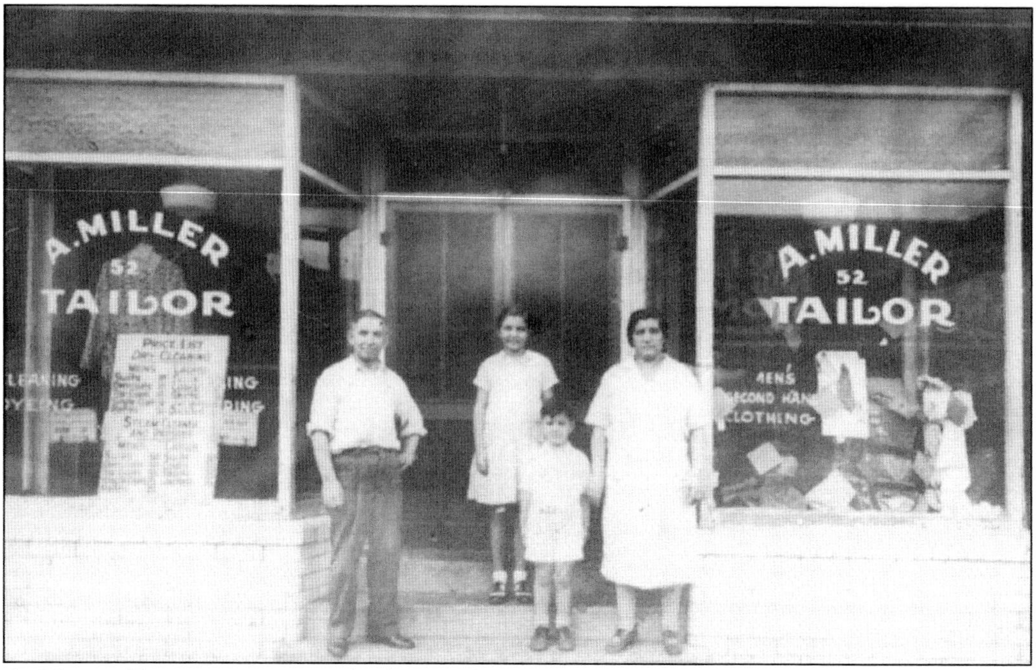

A. Miller Tailor, c. 1930. Abraham Miller stood in front of his store at 52 Throckmorton Street with his wife Lena and children Freda and Charlie. A group of small businesses thrived for a time on Throckmorton Street at a seemingly promising location, opposite the train station. (Collection of Carl N. Steinberg.)

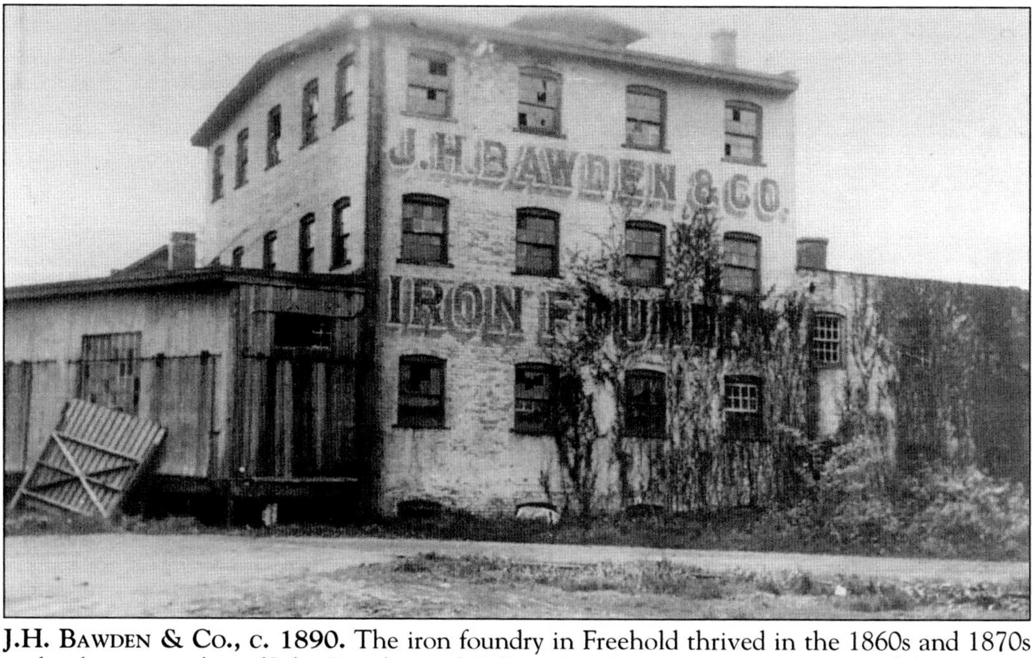

J.H. Bawden & Co., c. 1890. The iron foundry in Freehold thrived in the 1860s and 1870s under the partnership of John Bawden and Gilbert Combs. Ambitious and successful industrial ventures like this one enjoyed the prosperity that the railroad line brought to both commerce and agriculture when it was established in the 1850s. (Collection of Carl N. Steinberg.)

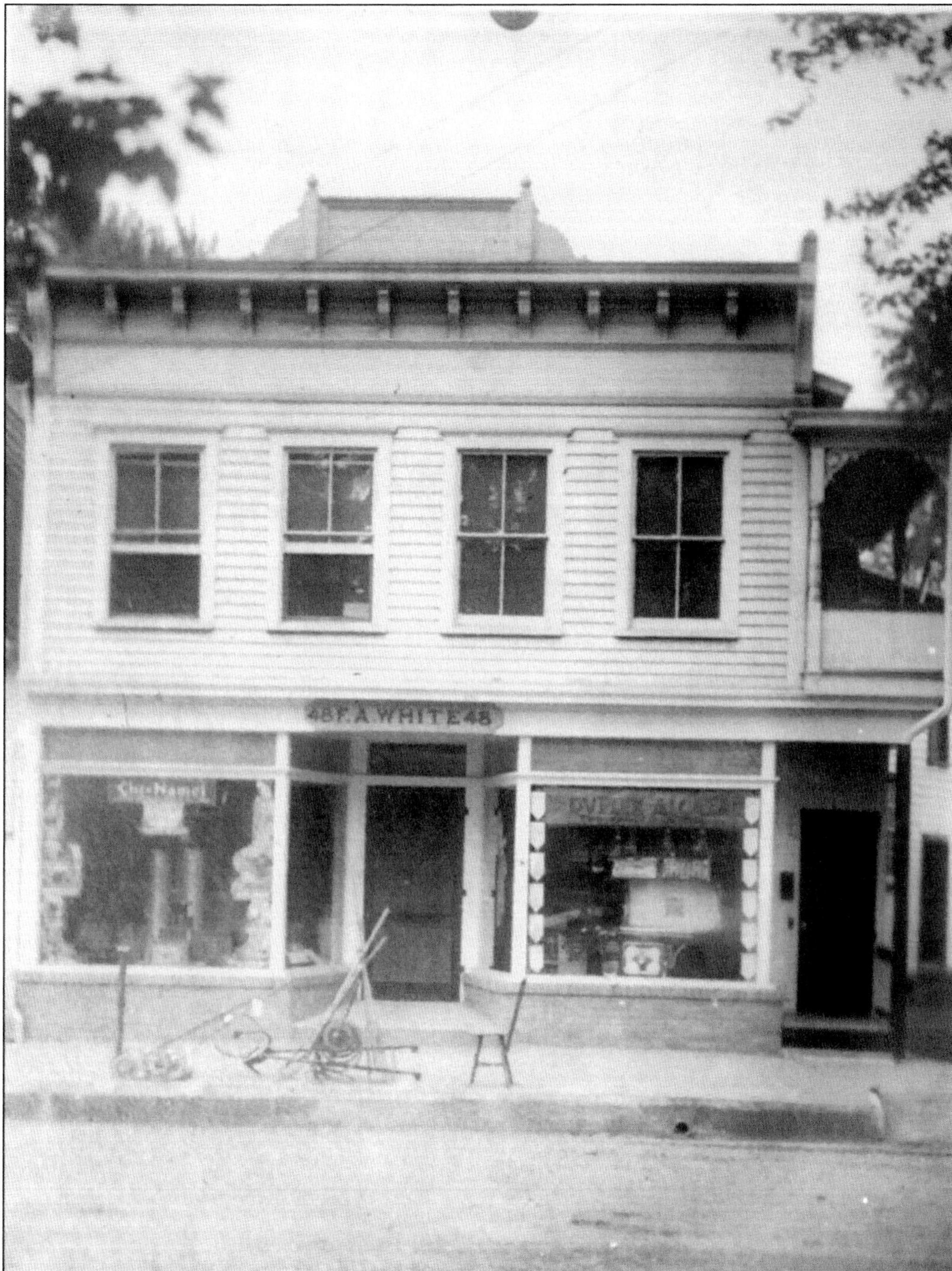

F.A. WHITE'S HARDWARE STORE, C. 1910. Frederick White assumed ownership of his father's tinsmithing and hardware business and supplied customers with agricultural equipment, enamel stoves, and sewing machines as well as smaller items. (Collection of Carl N. Steinberg.)

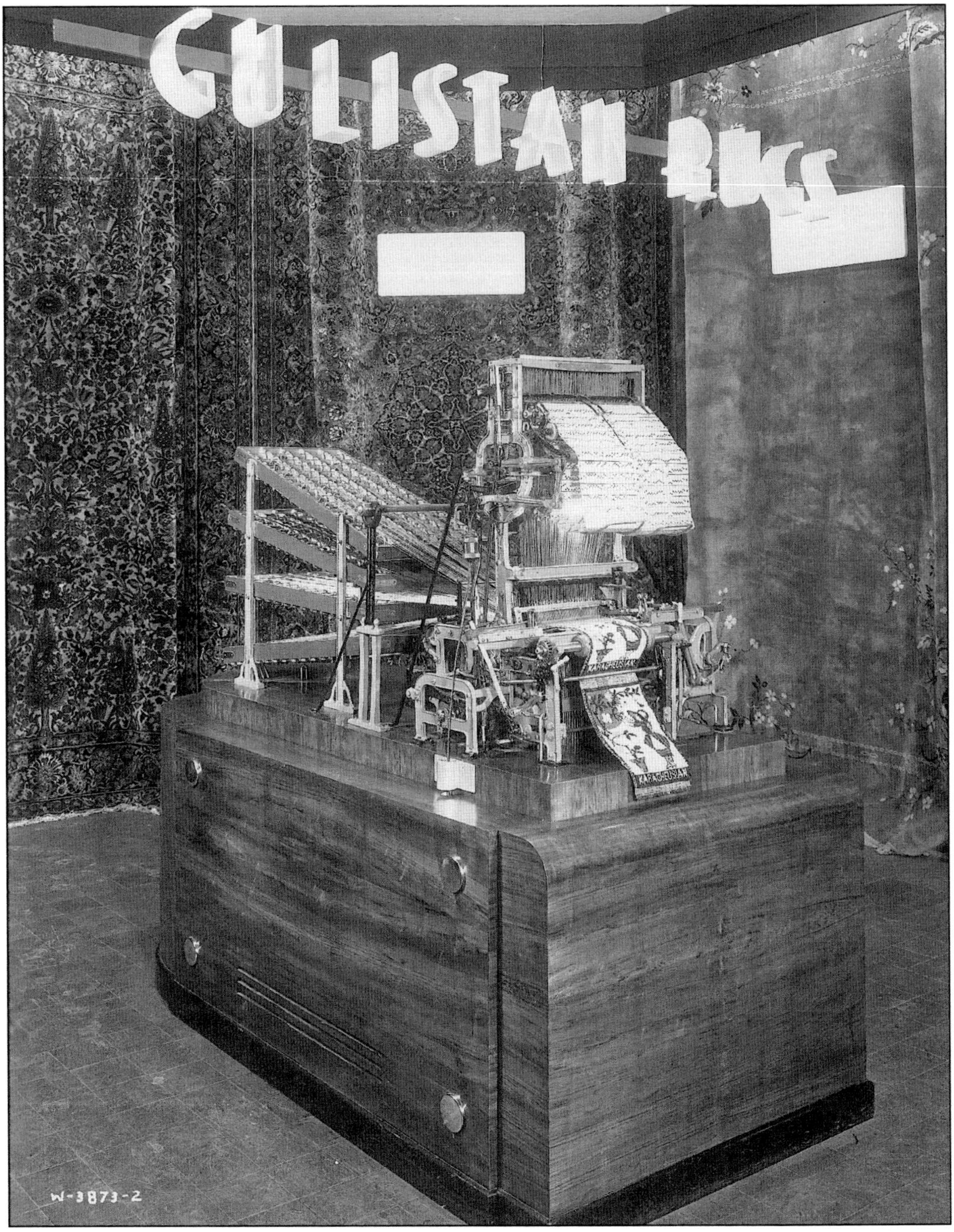

GULISTAN RUGS DISPLAY, 1933. A & M Karagheusian was represented at the Chicago World's Fair by a display of their Gulistan line of rugs and a miniature rug loom that worked to manufacture a small sample rug. (MCHA Archives FR457.)

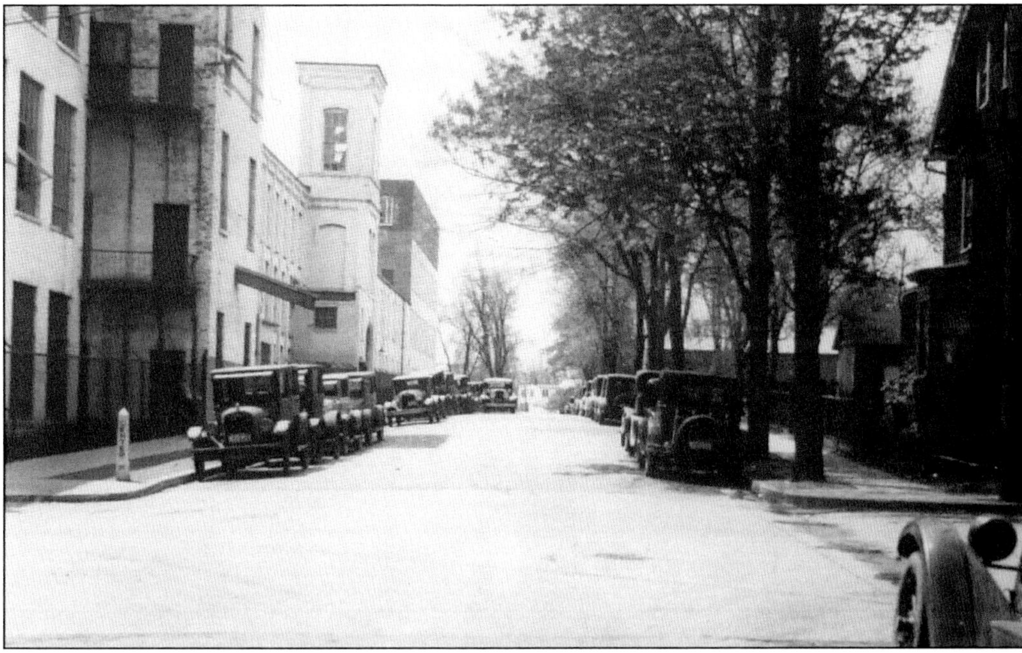

Karagheusian Rug Mill Buildings, late 1920s. The rug mill complex, which at one time employed more than half of Freehold's work force, stretched out along Jackson Street. The Rug Mill operated in Freehold from 1904 until the 1960s. (MCHA Archives FR423.)

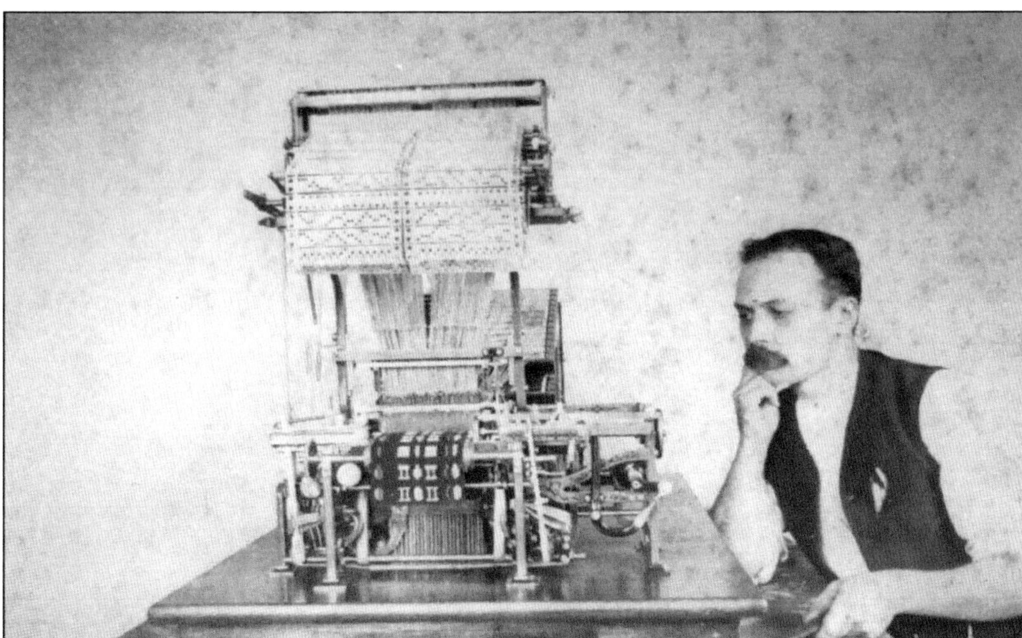

Miniature Rug Loom, c. 1930. Three miniature rug looms were made by Joseph Coley, shown with one of his creations, for use in expositions and displays like the one pictured on p. 82. One of those looms is in the museum collection of the Monmouth County Historical Association. (MCHA Archives FR456.)

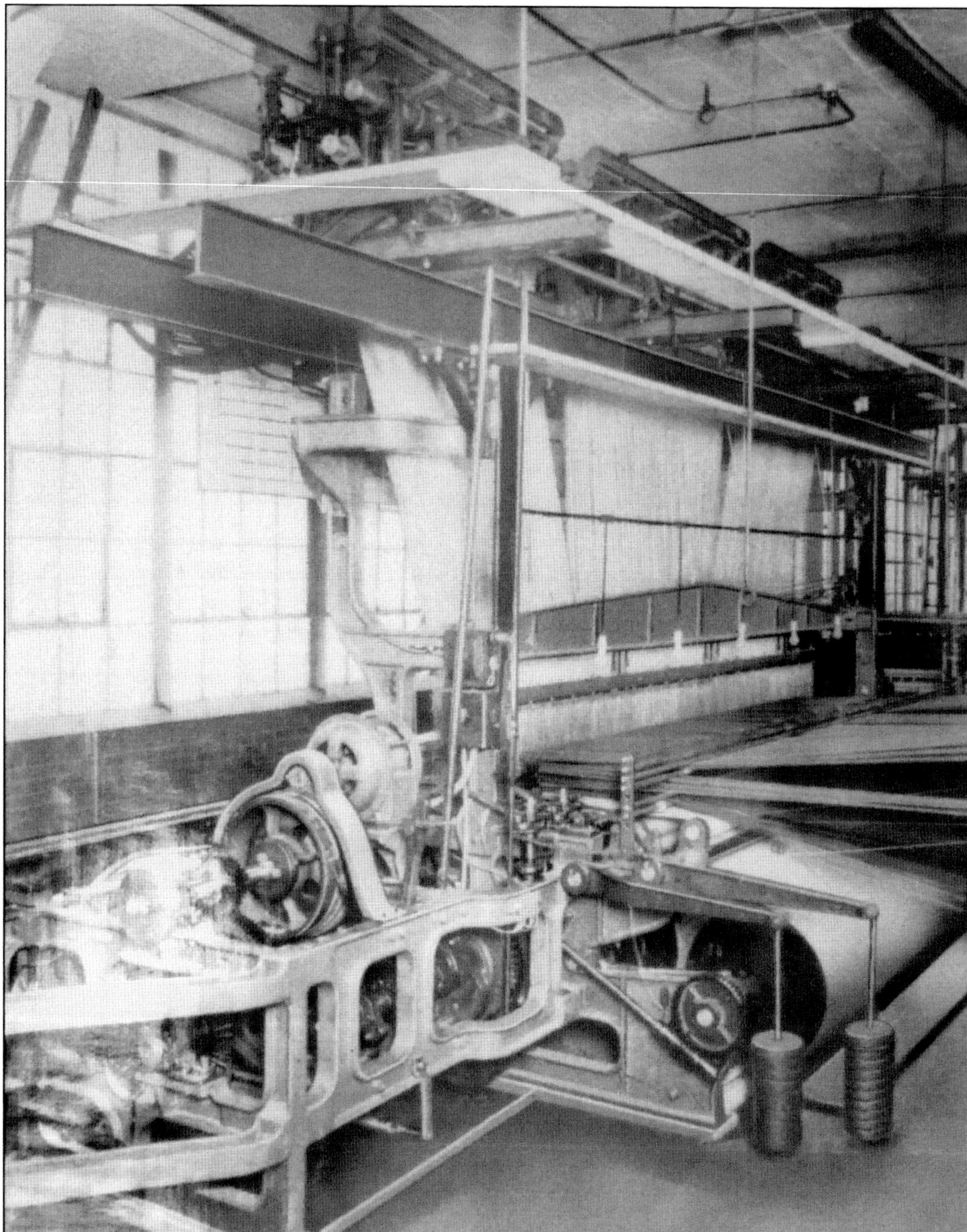

Broadloom, c. 1920s. This view of a broadloom in action shows the back where the yarn from the frames enters the loom to be woven into rugs. During WW II, the looms were adapted to weave duck cloth for the war effort. (Photographer, Barcey, Philadelphia. MCHA Archives FR430.)

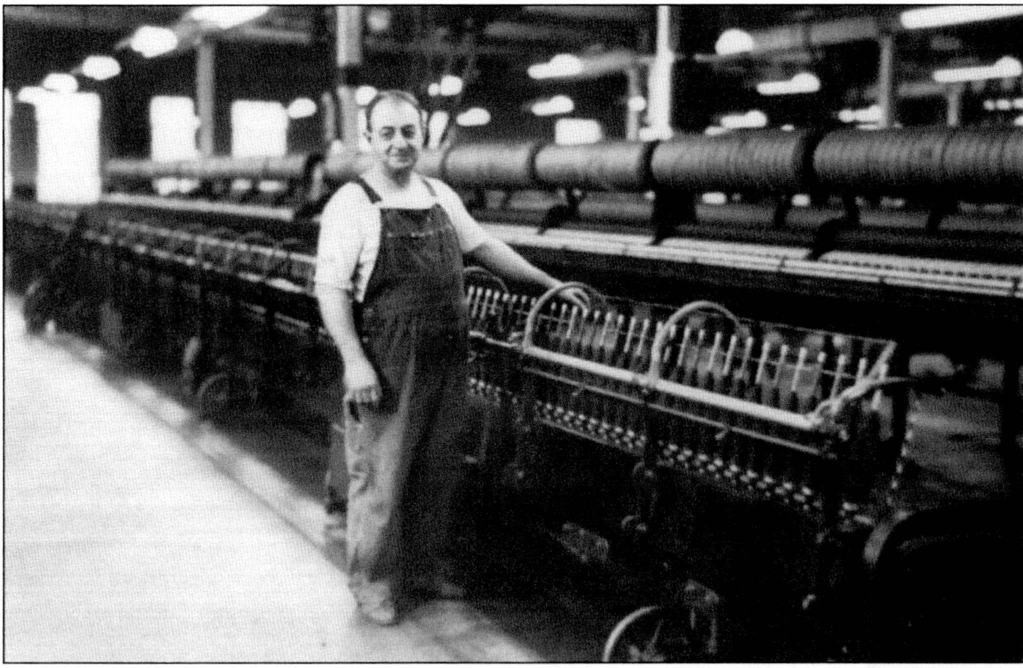

MR. ROSELLE, C. 1950S. This mill worker, identified only as "Roselle" on the reverse of the photograph, tends to the machinery at the Karagheusian Rug Mill. In the 1960s, economic and labor issues forced the business to relocate to North Carolina. (MCHA Archives FR437.)

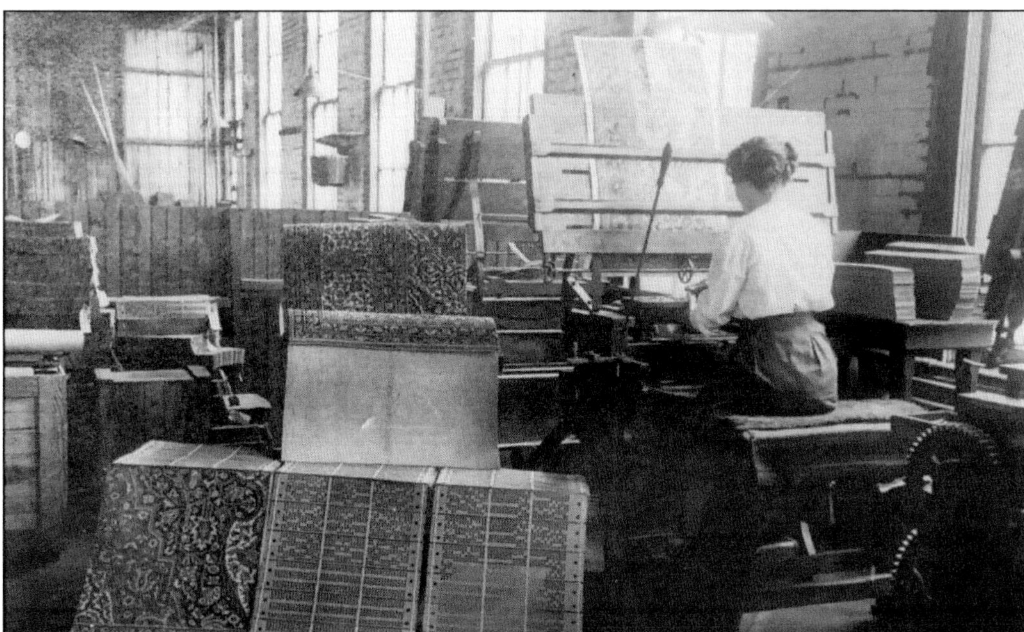

AT THE CARD LOOM, C. 1920S. An employee works with the punch cards that carried the elaborate oriental-rug patterns for which Karagheusian's Gulistan line was known. (Photograph by Hall Studio, Freehold. Collection of Carl N. Steinberg.)

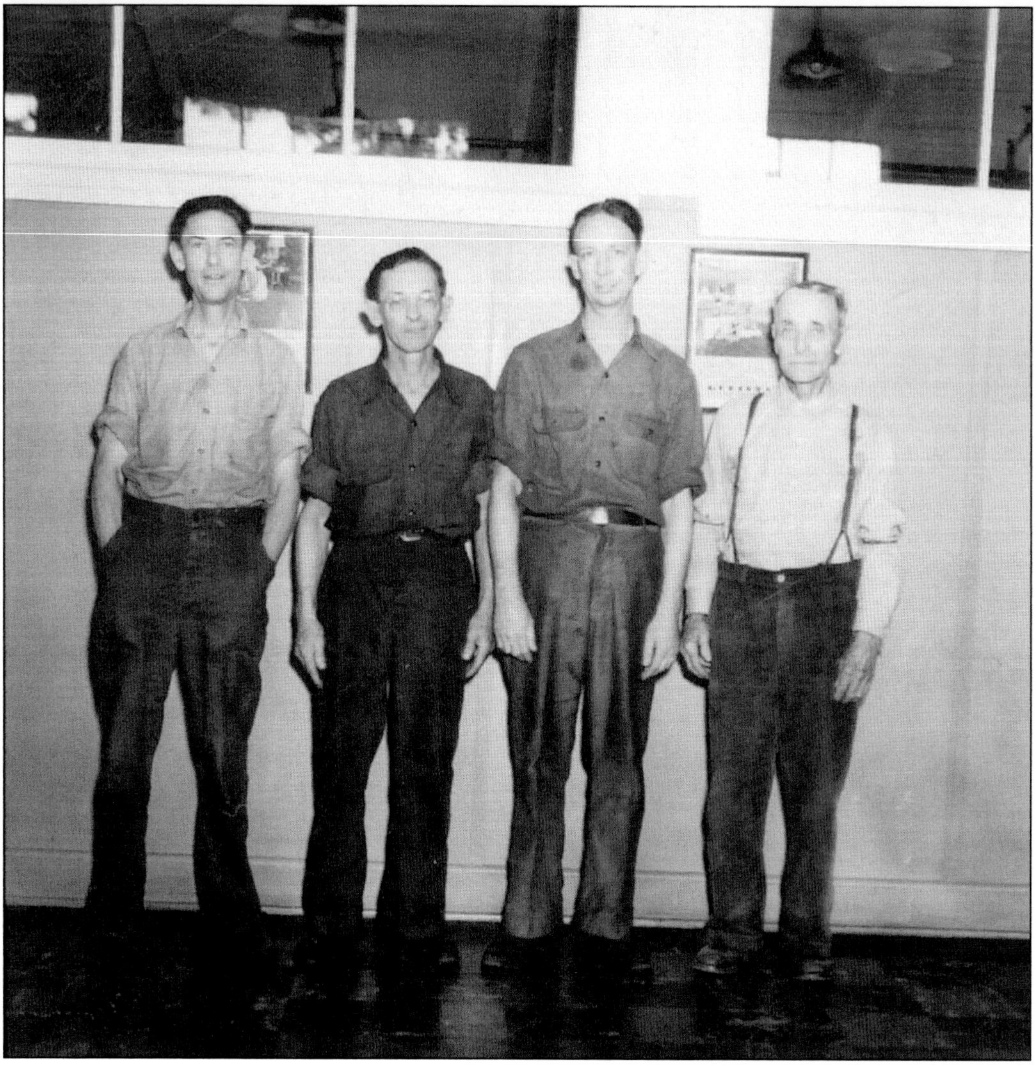

MILL FAMILY, 1950S. Three generations of the Anderson family worked together at the Karagheusian Rug Mill and were photographed for the mill's newsletter. They are, from left to right, Cortenus Anderson Jr., Conover Anderson, Carl Anderson, and Kortenus Anderson Sr. (Collection of Mary Jane Whalen.)

Seven
FAMILY PICTURES

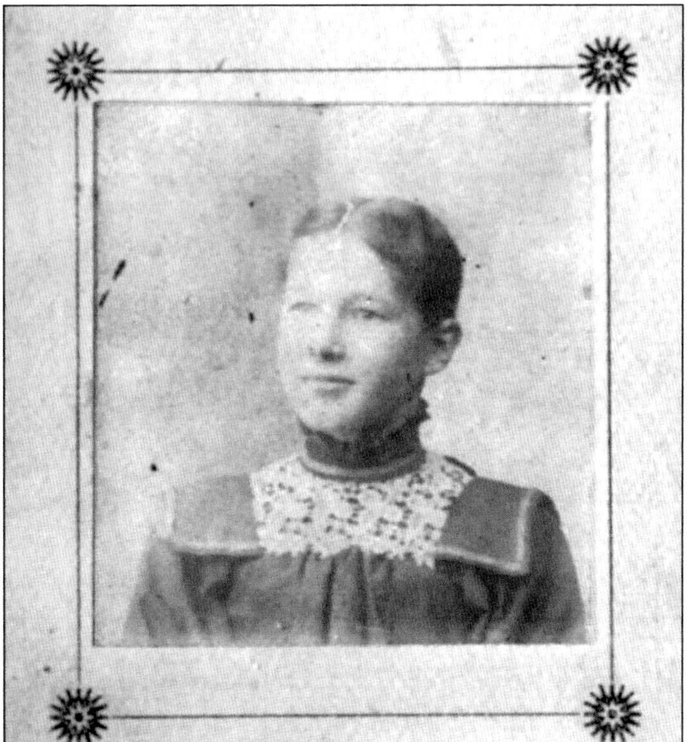

MARGUERITE RUE, C. 1905. Novelty photographs like this one evolved within the art and industry of portrait photography. The actual size of this "penny photograph" is 1 3/8" square. It was made by Pharr's of Mt. Holly and Freehold and probably held particular appeal to school age children who wished to give photographs to friends and family. This one is inscribed on the back to "Grandma." (MCHA Archives 1995.50.)

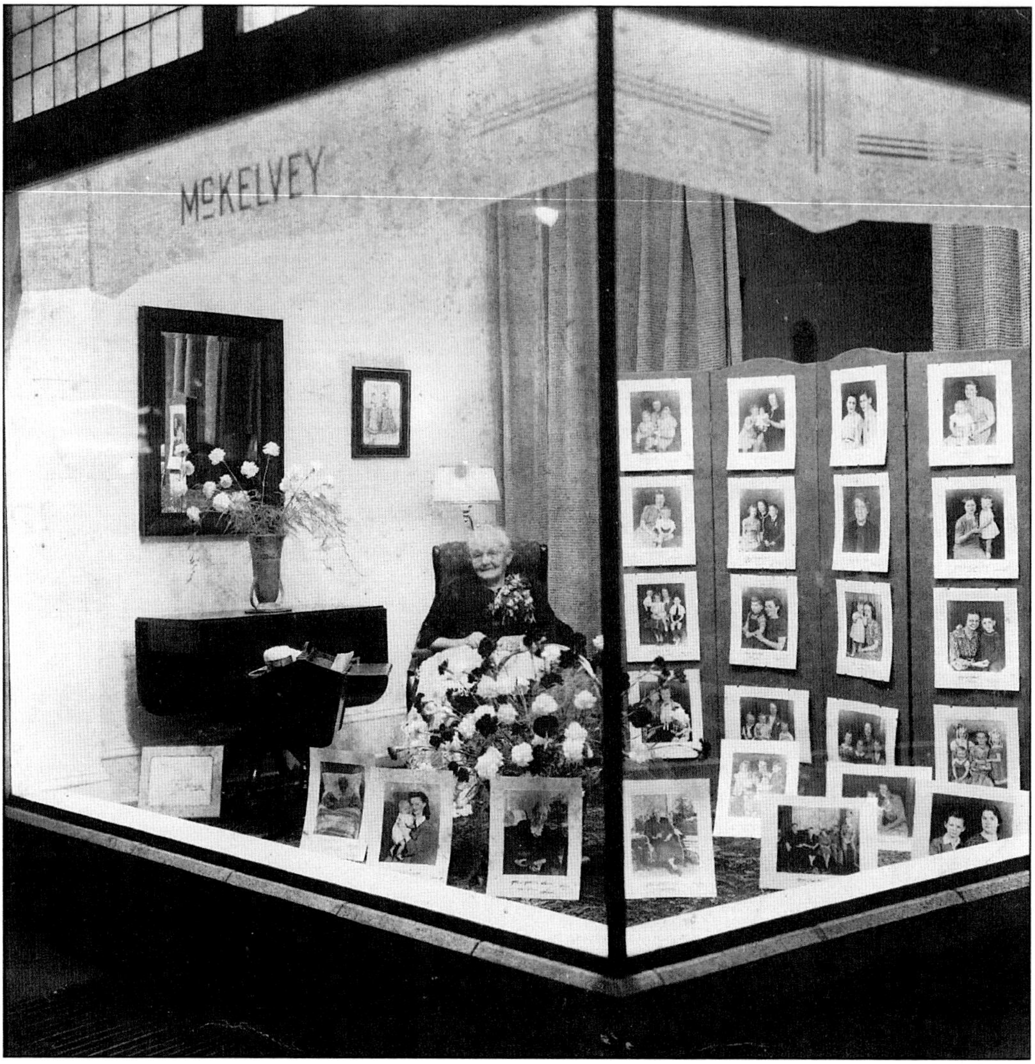

Mother's Day, c. 1939. McKelvey's store mounted the ultimate Mother's Day window display by arranging for a proud grandmother to sit in the storefront surrounded by family pictures. (Collection of Mary Jane Whalen.)

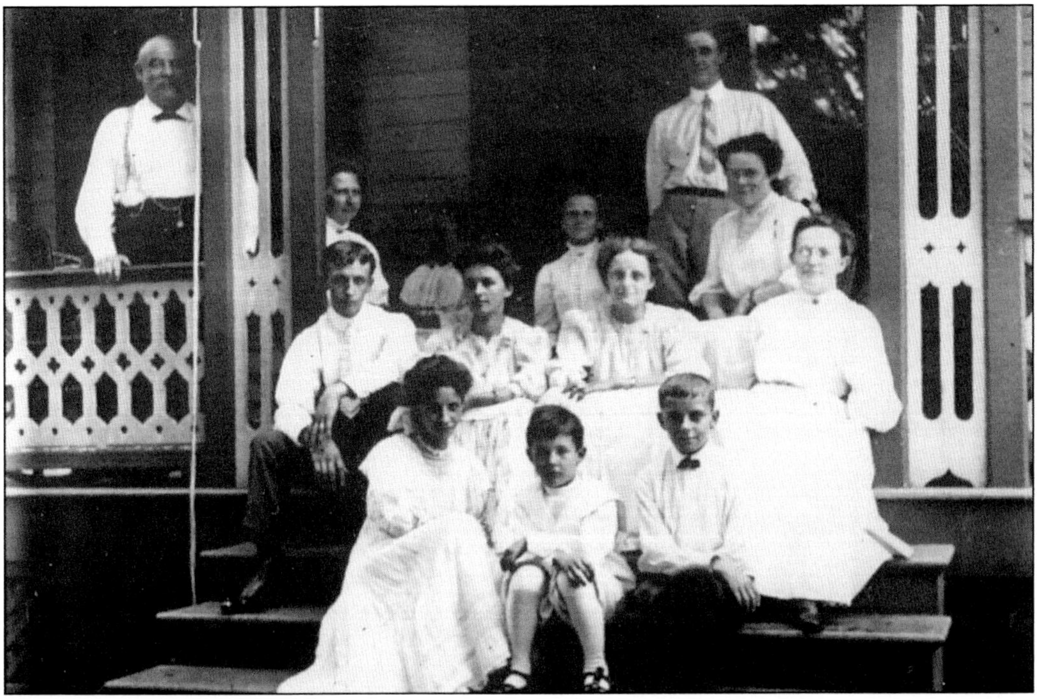

SIXTY-ONE SOUTH STREET, JULY 29, 1906. Family and friends—the Bacons', Muldoons', and Voorhees'—gather on a hot July day in their summer whites for a photograph on the porch. (Collection of Richard J. Dalik.)

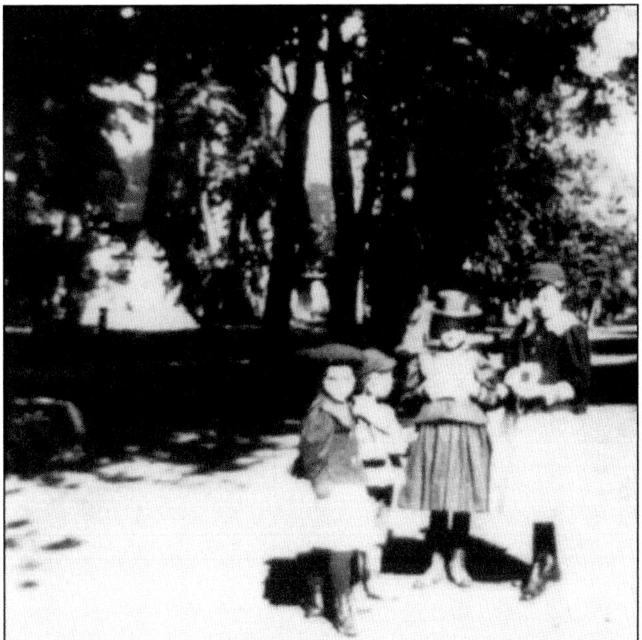

FRIENDS, C. 1900. Inscribed "Raymond Smith from Helen Mount," this photograph shows four young friends standing on Main Street. (MCHA Archives FR546.)

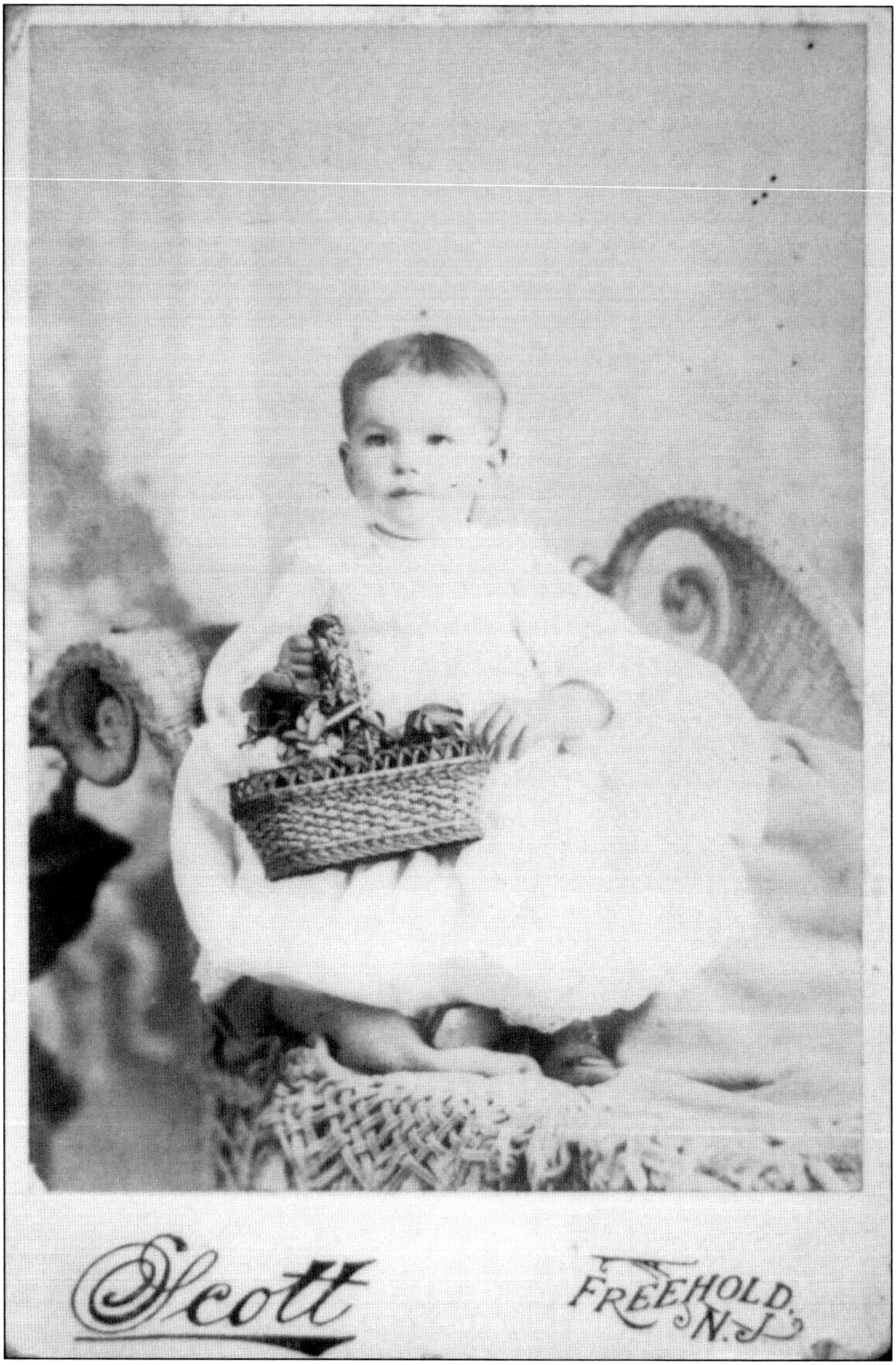

LILLIAN REID, C. 1895. The photographer, John Scott, gave baby Lillian a basket to play with as she sat on a wicker settee in his studio. (MCHA Archives 1995.50.)

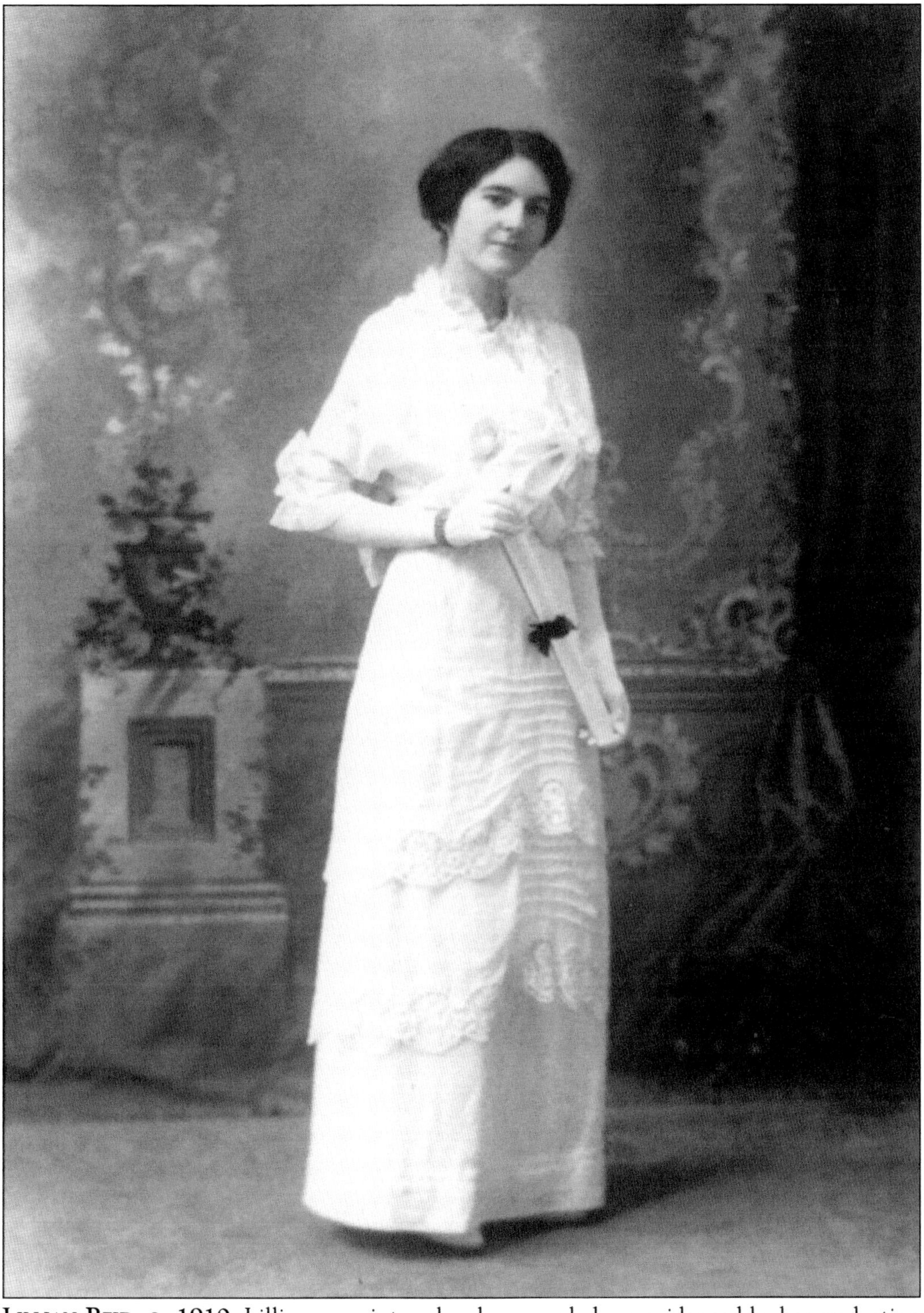

LILLIAN REID, C. 1910. Lillian grew into a lovely young lady as evidenced by her graduation photograph above. She dressed in a white dress with lace trim, holding her diploma, for the event. (Photograph by Hall Studio, Freehold. MCHA Archives 1995.50.)

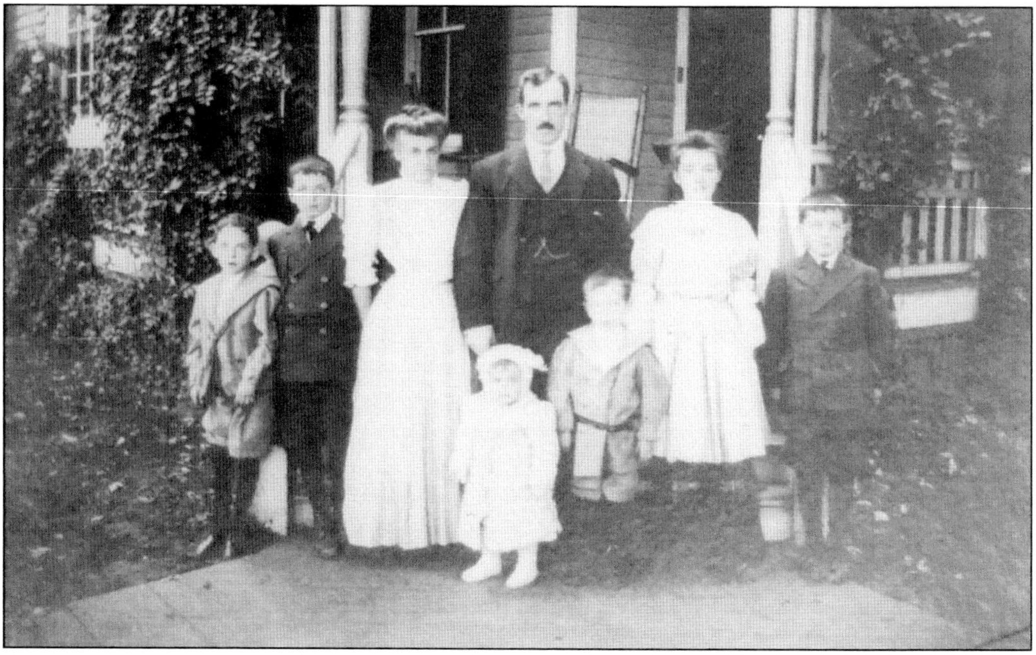

A Freehold Family, c. 1890s. A handsome but unidentified Freehold family gathered for their portrait. The six youngsters surround their proud parents standing at their front porch. (Photograph by Arthur Hall. MCHA Archives.)

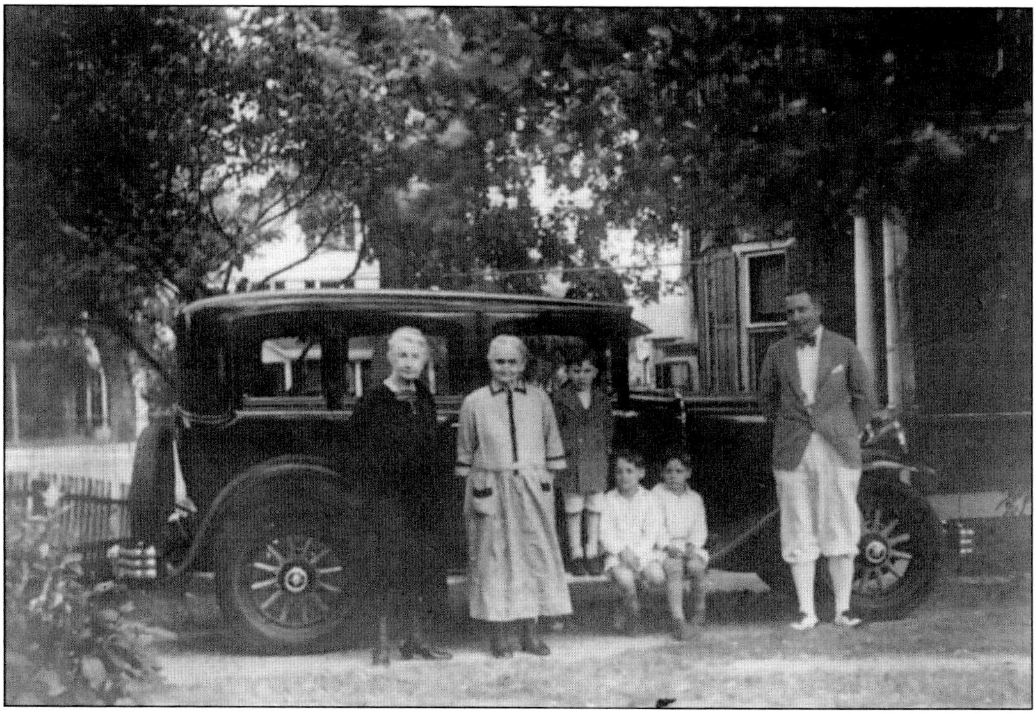

The McMahon Family, c. 1930. James A. McMahon owned a men's clothing store on Main Street in Freehold, as one might guess by his snappy outfit. The family resided on Main Street at Hull where they were photographed in front of their car. (Collection of Carl N. Steinberg.)

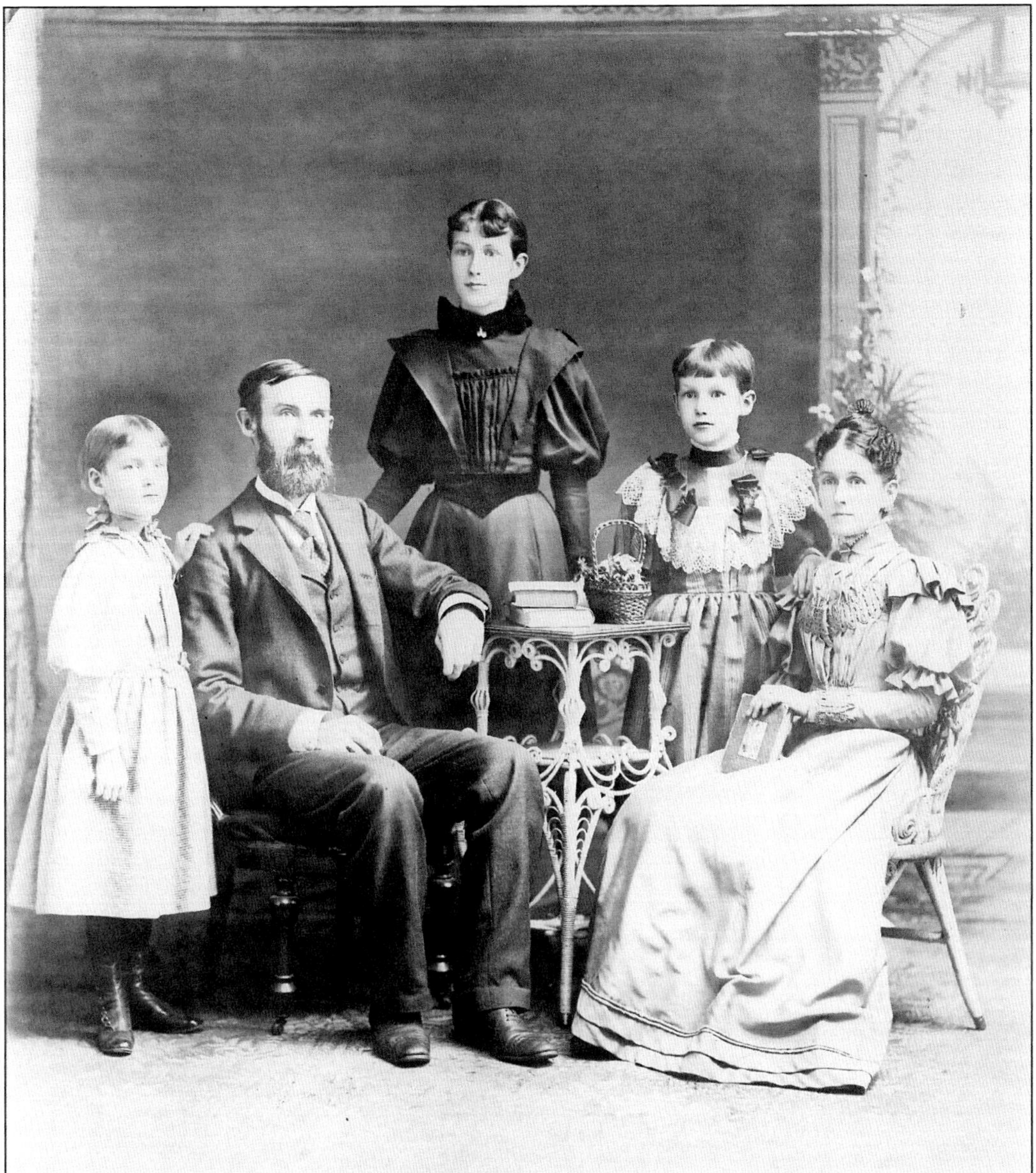

The Chalmers Rue Family, c. 1898. A large scale and formal portrait of this family is inscribed on the back, "The J. Chalmers Rue Family of Freehold, J. Chalmers Rue, Ariet Reid Rue, [and children] Mary Lou (center), Marguerite, and Myra Woodward Rue." (MCHA Archives, 1995.50.)

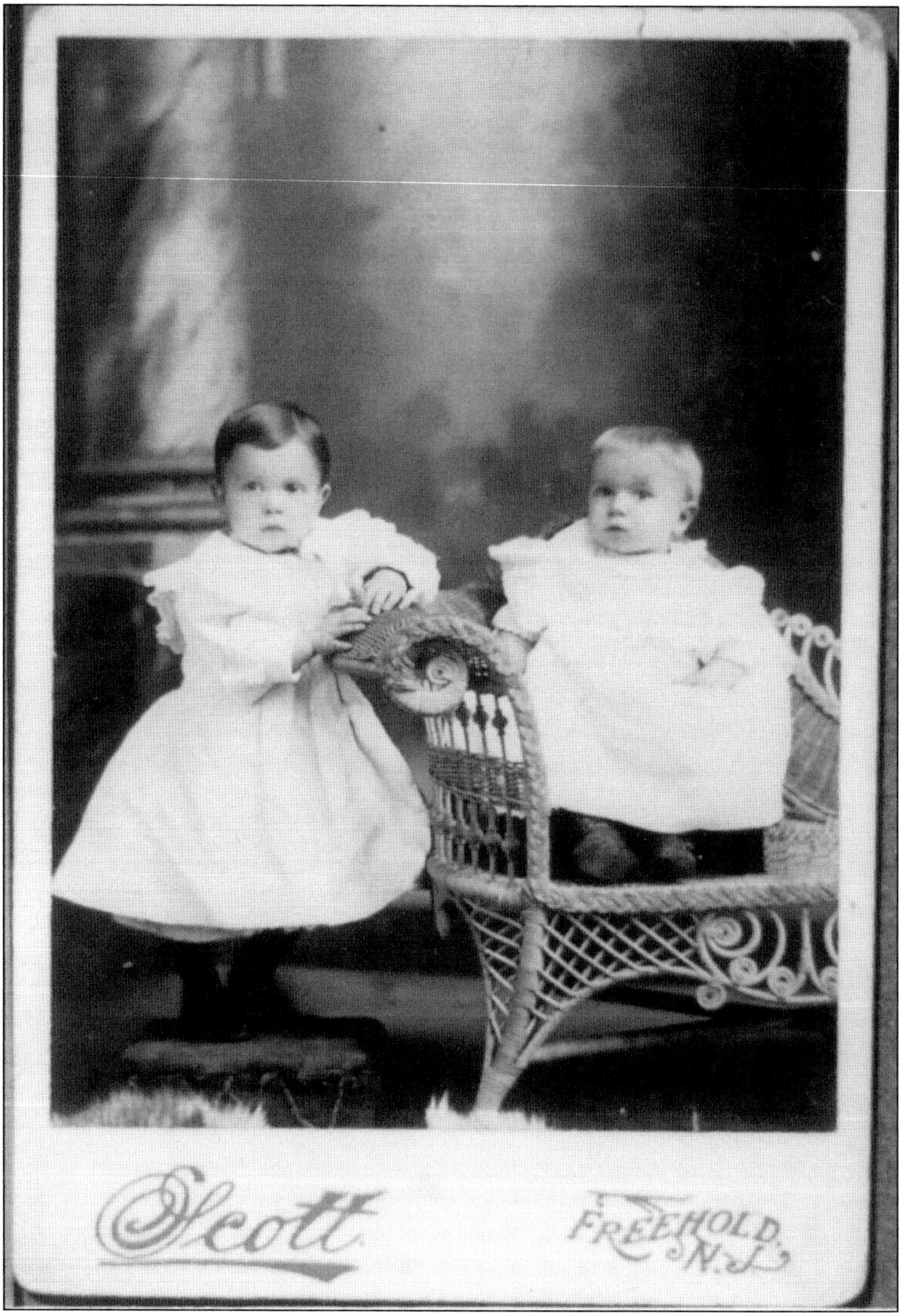

Woodward Brothers, 1896. Edward (left) and Harold (right) were the sons of Charles and Elizabeth Woodward. It was common practice in this era for little boys to wear dresses when they were very young. In this photograph taken in Scott's studio, they posed with the same wicker settee as baby Lillian Reid on p. 90. (MCHA Archives, 1995.50.)

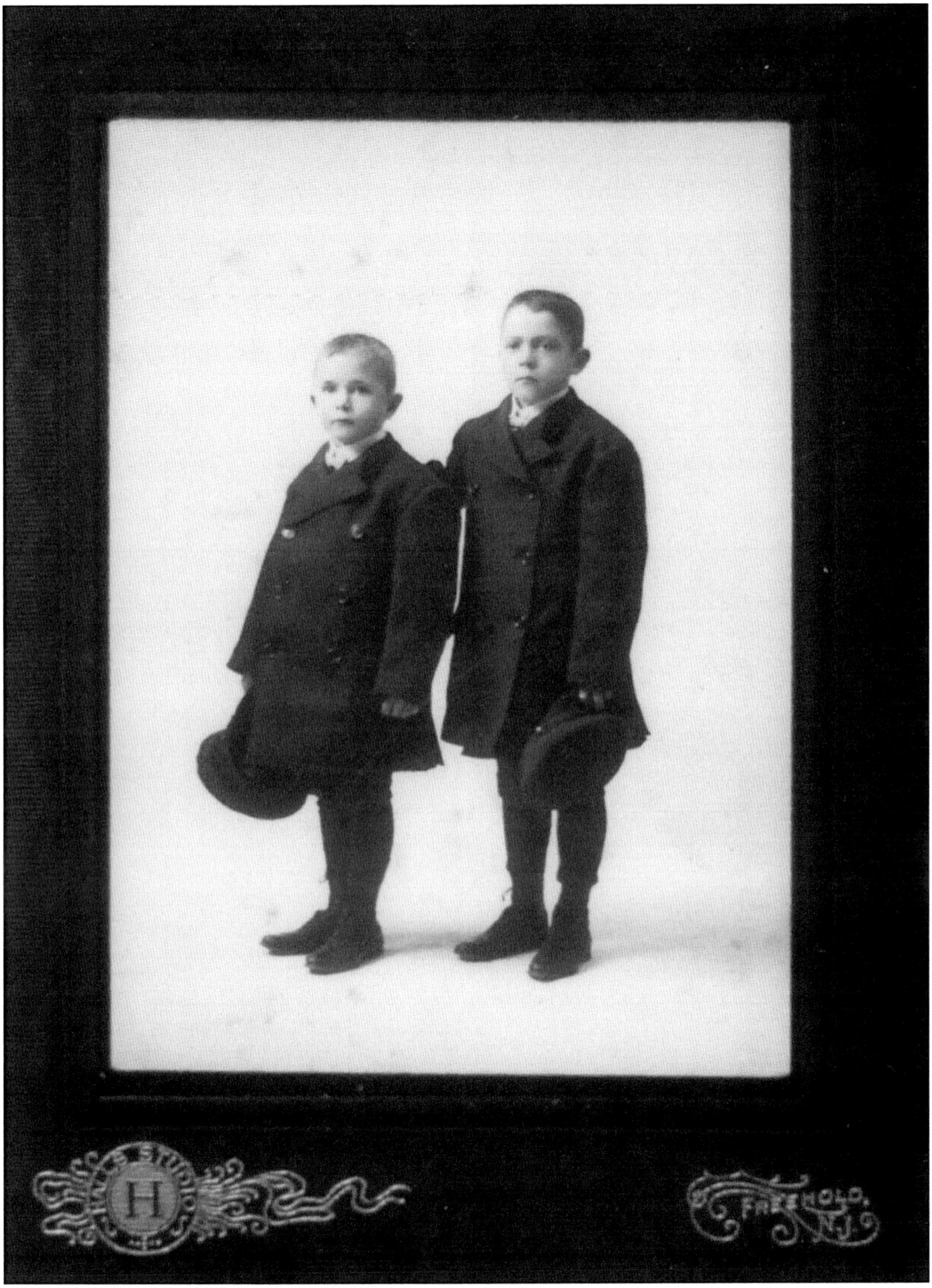

Woodward Brothers, 1902. Just a few years later, Harold and Edward were photographed in a strikingly different style, very contemporary in appearance. The two boys, dressed in black suits, stand for a full-length portrait without any props or background. (Photograph by Hall Studio, Freehold. MCHA Archives 1995.50)

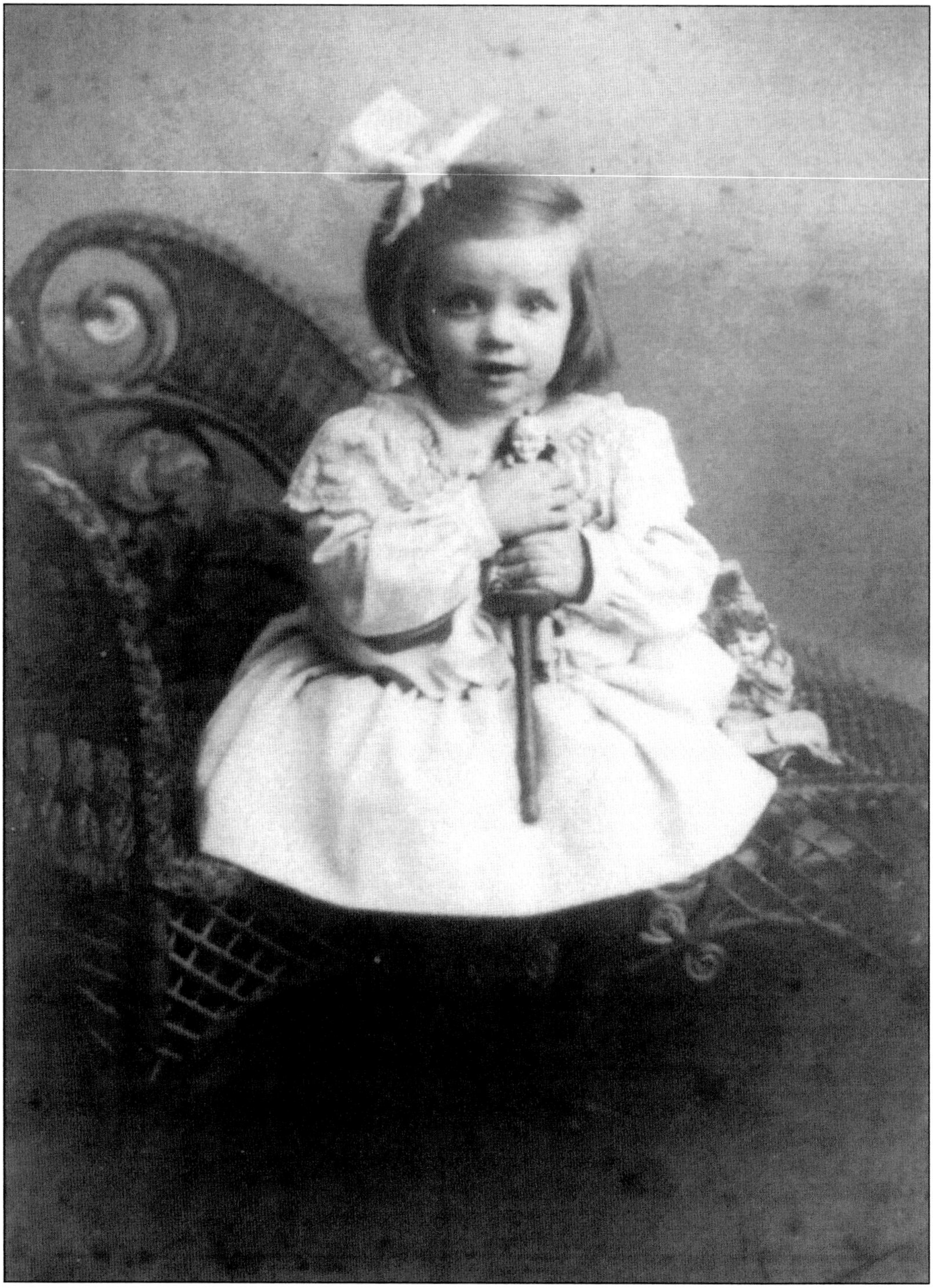

MARION BUCKELEW VOORHEES, 1905. Little Marion clutched a toy marionette and gazed in wonder at the photographer. The extravagant bow in her hair looks as though it might fly away at any moment. (Photograph by Rogers Studio, Freehold. MCHA Archives 1998.18.)

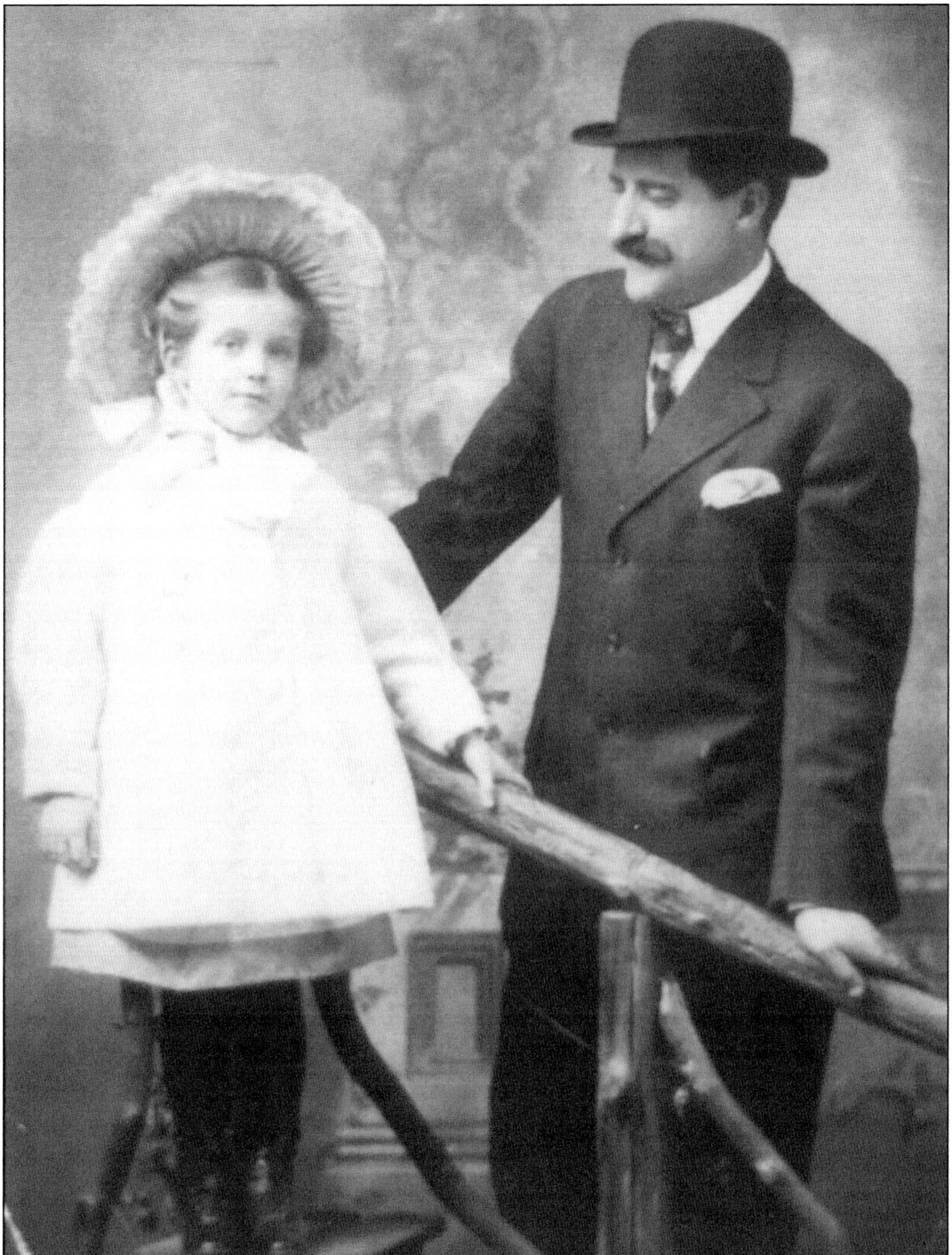

MARION BUCKELEW VOORHEES, C. 1910. Marion's portrait, taken a few years later with her father Frederick S. Voorhees, shows her dressed very smartly and wearing an elegant hat. This casual pose with a rustic fence prop is a charming image of an adoring father and his little girl. (MCHA Archives 1998.18.)

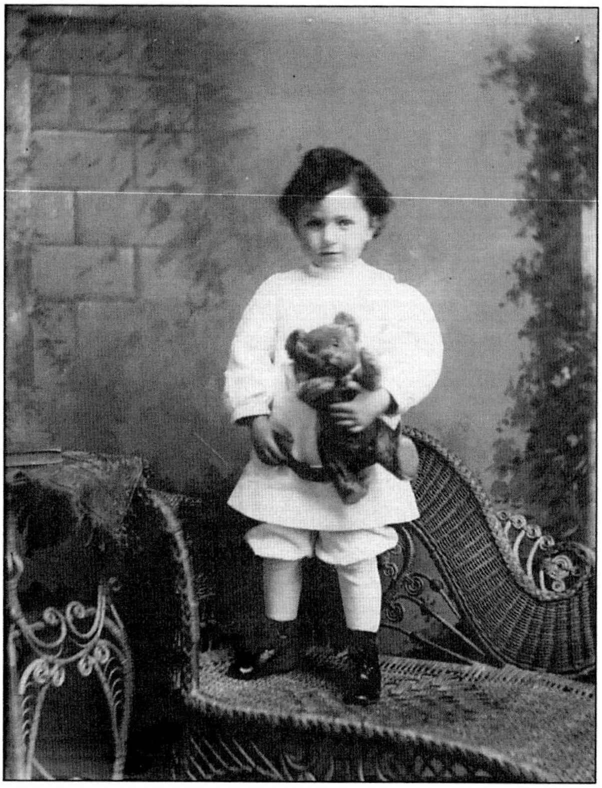

Leo T. Whalen, c. 1908. This little boy, photographed with his bear, is standing on a very familiar wicker settee. The photograph was made as a postcard and, presumably, a number was printed so that his parents could mail them to relatives. (Collection of Mary Jane Whalen.)

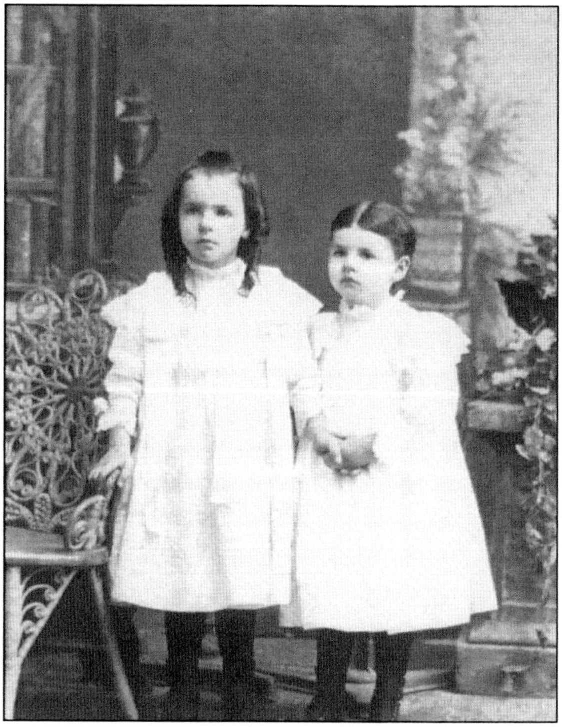

Symmes Sisters, c. 1900. "You can make me get my picture taken, but you can't make me smile." Dorothy and Marion Symmes were photographed with an elaborate backdrop and props. (Photograph by Scott Studios. MCHA Archives.)

Elsie Conover, 1911. The daughter of William Reid Conover and Laura May VanDerveer Conover, Elsie, died at the age of 19. (Photograph by Hall Studio, Freehold. MCHA Archives P771.)

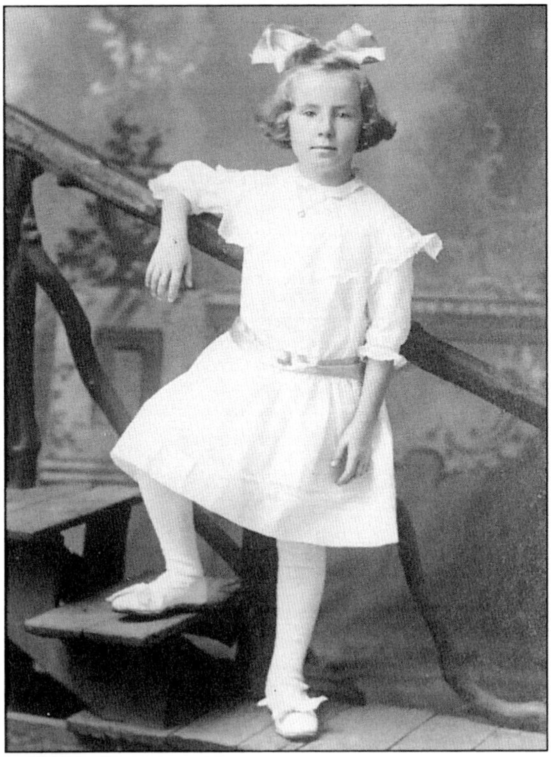

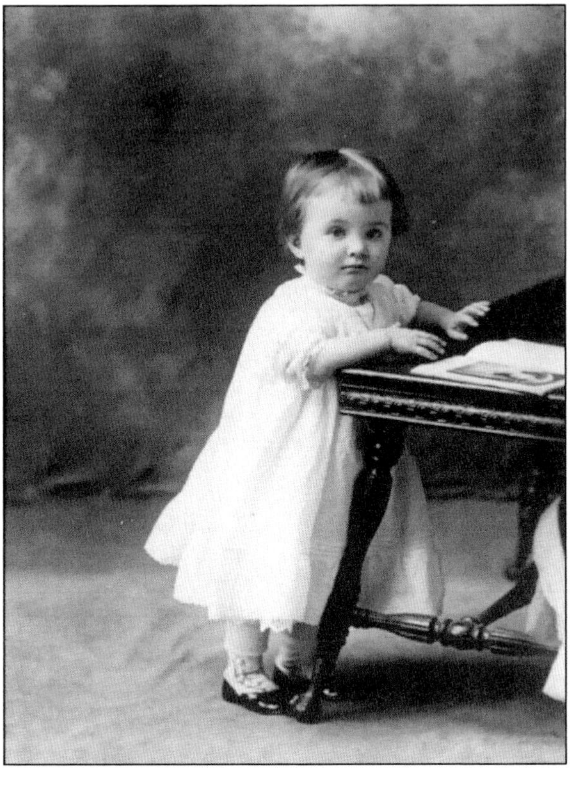

Frances V. Applegate, 1914. Little Frances, aged 19 months, needed that table to steady himself even with his fancy shoes and spats. (Photograph by Hall Studio, Freehold. MCHA Archives P456.)

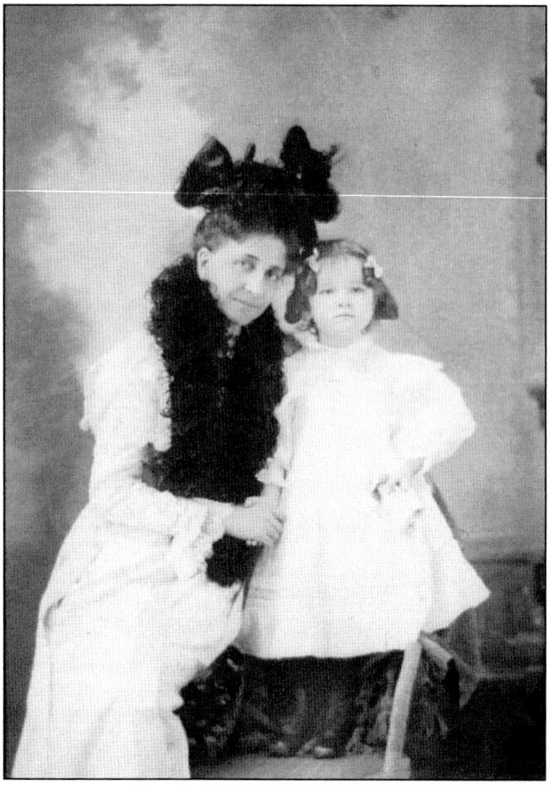

MOTHER AND CHILD, 1898. Matilda (Mrs. John P.) Walker and her little girl, Winnie, posed for this portrait at Christmastime 1898 according to the inscription on the reverse. (Photograph by Hall Studio, Freehold. MCHA Archives P2059.)

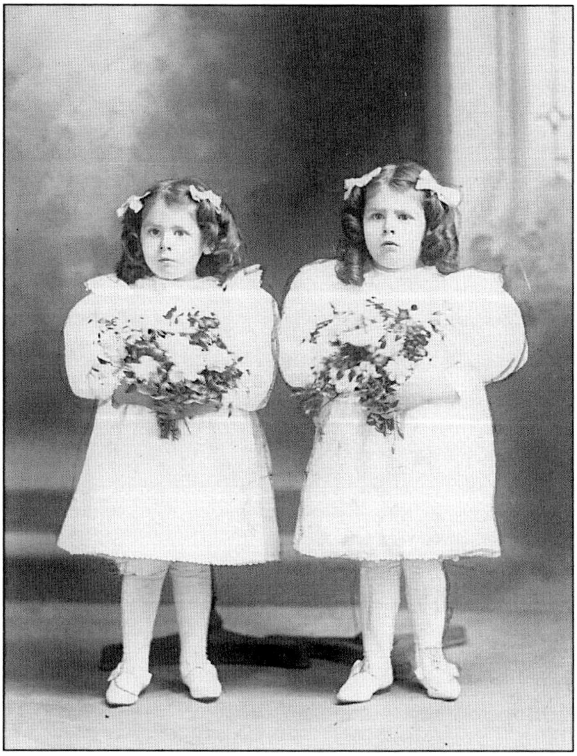

FIRST COMMUNION, C. 1900. Two unidentified girls were ready for their first communion. (Collection of Kevin Coyne.)

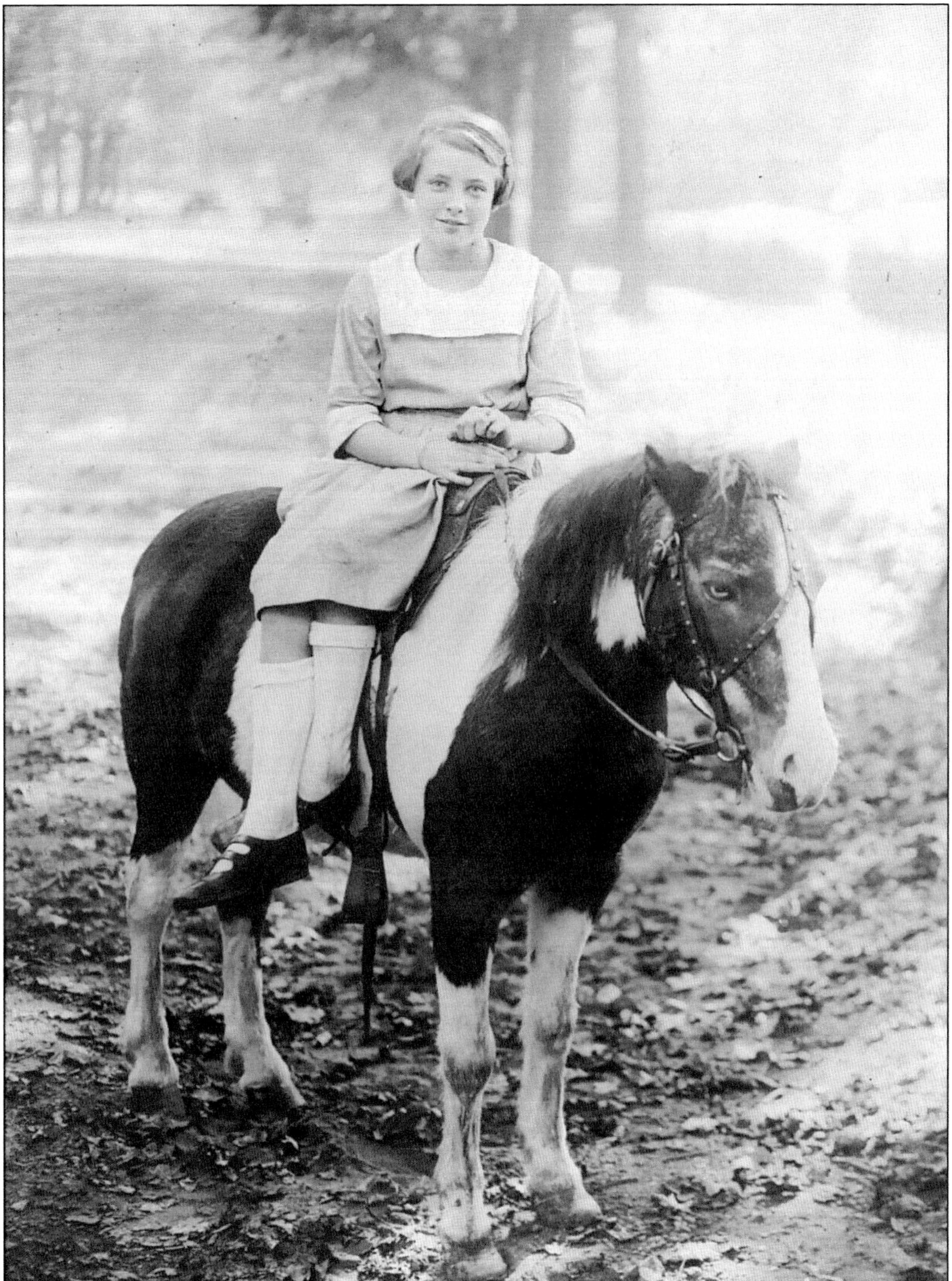

MARY ANDERSON, C. 1920. The sitter recalls that an itinerant photographer brought this pony around the neighborhoods of Freehold and offered to make portraits of the local children riding it. The pony looks as if he has seen it all. (Collection of Mary Jane Whalen.)

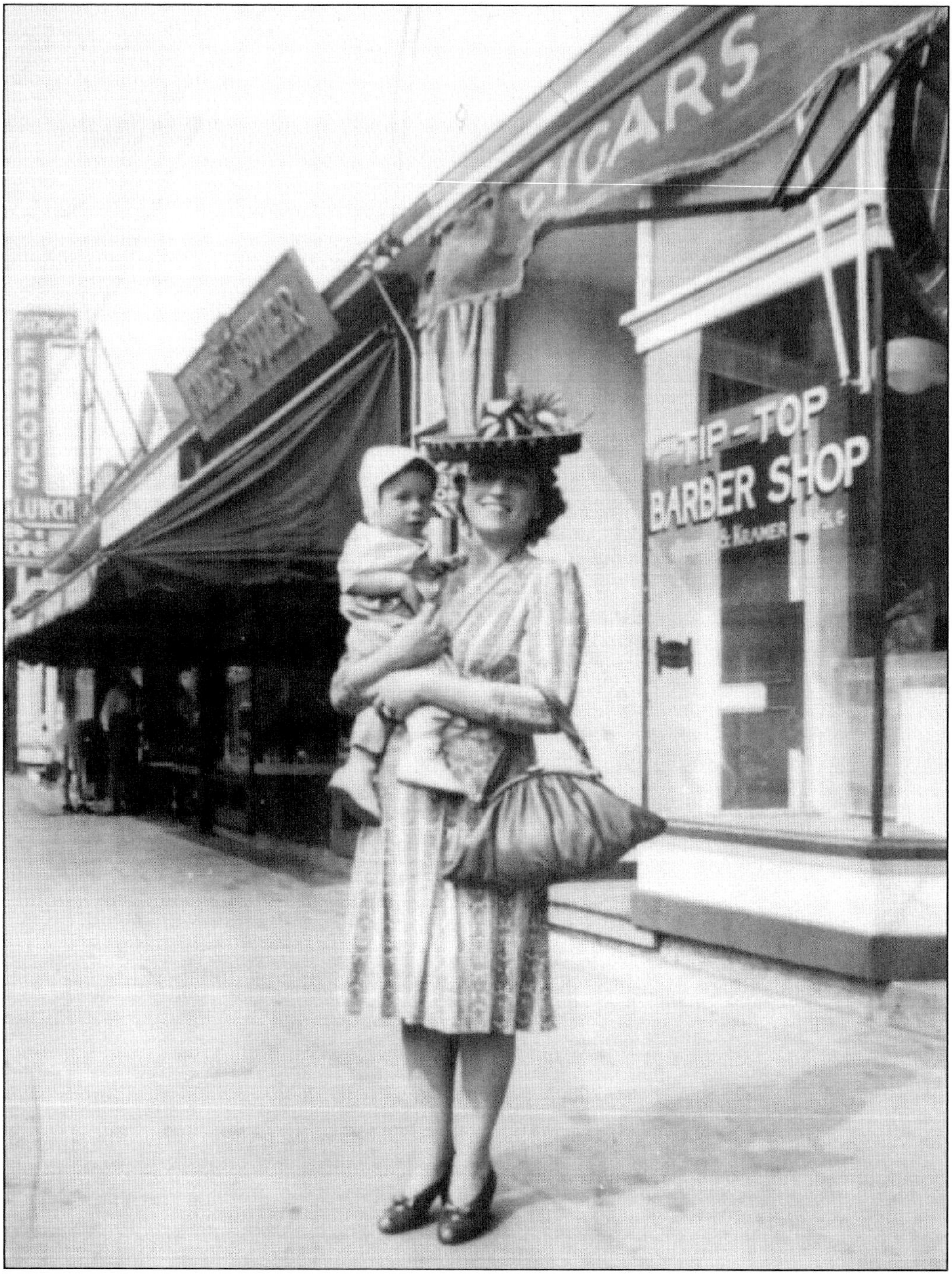

MRS. EHLIN AND STANLEY, C. 1945. Marian Ehlin holds her son Stanley. She is dressed and accessorized in the latest style, from her hat to her shoes. Her husband owned Woods Pharmacy at the corner of South and Mechanic Streets just up the street from where she is standing. (Collection of Carl N. Steinberg.)

Eight
DISASTERS

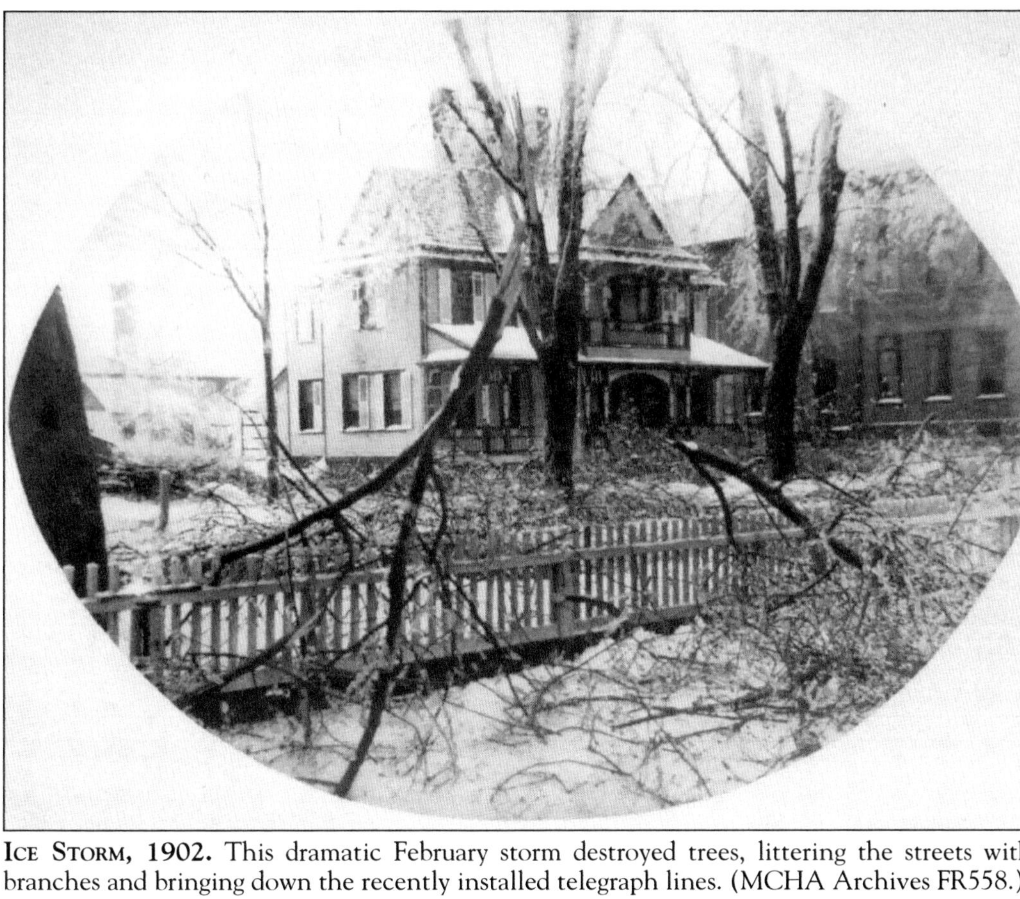

ICE STORM, 1902. This dramatic February storm destroyed trees, littering the streets with branches and bringing down the recently installed telegraph lines. (MCHA Archives FR558.)

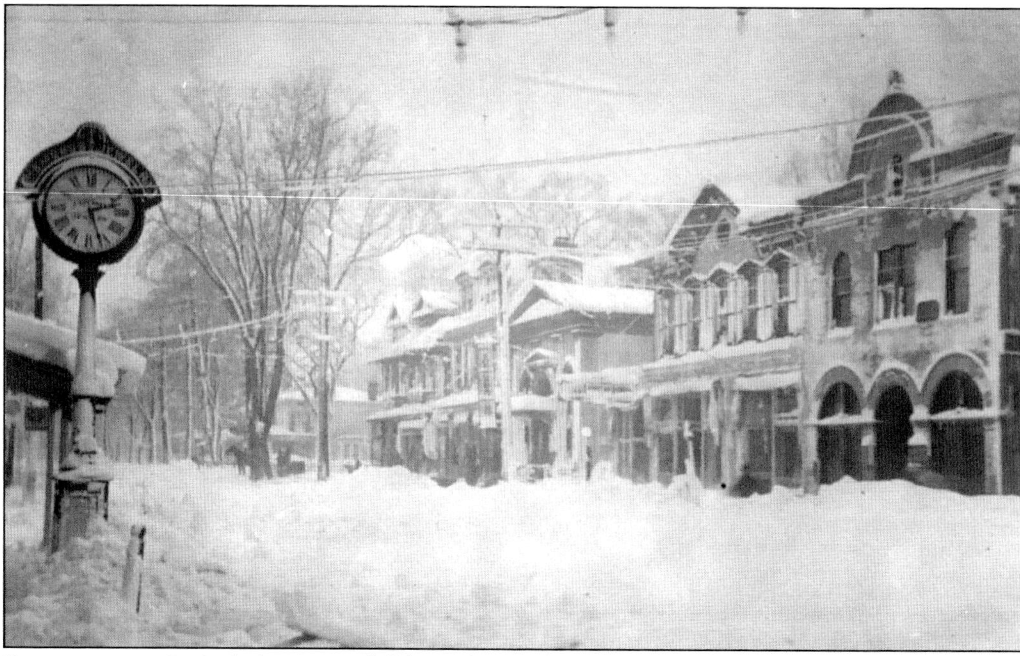

Snowstorm, 1914. A deep snowfall brought Freehold's business district to a halt on March 1, 1914. (Collection of Richard J. Dalik.)

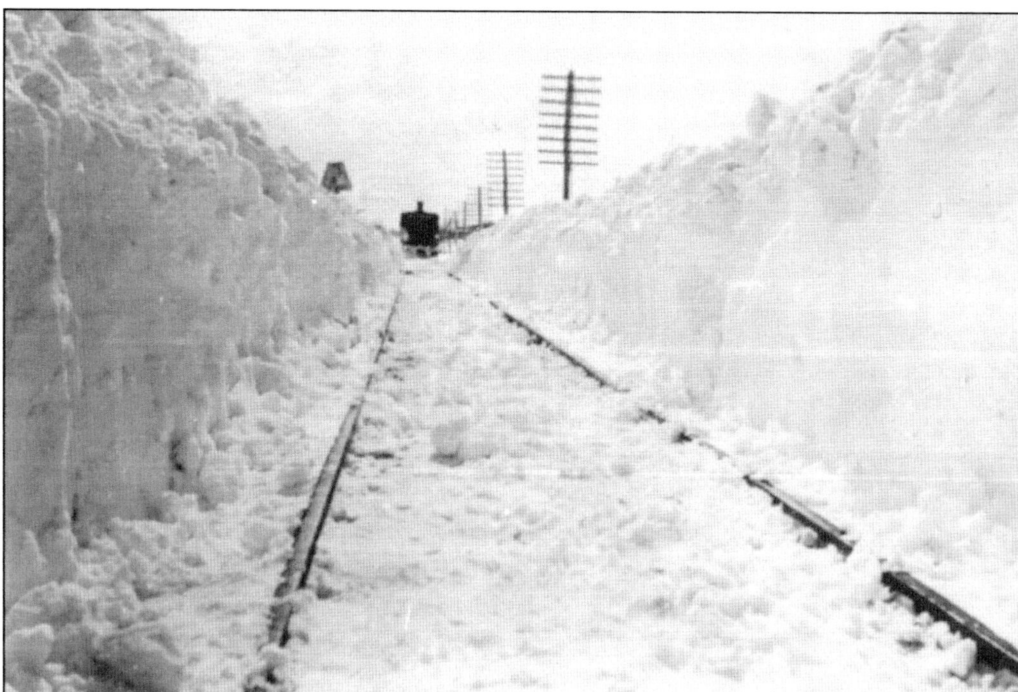

Cleared Tracks, 1914. That same snowfall stopped rail traffic until the tracks could be cleared. The inscription on the reverse reads, "First train on Central R. R. March 4, 1914. Lucy was aboard having been stalled at Manalapan since March 1." (Collection of Carl N. Steinberg.)

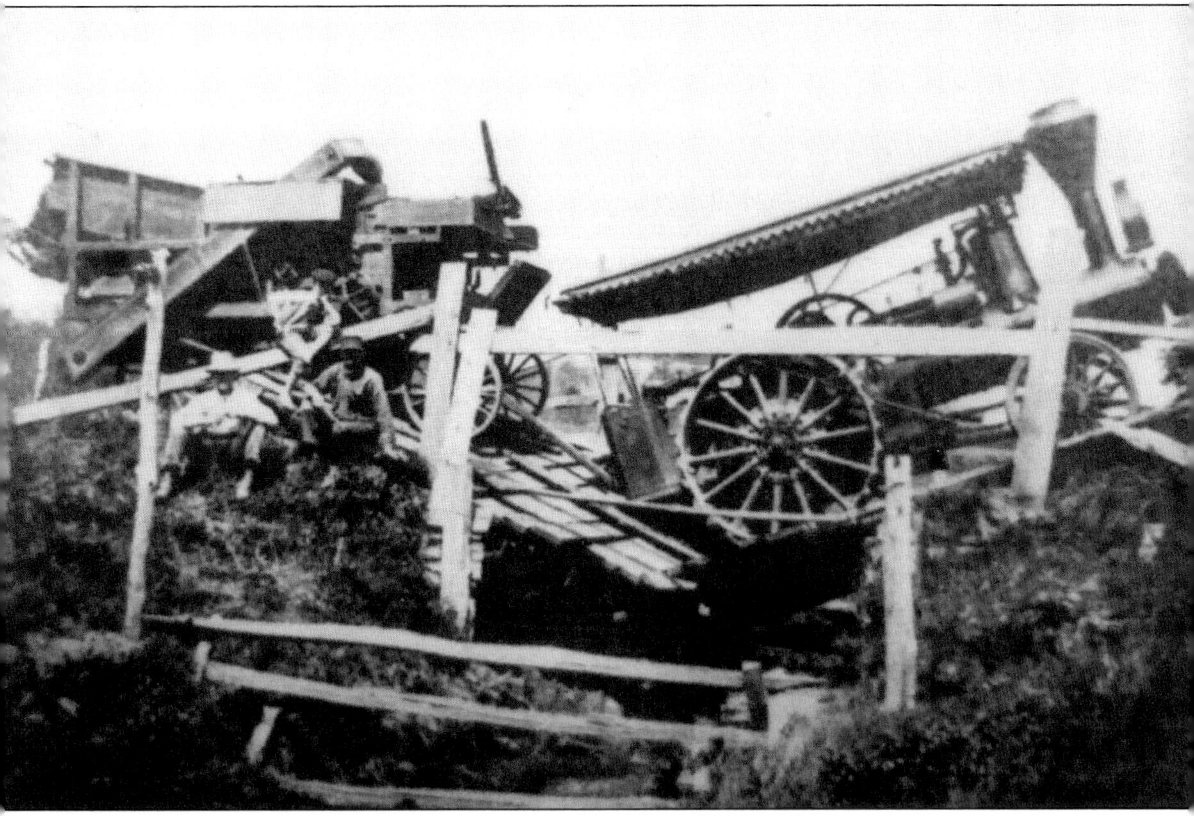

ACCIDENT AT APPLEGATE'S CREEK BRIDGE, C. 1913. Cornelius Hendrickson's wheat thrashing machine and the steam engine that pulled it were too heavy for the wooden bridge at Applegate's Creek as documented by this photograph. Hendrickson and Charles Applegate sit in the foreground. (MCHA Archives 1998.30.)

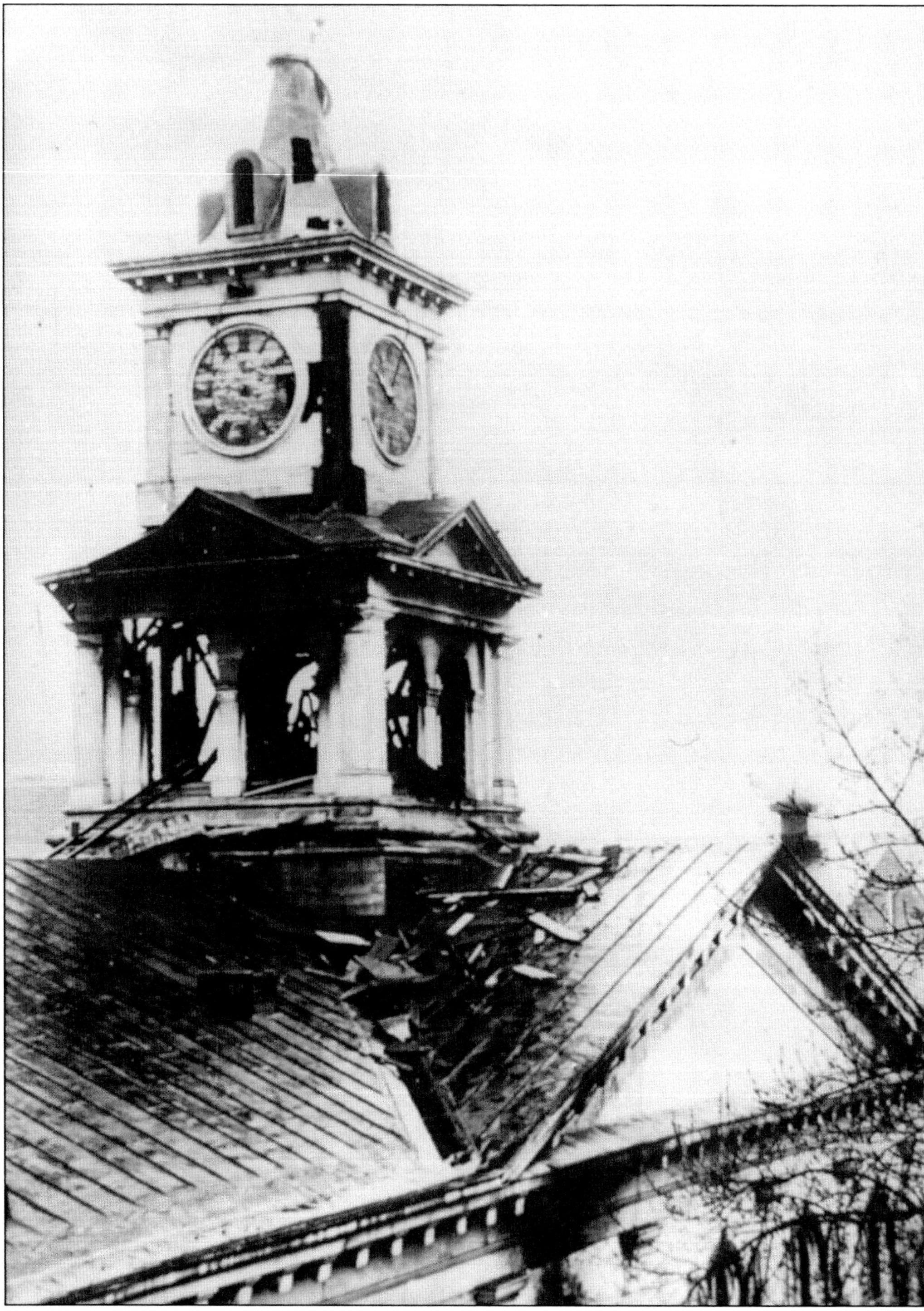

COURT HOUSE FIRE, 1930. The cupola of the County Court House (now the Hall of Records) burned on several occasions. On April 19, 1930, the cupola was apparently hit by lightning and burned. Fortunately, the main structure was saved. (MCHA Archives.)

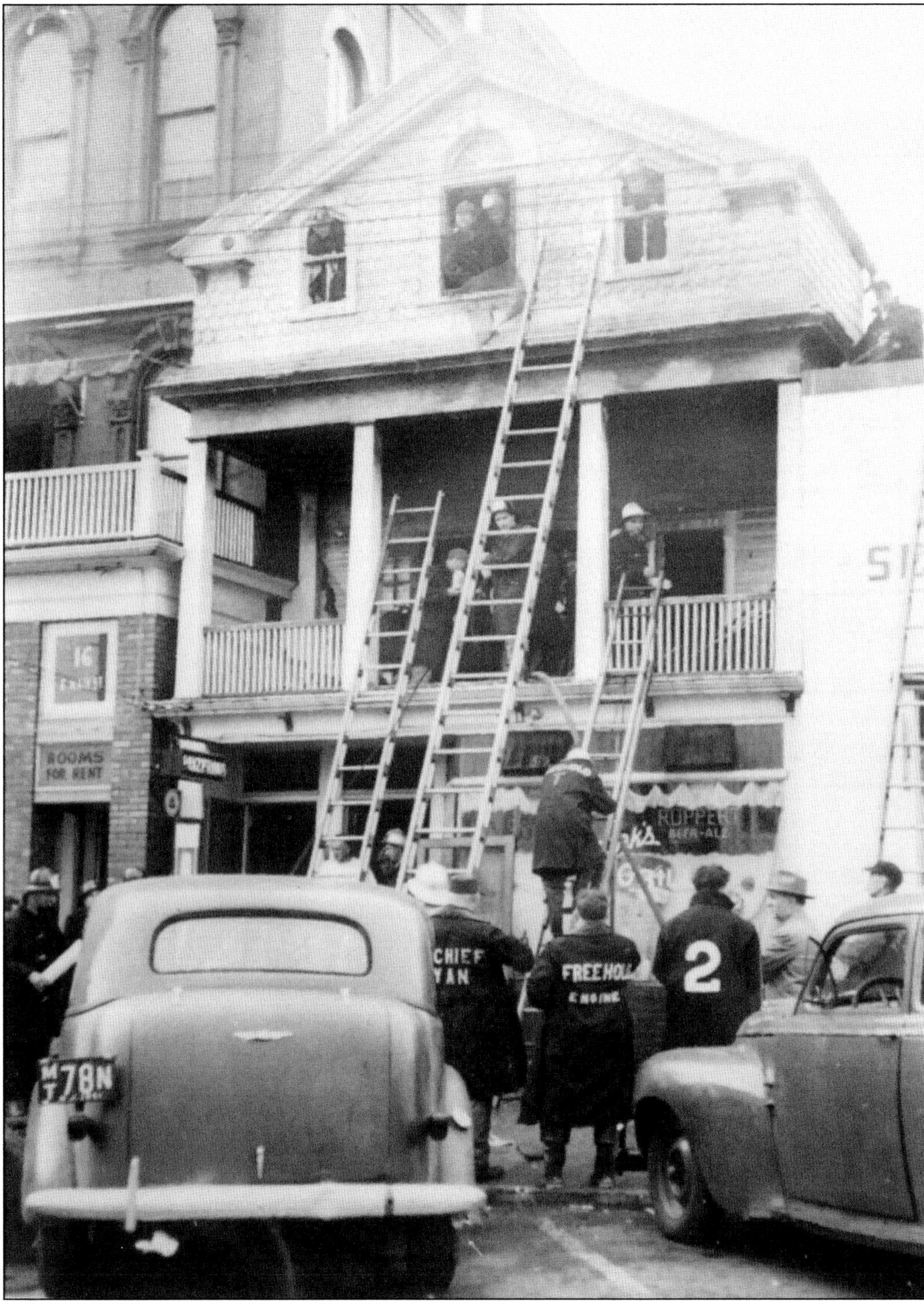

FIRE AT FEDERICI'S, C. 1950. A fire at Federici's (the old site of the Wolcott Saloon) did a good deal of damage to the interiors of the second and third floors. Chief Ryan is in front of the building. (Collection of Carl N. Steinberg.)

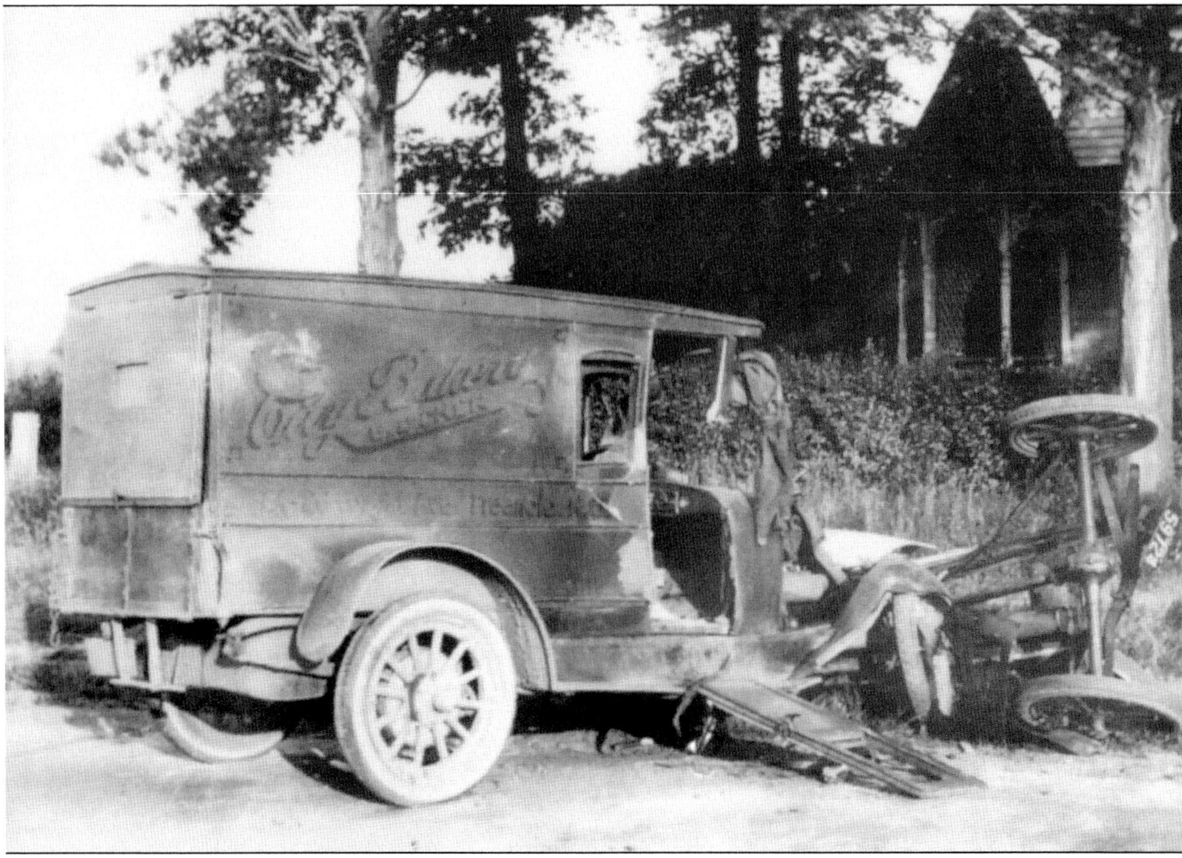

Collision, c. 1930s. The City Bakery truck seems to have had a run-in with another vehicle in the photograph taken by Ladd Studio. Located at 26 Vought Avenue, City Bakery was one of several bakeries that served Freehold. (Collection of Carl N. Steinberg.)

Nine
Transportation

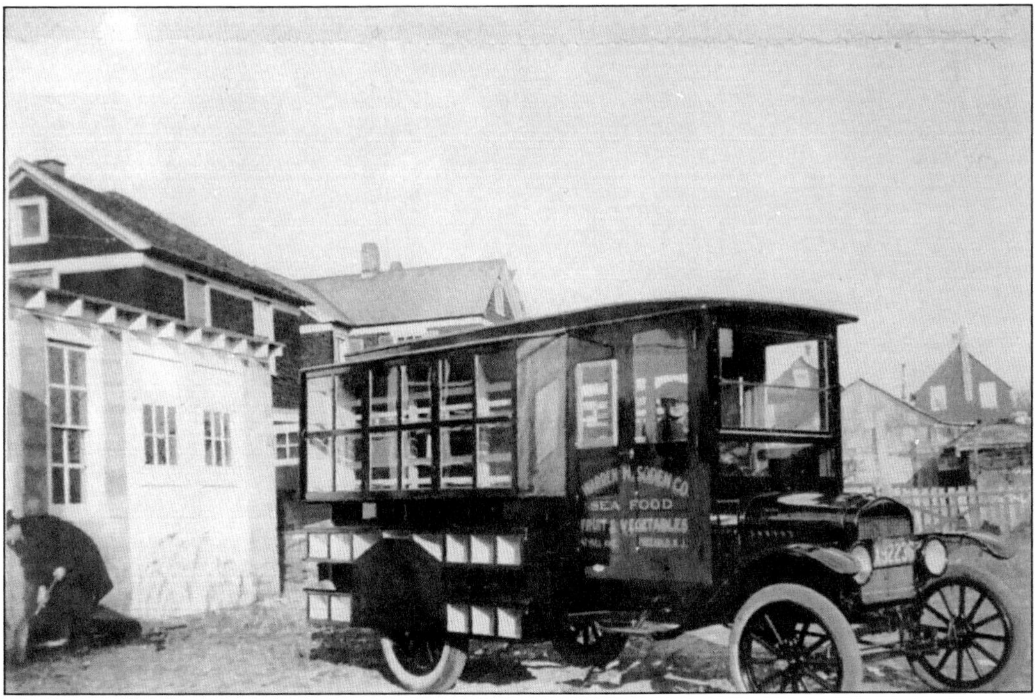

Delivery Truck, 1930s. Located at 40 Hull Street, Warren H. Soden Co. sold seafood as well as fruit and vegetables. This truck seems to have been outfitted for produce sales with all of its compartments. (Collection of Richard J. Dalik.)

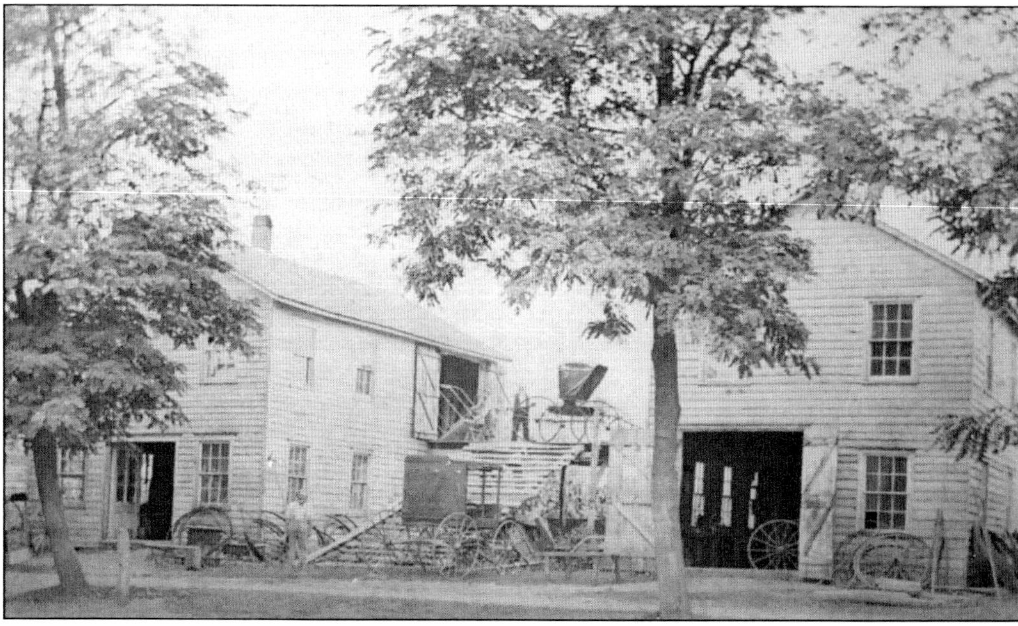

Shop of Amos Haviland, Blacksmith and Coach Builder, c. 1860. Located behind the shops on South Street near Mechanic, this thriving business served Freehold's "carriage trade." Evidence of those times can be seen in the size of many of Freehold Borough's lots, which were deep enough to accommodate a carriage house. (Collection of Carl N. Steinberg.)

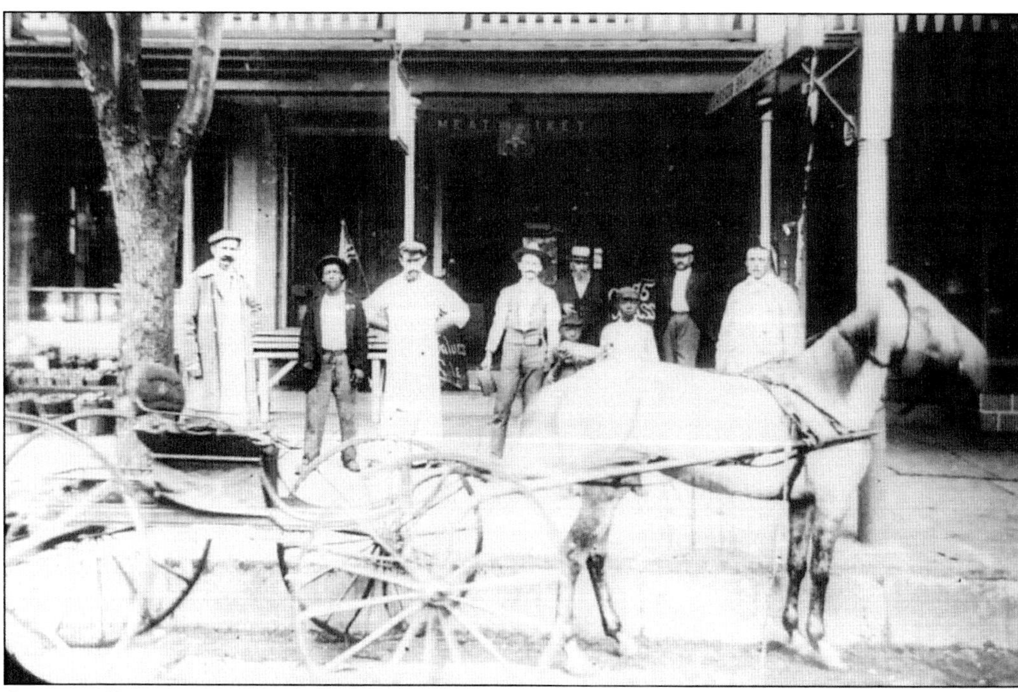

Carson Brothers Meat Market, c. 1890. The storefront of this butcher shop was photographed with their horse and carriage. The shop was located on Main Street near the Courthouse where the Strand Theatre was. (MCHA Archives.)

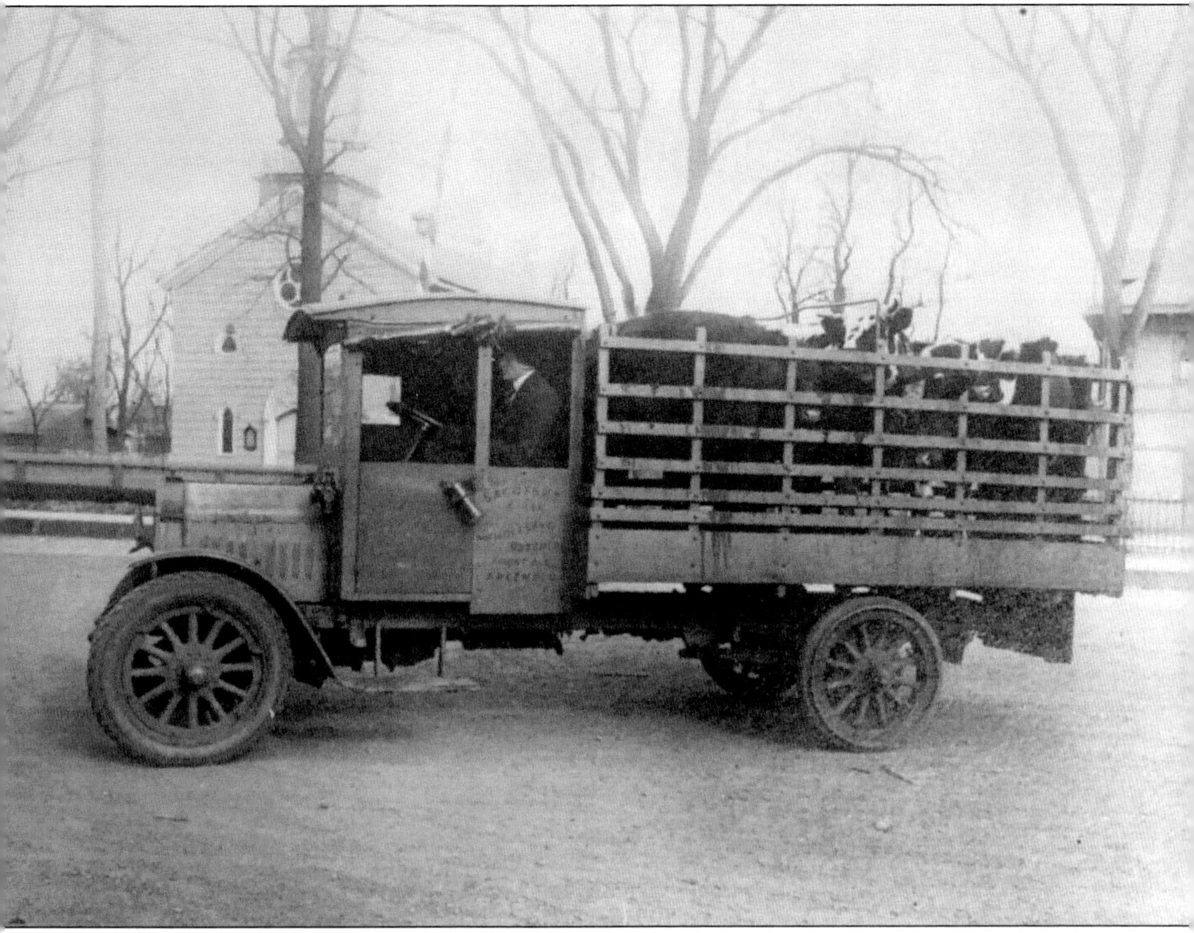

Sagotsky & Son Truck, c. 1920s. This truck carried livestock to be slaughtered and butchered at the Sagotsky's butcher shop. In the background is St. Peter's Church on Throckmorton Street. (Collection of Carl N. Steinberg.)

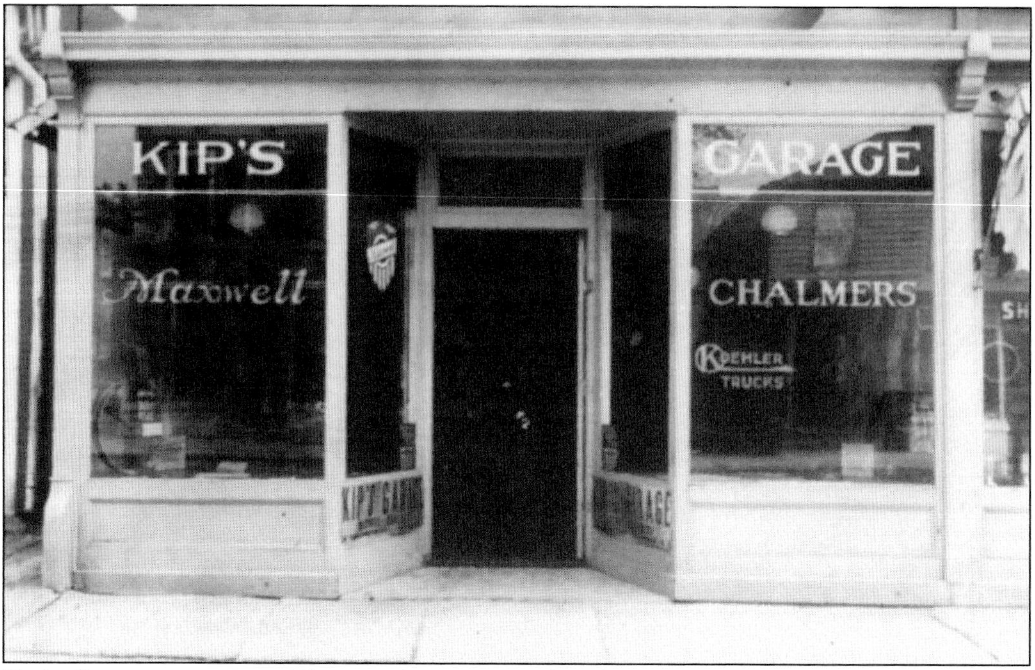

Kip's Garage, c. 1920. The storefront at 49 Throckmorton Street of Kip's Garage shows that they dealt in Maxwell and Chalmers vehicles, as well as Koehler trucks. (Collection of Carl N. Steinberg.)

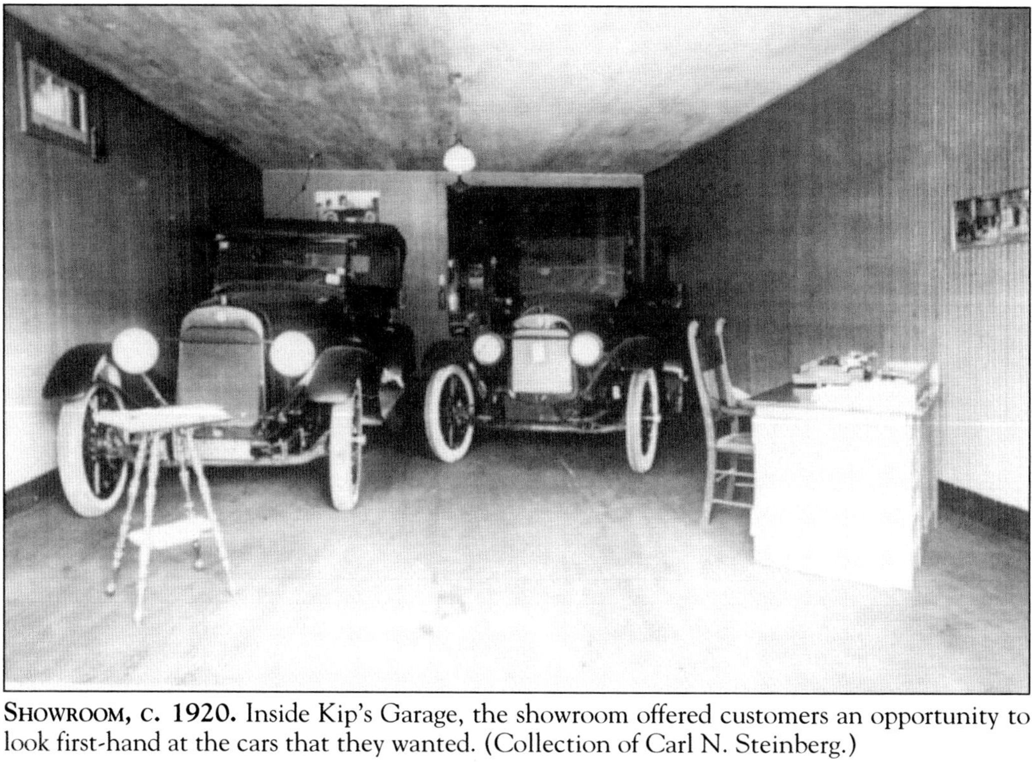

Showroom, c. 1920. Inside Kip's Garage, the showroom offered customers an opportunity to look first-hand at the cars that they wanted. (Collection of Carl N. Steinberg.)

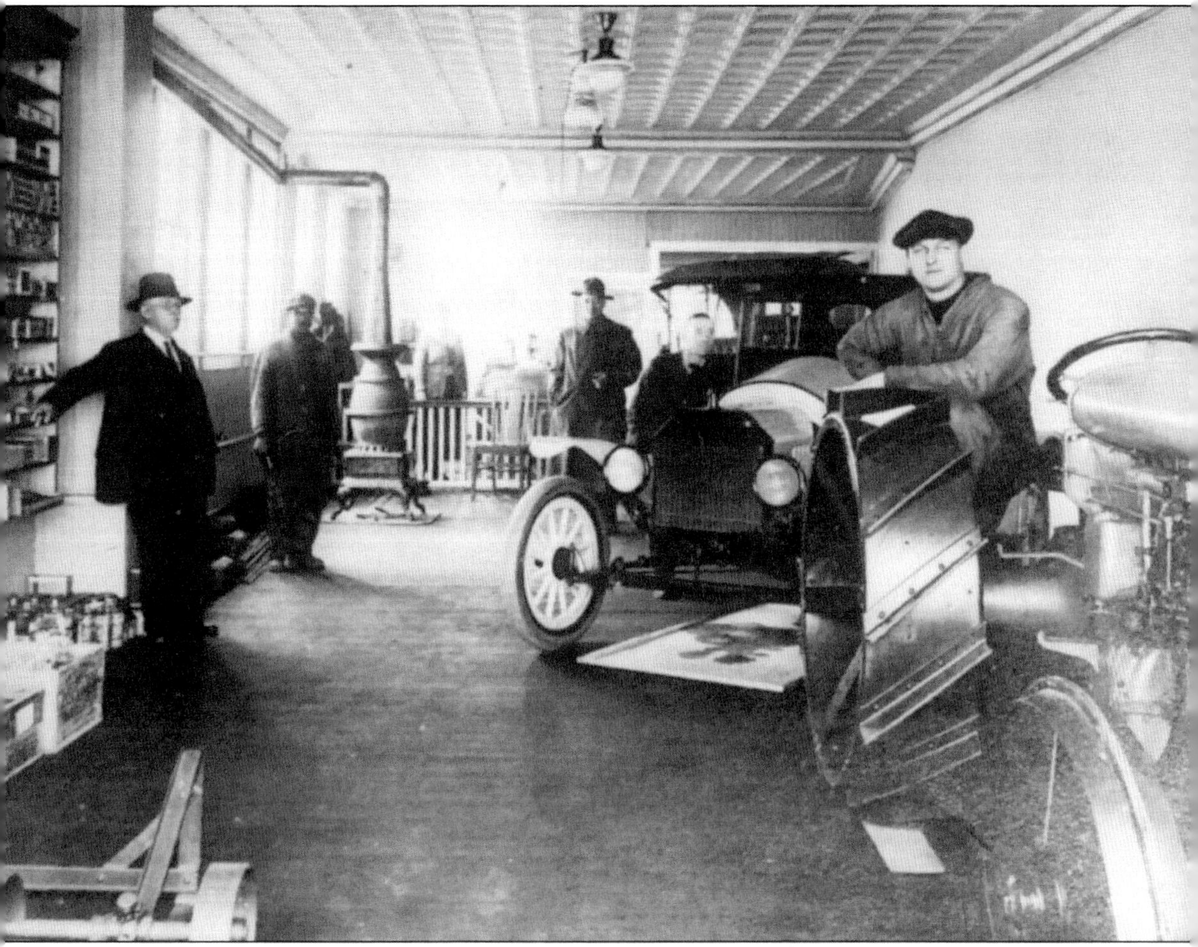

CHILDS-MCGRATH MOTOR COMPANY, 1919. Located at 17 South Street, this showroom featured a car (that required a drip pan!) as well as a tractor. Shown here are, from left to right, Mr. Childs, Alonzo, Lester Kip, Mr. McGrath, and Lester Grenville. (Collection of Carl N. Steinberg.)

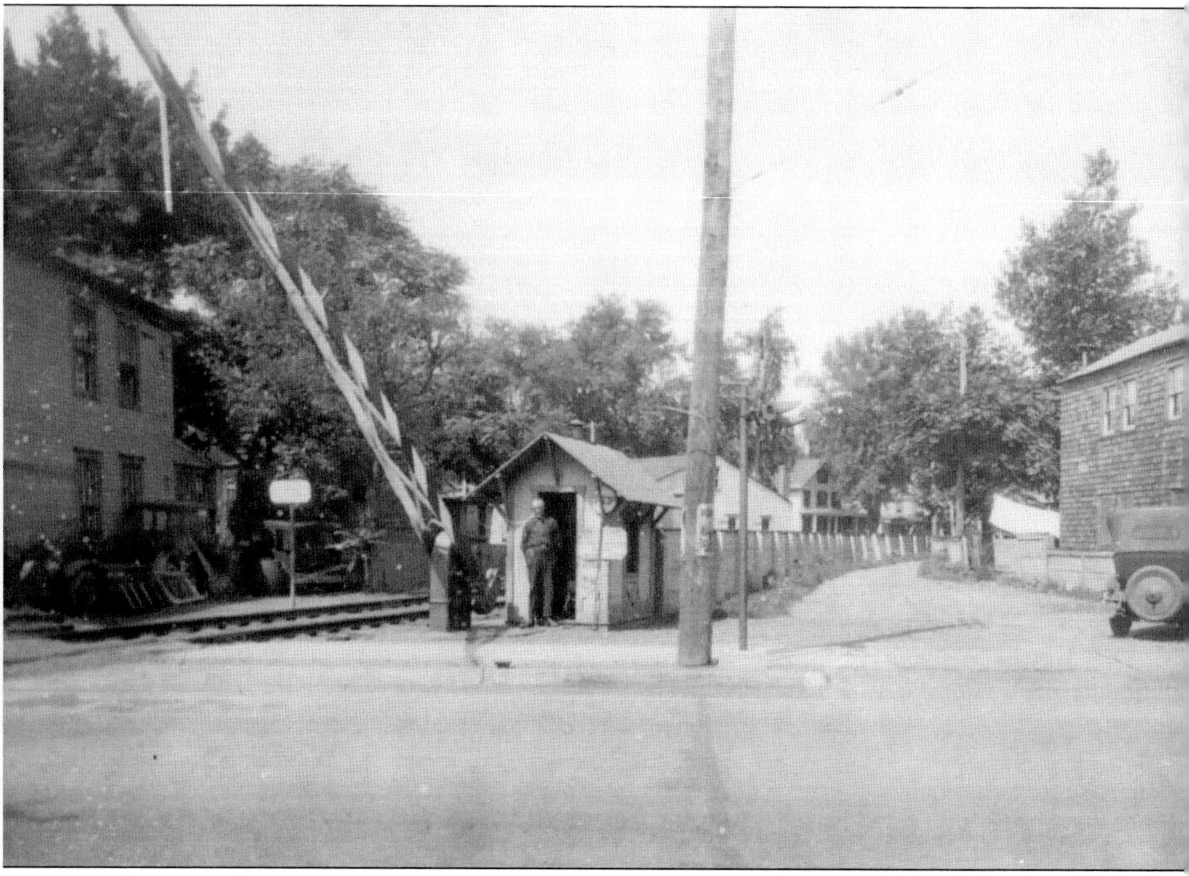

Railroad Shanty, c. 1920s. At every crossing of the railroad, a shanty was set up so that a watchman could safeguard the motorists (carriages in earlier days) and pedestrians. (Collection of Carl N. Steinberg.)

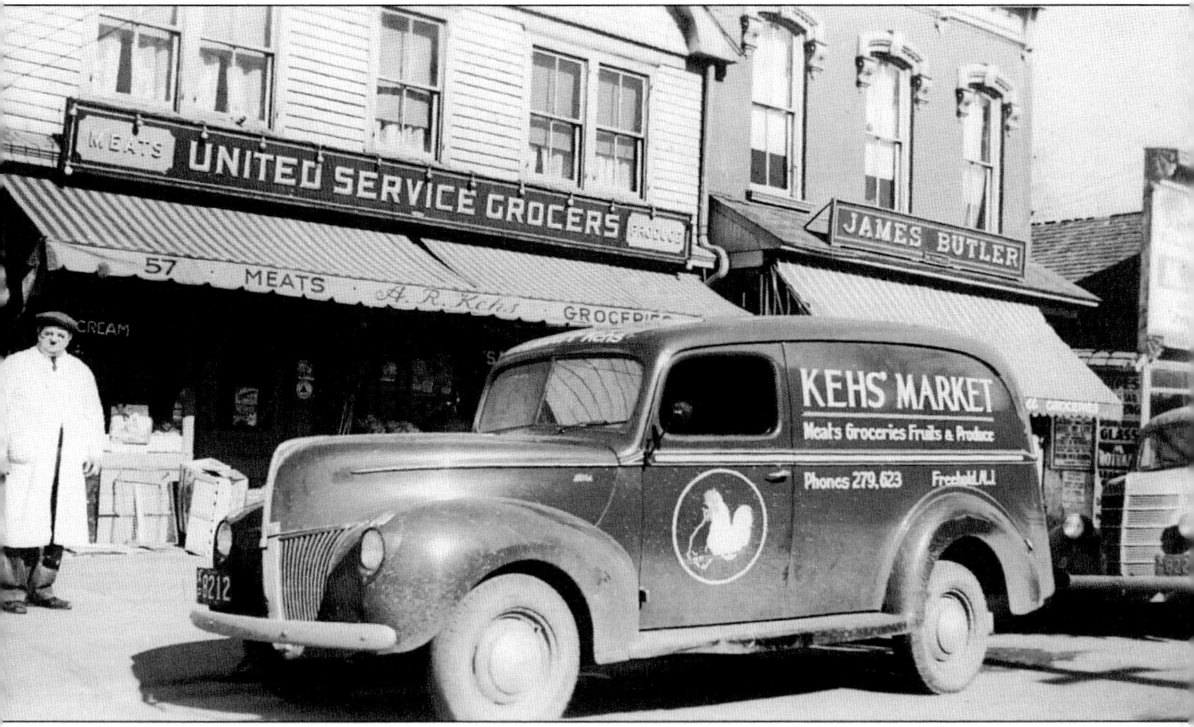

KEHS' MARKET DELIVERY TRUCK, 1930S. Kehs' Market was located at 57 Throckmorton Street next to the old fire department building. The owner, A.R. Kehs, stands in front of his shop, which offered home delivery of grocery orders—a common practice in the past now enjoying a revival. The building now houses a motorcycle parts shop. (Collection of Carl N. Steinberg.)

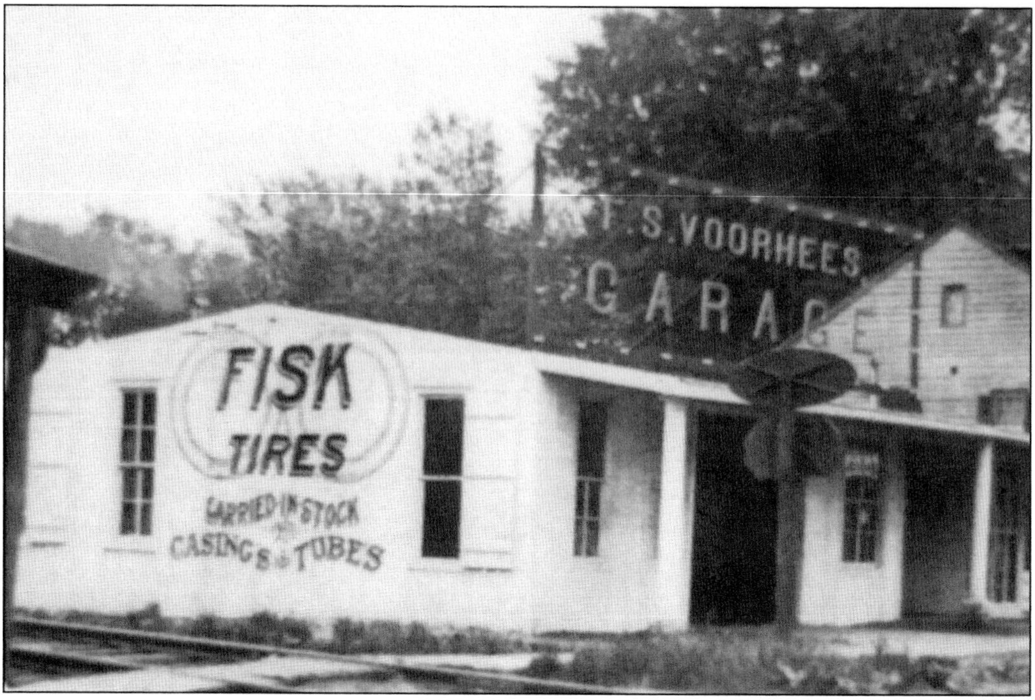

VOORHEES GARAGE, c. 1920s. Located at 43–45 South Street, this garage was owned by Frederick S. Voorhees, whose picture appears on p. 97 with his daughter Marion. This photographic postcard was sent to Marion in fun with the message, "Do you know what place this is? Papa." (MCHA Archives 1998.18.)

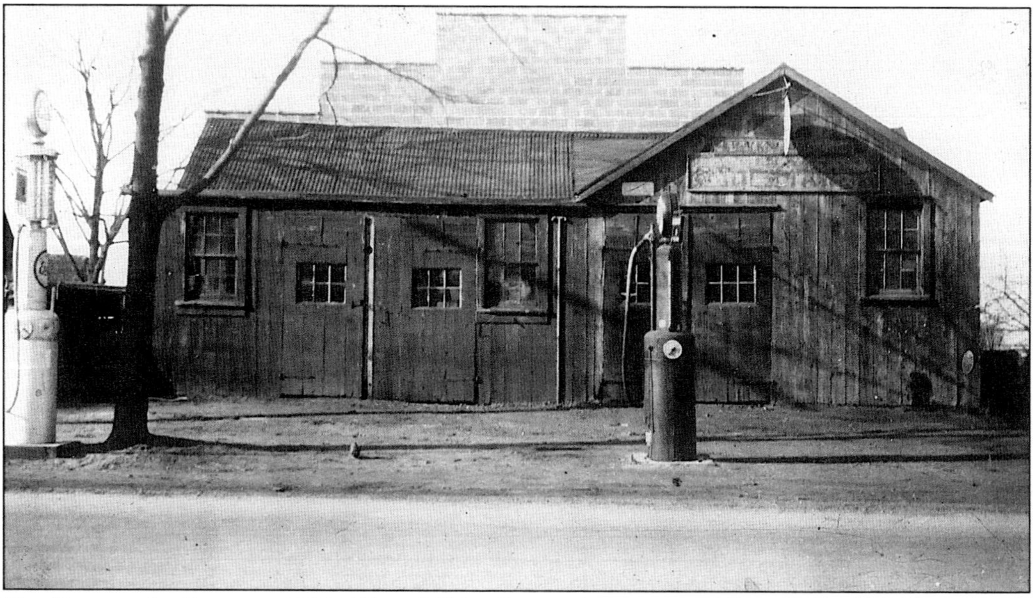

VANDERVEER'S GARAGE, 1927. The old VanDerveer's garage in West Freehold is shown with the new building being erected right behind it. The business was owned by J. Elmer and Howard I. VanDerveer, and the new building, with its stepped façade, is still in place. (Collection of Carl N. Steinberg.)

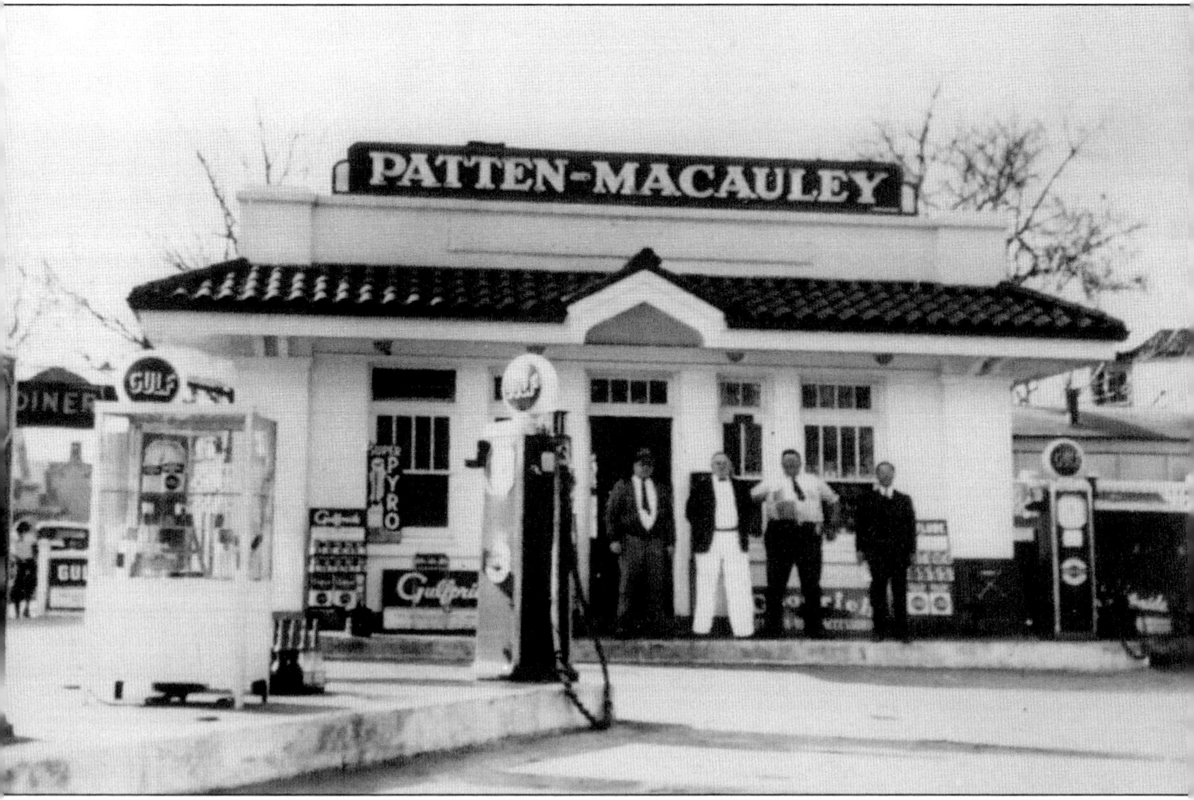

Patten-Macauley Gulf Station, c. 1940s. At the corner of East Main and Spring Streets, this Gulf Station had a prime location at the east end of Freehold's business district. You can see the sign for the Freehold Diner next door. (Collection of Carl N. Steinberg.)

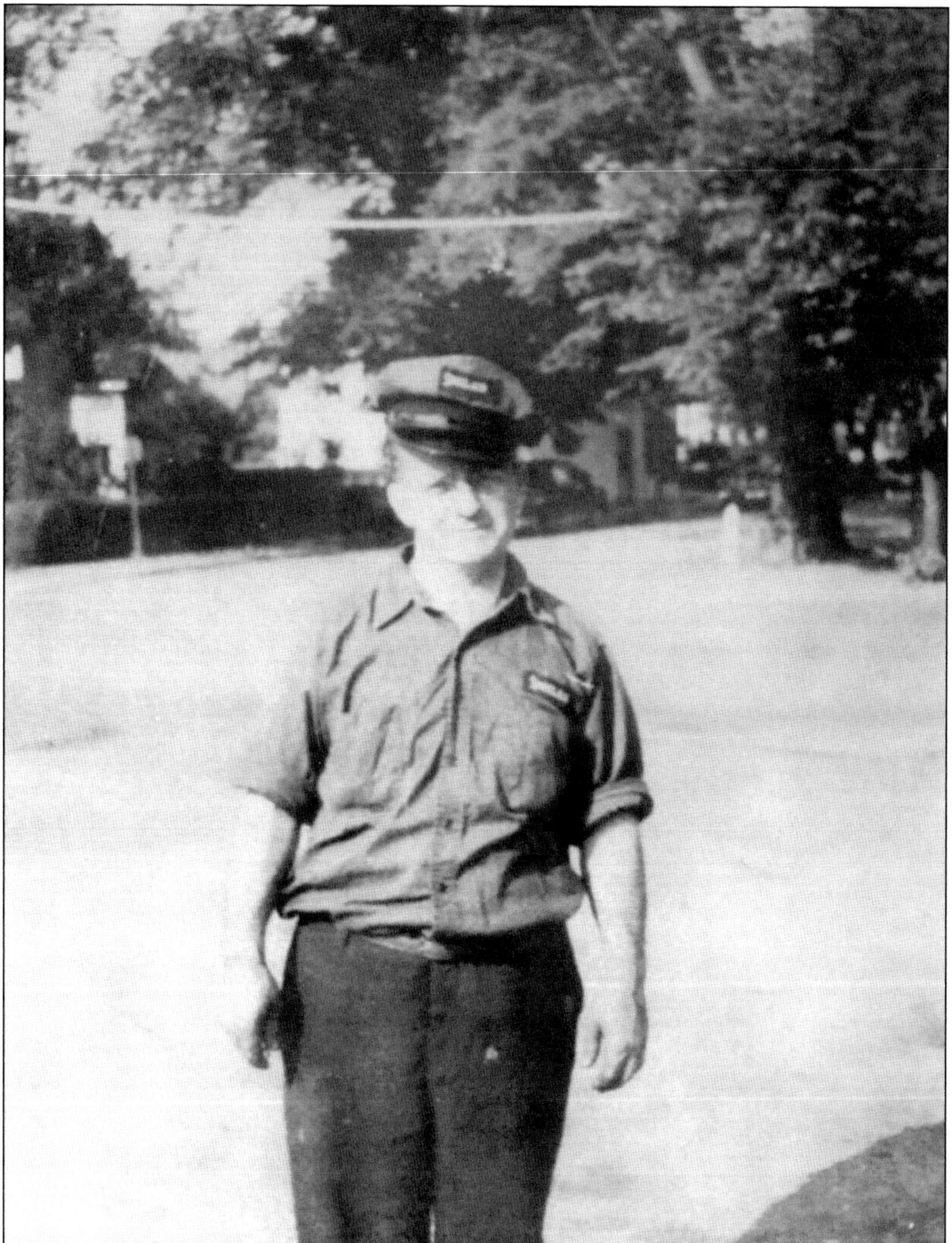

James Slattery, 1950s. James "Ducky" Slattery owned the Sinclair station at 58 South Street. The Slattery brothers owned a number of service stations in Freehold Borough. (Collection of Carl N. Steinberg.)

Ten

PARADES

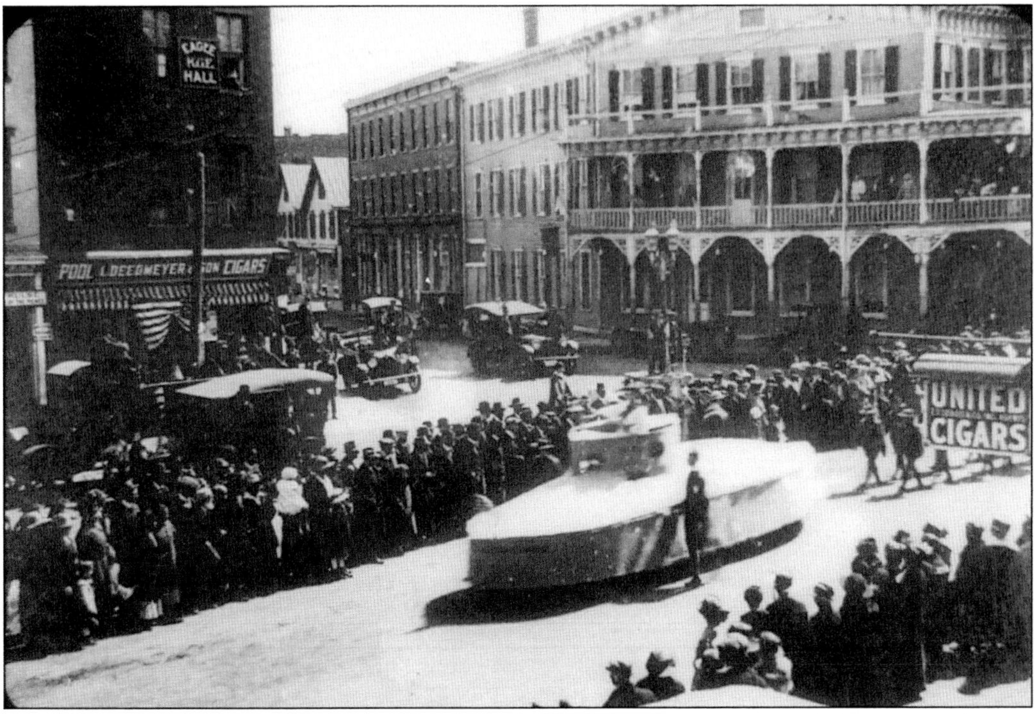

WAR BOND DRIVE, 1918. A parade for the War Bond Drive for WW I proceeded up Main Street, at the corner of South Street. The Belmont Hotel is visible in the background. (MCHA Archives.)

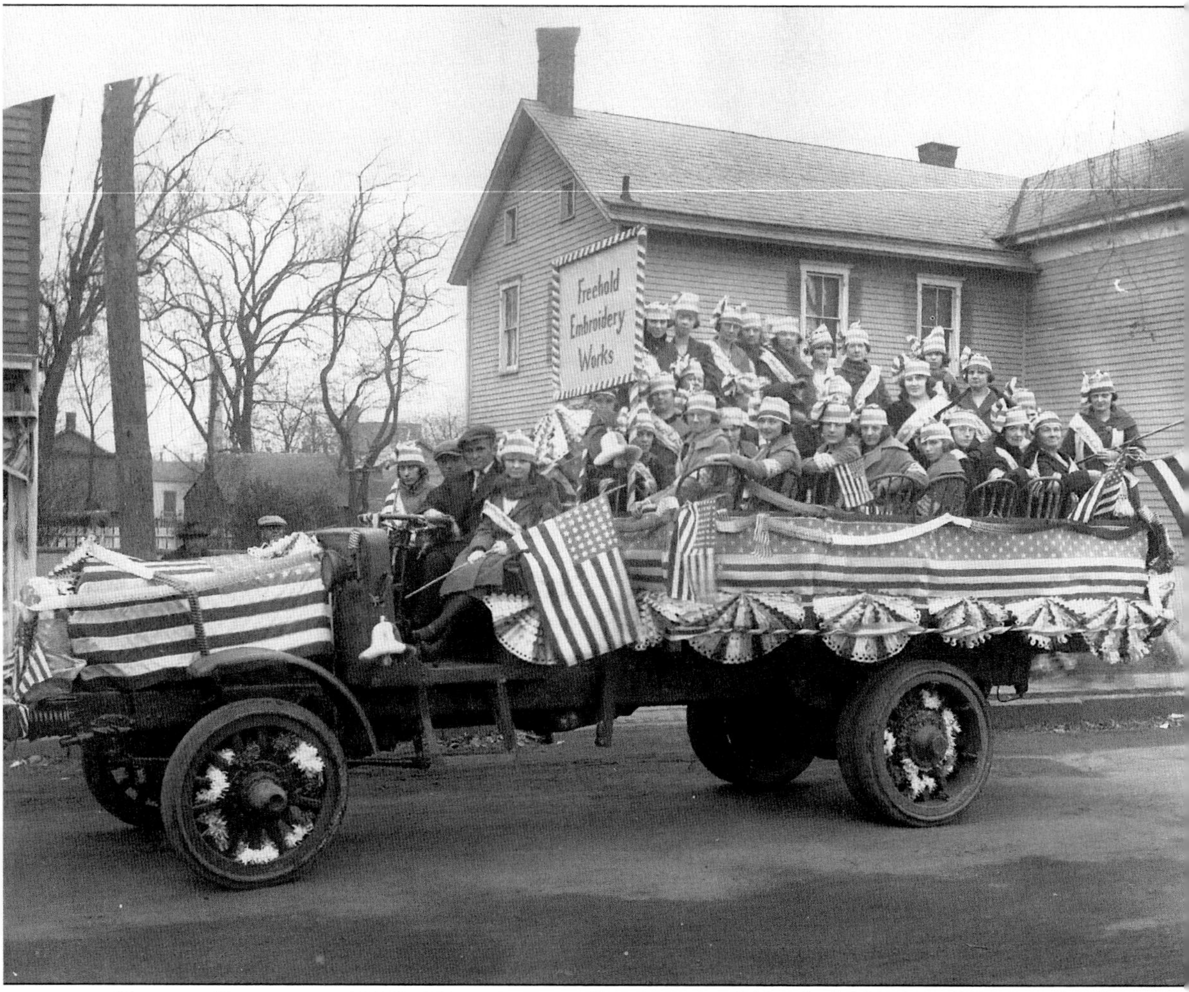

Parade Float, c. 1925. The patriotically decorated Freehold Embroidery Works float passed the rectory of St. Peter's Church on Throckmorton Street. One of many small industries in Freehold, the Embroidery Works had their employees fill the float. (MCHA Archives 1997.18.)

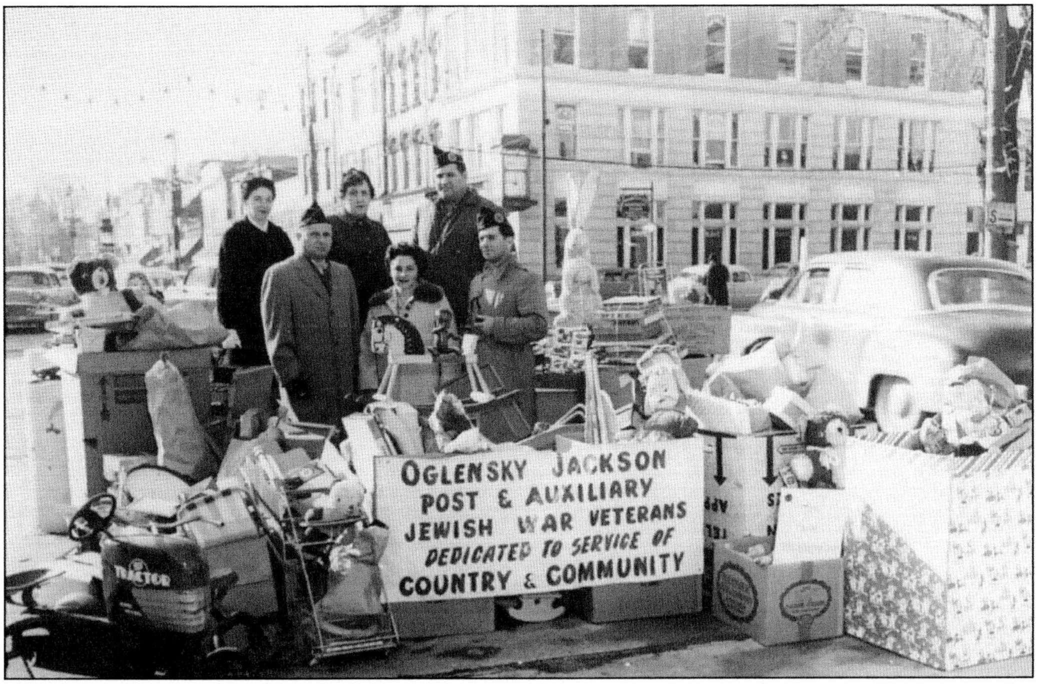

TOY COLLECTION, 1950S. The Jewish War Veterans gathered toys for needy children in the intersection of Main and South Streets. At that time, there were barricades in place to create a center island. (Collection of Carl N. Steinberg.)

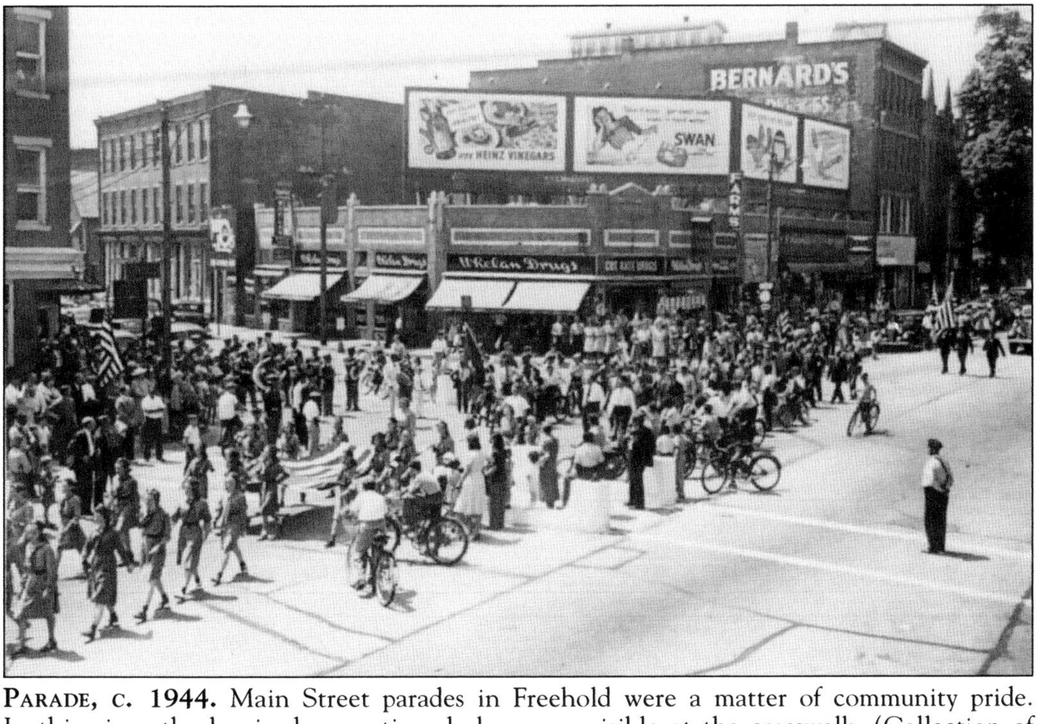

PARADE, C. 1944. Main Street parades in Freehold were a matter of community pride. In this view, the barricades mentioned above are visible at the crosswalk. (Collection of Carl N. Steinberg.)

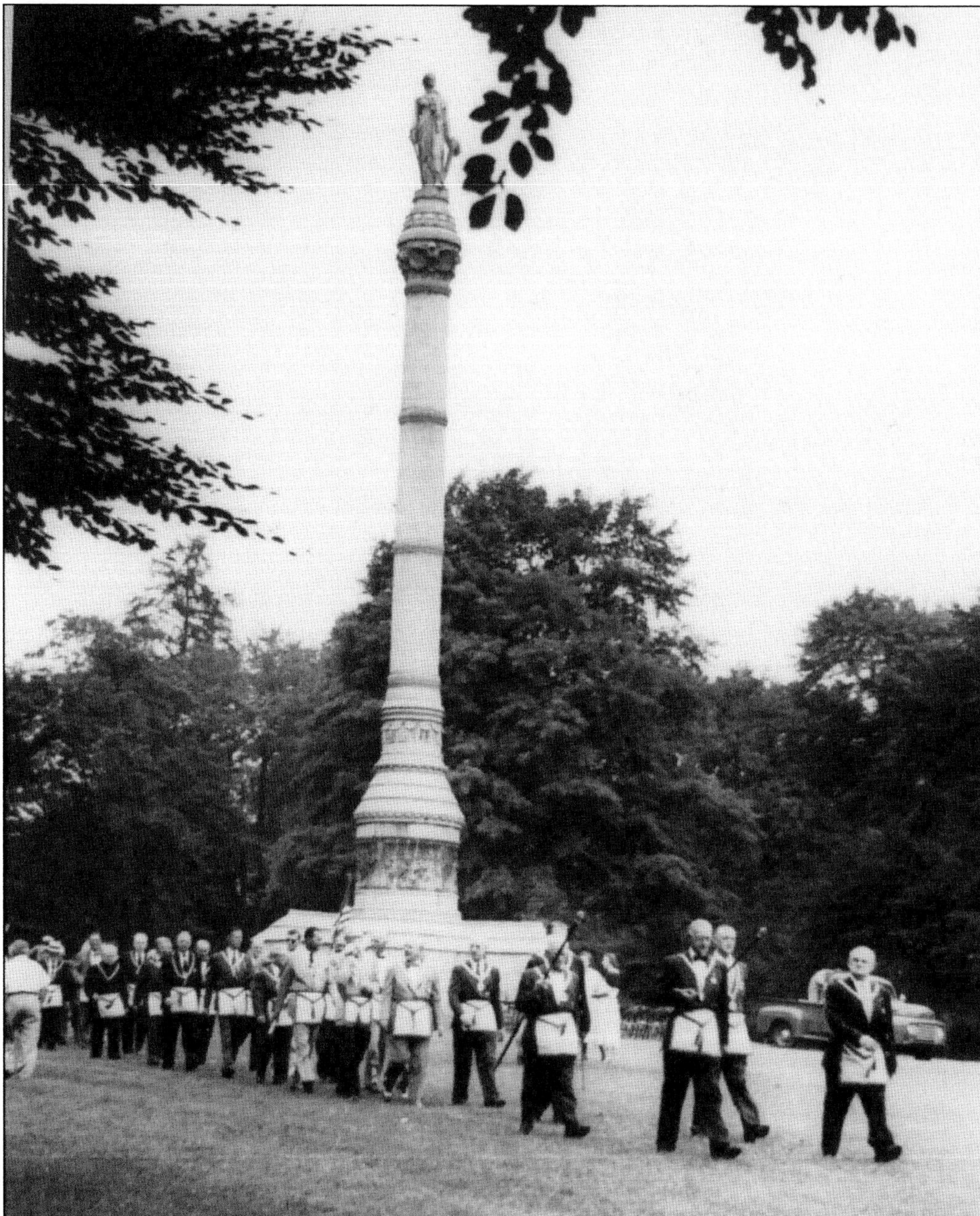

MASONIC LODGE, 1953. The Freehold Lodge of Masons, formally dressed with their Masonic aprons, marched in the 175th Anniversary Parade for the Battle of Monmouth. They passed the Battle Monument, in this photograph. (Photograph by Arthur Schreiber. MCHA Archives FR74.)

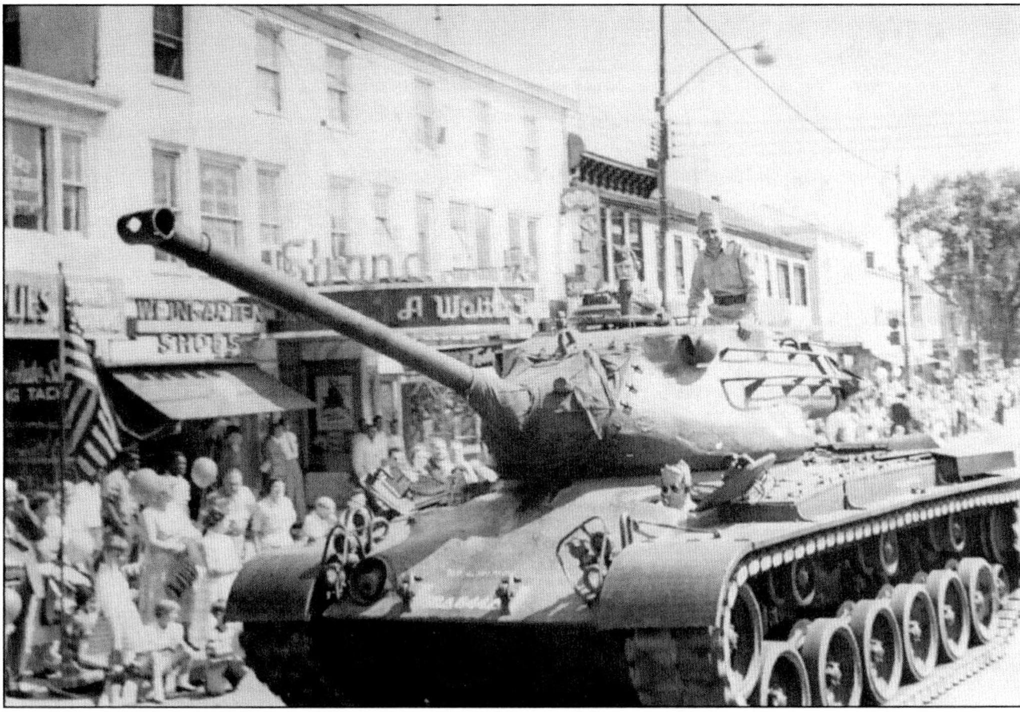

A Tank on Main Street, 1953. The 175th Anniversary Parade for the Battle of Monmouth was one of the largest ever and included a number of military groups. Several military tanks were among the attractions. (Collection of Carl N. Steinberg.)

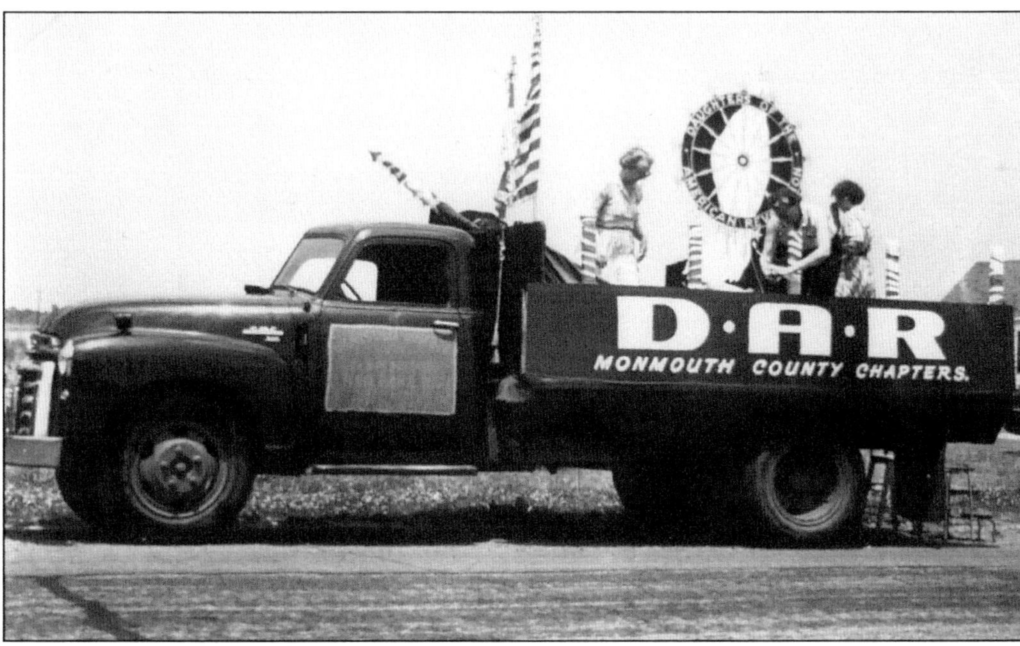

DAR Float, 1953. The Monmouth County Chapters of the Daughters of the American Revolution sponsored a float in the 175th Parade. They rode in a truck supplied by Blaisdell Lumber Company of Red Bank. (Photographer, Arthur Schreiber. MCHA Archives FR94.)

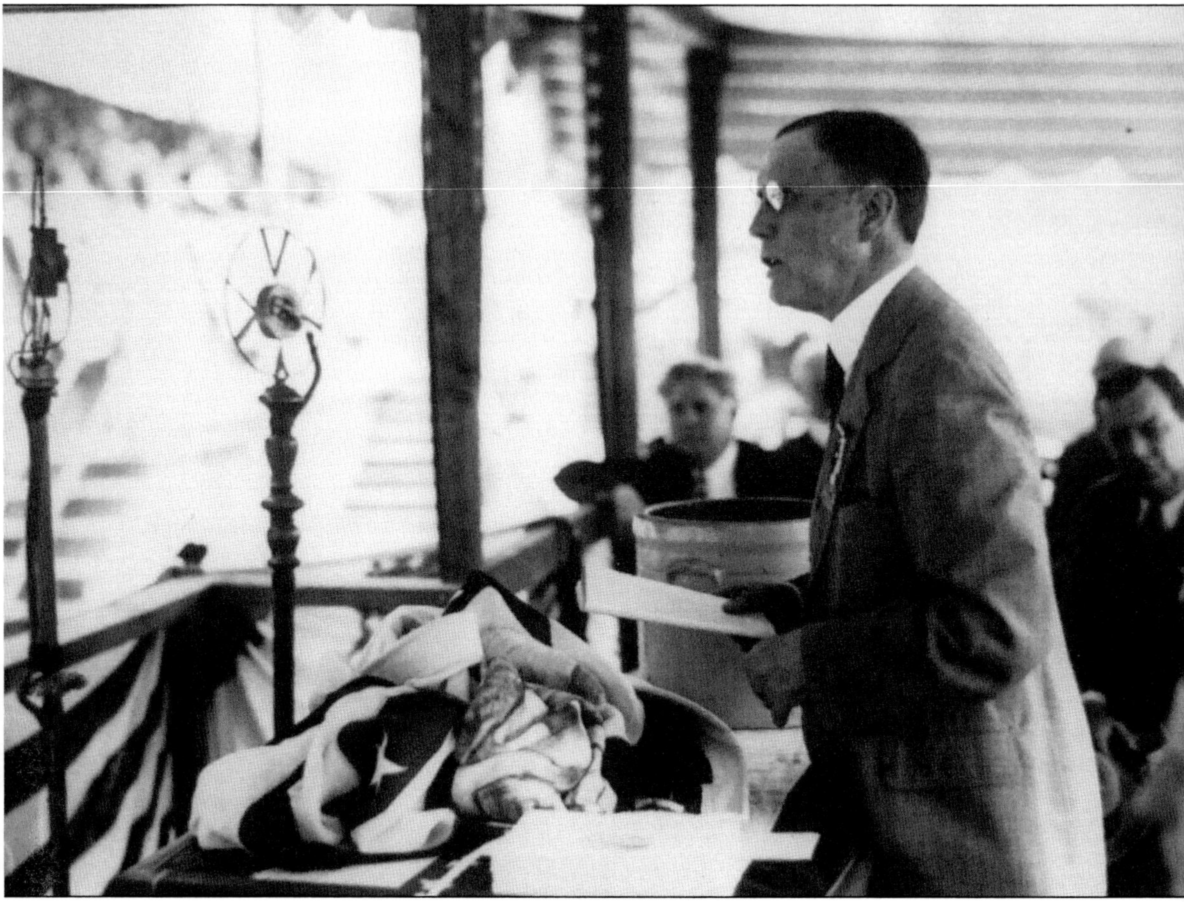

Samuel Craig Cowart, 1928. The ceremonies for the sesqui-centennial (150th) celebration of the Battle of Monmouth included a radio address by Samuel Craig Cowart, Historian of the Monmouth Chapter of the Sons of the American Revolution and Freehold native. (MCHA Archives FR32.)

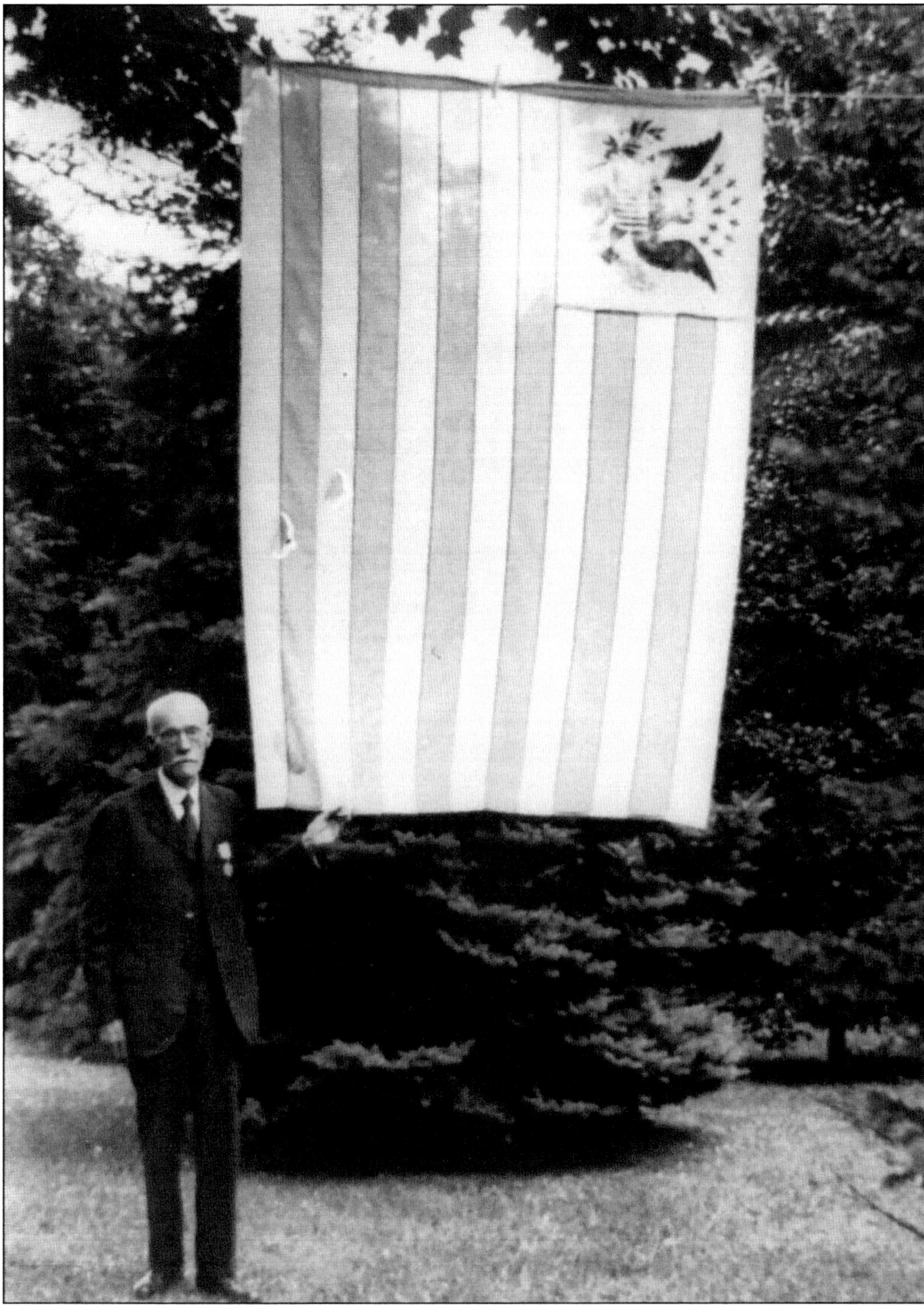

J.W. Campbell, 1928. Also present for the sesqui-centennial celebration was J.W. Campbell, president of the New Jersey Society of the Cincinnati, with the only Cincinnati flag in the state. (MCHA Archives FR3.)

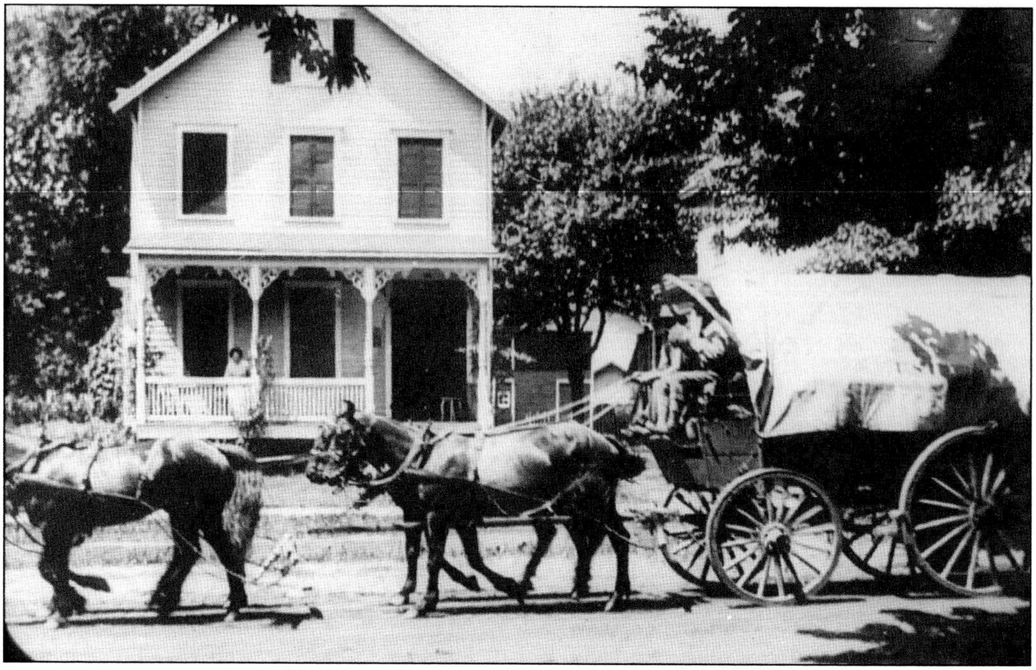

Signal Corps, c. 1901. The Signal Corps wagon from the Spanish-American War proceeds down Conover Street. (MCHA Archives.)

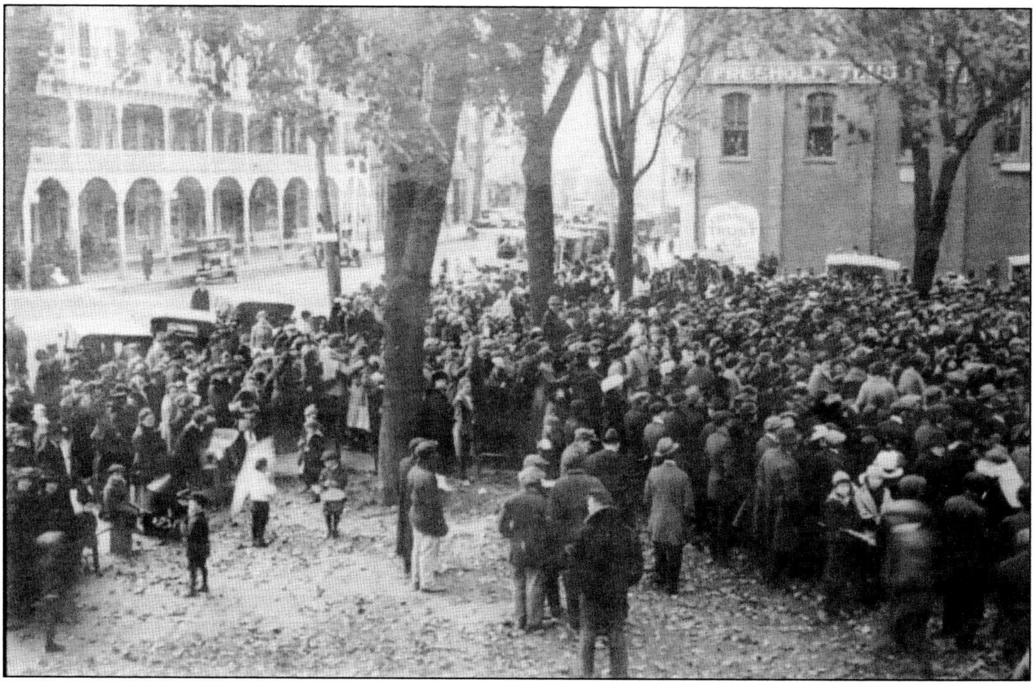

Court House Yard, c. 1930s. A crowd assembled outside of the County Court House, perhaps to hear a political speech or election results. On the corner building, a sign indicated that the Freehold Trust would soon be occupying the building. (Collection of Carl N. Steinberg.)

PARADE, C. 1930S. This photographer found a perch on the second floor of the Courthouse to view the passing parade, which at this point included a horse-drawn float. (Collection of Carl N. Steinberg.)

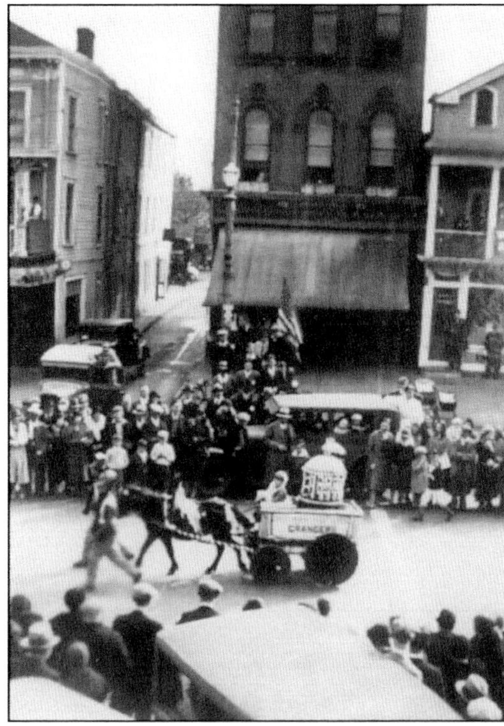

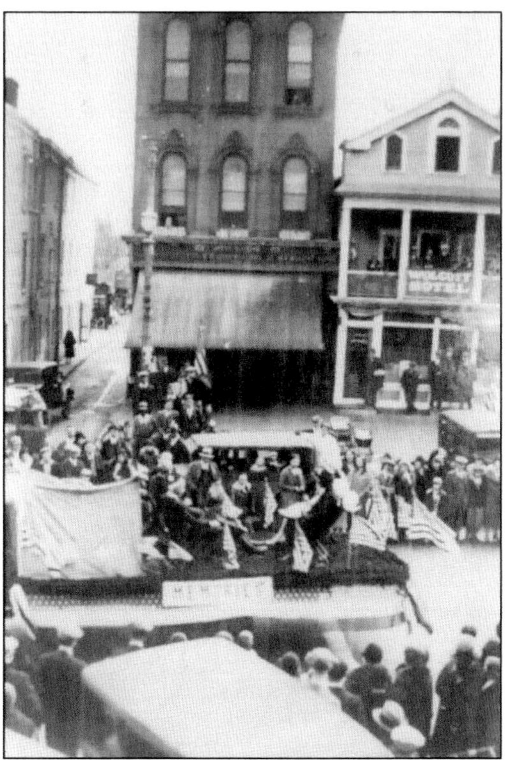

PARADE, C. 1930S. A larger float entitled, "Memories" (pre-*Cats*), passed with the Wolcott Hotel clearly visible behind. (Collection of Carl N. Steinberg.)

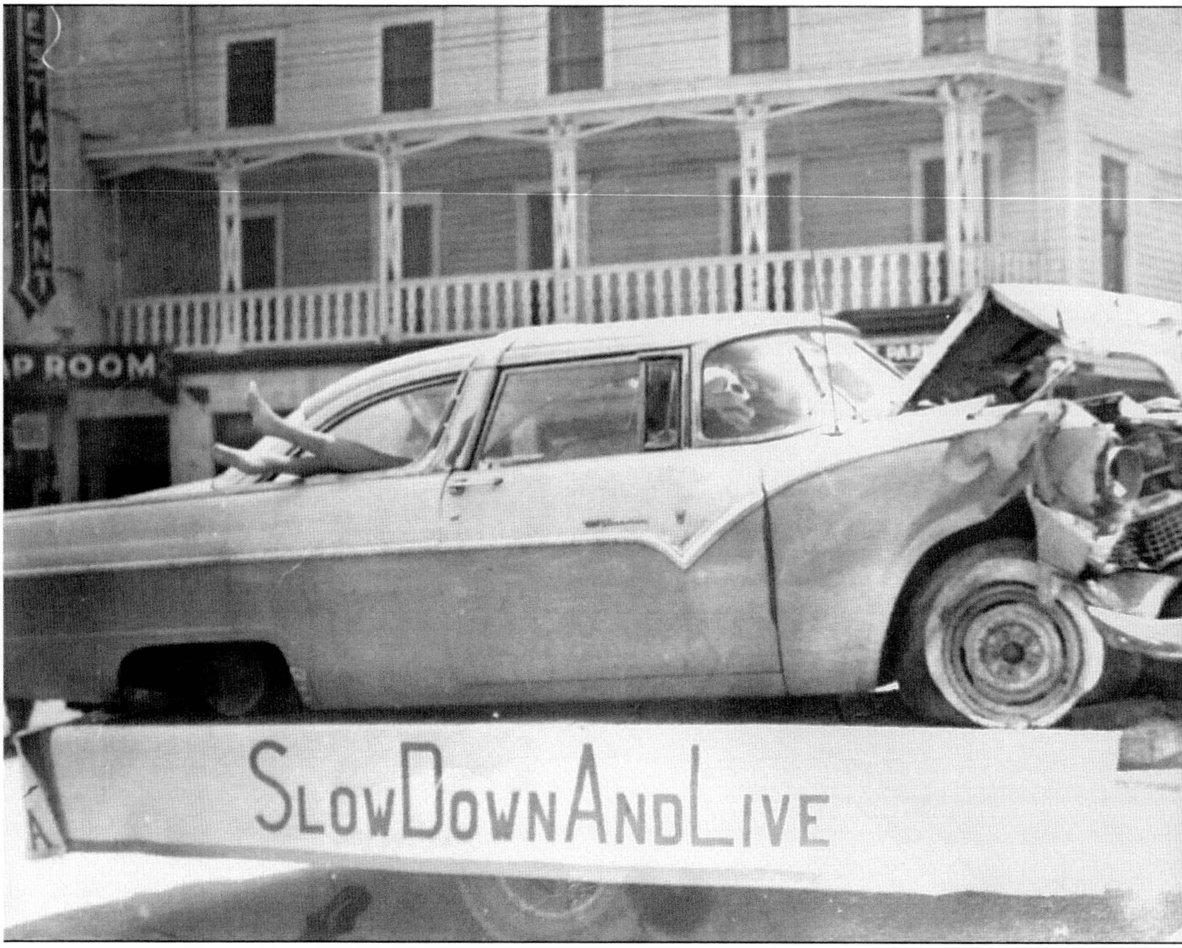

"SLOW DOWN AND LIVE," C. 1950. This slightly gruesome float featured a 1948 Ford Fairlane that had been in a head-on collision, with an added admonition about safe driving. The American Hotel is in the background. (Collection of Carl N. Steinberg.)